Choosing Life
or Death

Choosing Life or Death

A Guide for Patients, Families, and Professionals

William J. Winslade
Judith Wilson Ross

FP

THE FREE PRESS
A Division of Macmillan, Inc.
NEW YORK

Collier Macmillan Publishers
LONDON

The Free Press
A Division of Macmillan, Inc.
866 Third Avenue, New York, N.Y. 10022

Collier Macmillan Canada, Inc.

Printed in the United States of America

printing number

1 2 3 4 5 6 7 8 9 10

Library of Congress Cataloging-in-Publication Data

Winslade, William J.
  Choosing life or death

  Bibliography: p.
  Includes index.
  1. Medical ethics.   2. Medical care—Decision
making.   3. Medical personnel and patient.   I. Ross,
Judith Wilson.   II. Title.
R726.W56   1986   174'.24   85–16299
ISBN 0–02–934720–3

To Al Stern

Contents

Preface

Serious illness almost always creates a crisis for patients and for their families and friends. It is bad enough to have one's capacities and even life threatened, but modern medicine can make the crisis worse because it magnifies moral dilemmas for patients, as well as for health care professionals and policy makers. In a time of double crisis, it may be asking too much to expect patients to be rational, thoughtful, and decisive. Yet, if patients are to exert some control over their own lives and their own deaths, they must be able at least to aspire to those goals. It is difficult. It is not impossible.

Many persons are intimidated by technological medicine and by massive medical bureaucracies. Moral choices become confusing; legal issues are in flux; economic problems threaten. The physician-patient relationship is strained by threats of litigation on the one hand and economic pressures on the other. Patients, professionals, hospitals, communities, insurance interests, governments, and others have different interests, values, and obligations. Political differences and ideological controversy further complicate the situation. When faced with a medical crisis, what is a patient to do? This book attempts to answer that question.

We write for the general reader: for the present and future patient. We hope (1) to help those readers understand why it is hard for patients to function as equals in health care, (2) to convey to them how health problems create emotional pressures that impair decision-making capacities, (3) to explain the legal, ethical, and medical dimensions of these problems so that they can make better choices about what they themselves want in the face of difficult choices, and (4) to offer them practical strategies that will increase the probability that their own values and preferences will be honored when they are ill.

The book is intended to give present and future patients some sense of how, with this information in hand, they can make decisions about their own health care and see that these decisions are carried out. By providing practical suggestions, we hope to encourage people to take action, either for themselves (for example, by signing a natural death act or a living will) or for their community (for example, by writing to legislators and urging that durable power of attorney for health care legislation be passed). Becoming an effective patient is not an easy task because the health care system is not designed for mutual participation. Control over one's choices is possible, but it takes concerted effort on the part of patient as well as physician. Many books have been written to explain to health care workers how they can better relate to patients. This book is intended to help patients make their preferences clearer to physicians in particular, but also to other health care workers with whom they come in contact.

Even persons who are familiar with modern health care through professional or personal experience often forget what they know when caught in a crisis. It is tempting to let yourself be swept along by the momentum of a medical emergency and the powerful forces of the modern hospital bureaucracy. It is easy to have your personal preferences swept away before you realize what has happened. Physicians who become patients often develop a new appreciation of the patient's plight. This book is designed to remind professionals of the patient's perspective, for it may also become their own.

Each chapter begins with background material to establish the setting out of which the problems arise. We present detailed and dramatic cases to illustrate dilemmas that confront patients and their families. Most bioethical and medical writing presents only brief case vignettes; we believe that more complete case presentations are needed to bring out the richness and the difficulties of real personal choices. Our illustrative cases are composites created from aspects of actual cases; the names are fictional. The perspectives and interests of relevant professionals are briefly identified to frame the issues. Finally, practical guidance is offered to patients. The suggestions are not in the form of recipes or an instruction manual; rather

we attempt to clarify the choices and identify the factors that patients or families must take into consideration to act on their own
behalf. We recognize that many forces converge to prevent or minimize individual choice. Nevertheless, we believe that many persons,
even if not wholly masters of their own fate, desire to exercise control, and can do so, if only within certain limitations.

We have chosen a variety of health care issues that represent the
kinds of situations in which patients and their families may have difficulty controlling personal decisions or may not fully consider the
implications of decisions.

We begin with the problem of kidney dialysis, a scarce resource
   until 1972, when the federal government guaranteed public
   payment for all treatment needed by Americans suffering
   from end-stage renal disease. As our government's first foray
   into the dark labyrinth of resource allocation, it was in part a
   failure, despite the many lives it saved and sustained, for it resulted in treatment being provided *because* it was paid for,
   even if patients did not want it.

Terminating treatment combines conflicts about individual attitudes toward the value of life with questions about fair allocation of resources for those who have lived out the healthy, productive portion of their lives but are still among us. As the
   population ages and chronic disease in the elderly becomes
   more prevalent, the resource question will increase in importance, even to the point, perhaps, of altering social values.
   The cost issue may make it easier for patients to control decisions as long as they—or their families—are asking for less
   treatment or for less expensive treatment.

Genetic screening is a relatively new area wherein individual
   choice may be seriously hampered by medical or other expert
   authority. Inconsistent social attitudes about the definition
   and value of human life make screening a very complex activity. Usually, the judgments are more complex than the counselors acknowledge and the patients understand.

The problems of embryo transfer (the results of which are sometimes mistakenly called "test-tube babies") are very new and
   likely to increase, given the current rate of infertility and infertile couples' desires to have only the kind of child they
   choose. Here, personal choice is very risky. The risks do not always come from the medical procedures (although those risks

can be considerable). Equally important is the absence of social regulation and of social conventions that tell us how to
think about children who can have as many as six different
parents (biological, gestational, and rearing mother and father).

The treatment of handicapped newborns has recently been the
subject of extensive government activity. New laws go a long
way toward eliminating individual choice about appropriate
medical care. Perhaps no other area of health care is more
controversial than this, and the government has only served to
make it more difficult, in many instances, for parents to decide when the available medical treatment may be excessive.

Organ transplantation has all the problems of experimental therapeutic research combined with the problems of dependence
upon others for the donated organ. How patients can take for
their own a part of another human raises complex psychological, emotional, medical, and legal issues.

Bone marrow transplantation is a specialized and harrowing
procedure that is still experimental. The use of bone marrow
transplants dramatically illustrates the potential conflicts between the patients' best interests and the scientists' needs to
add to their store of knowledge in order to advance medical
science and technology. Patients who choose to enter therapeutic research are at extra risk.

We conclude with a discussion of how financial factors in health
care will affect patients' opportunities to act on their preferences in the future. Financial considerations will restrict options and influence choices not only at the level of public policy but also in clinical situations involving individual patients.
Although financial considerations are more technical and less
humanly engaging than other kinds of health care dilemmas,
patients must be aware of these economic constraints because
these, too, will limit their choices.

Many other topics could have been selected. Many other cases
could have been chosen. We believe these typify the problems that
individuals now face in the health care system. In considering them,
it is necessary to continue to look simultaneously at the still unresolved conflicts among social values and among individuals' preferences and at the need for cost reduction and the allocation of scarce
resources. We may be on a collision course as long as the public con-

tinues to believe that they have a right to all available health care, even if it means that more than they want is sometimes inflicted upon them.

This book also grew out of our conviction that many persons, including health professionals, want a nontechnical introduction to pressing issues in and ways of thinking about health care and bioethics. Our views were shaped by several related experiences. With the support of the National Endowment for the Humanities, we taught an interdisciplinary survey course at UCLA called "Medicine, Law and Society" from 1977 to 1984. The hundreds of undergraduates and the sprinkling of graduate and professional school students who took the course usually entered it with little information and many misconceptions. We believe that many of them left the course better informed, more thoughtful, and more sensitive to the perplexing issues concerning personal choice as well as public policy in health care. Often they expressed their appreciation for being given the opportunity to learn about something that related, as they would say, "to the real world." These students are representative of a large segment of the general public who are very interested in the current conundrums of bioethics as illustrated in dramatic news stories but uncertain how they might personally cope with such situations.

We have also been engaged as consultants for clinicians, patients, and policy-making agencies. We have undertaken scholarly research, given numerous lectures, served on committees, written editorials, participated in conferences, and talked with many colleagues in science, medicine, law, and the humanities about problems in bioethics. Drawing on these varied experiences, we have tried to convey to our readers a sense of what goes on in hospitals, in the personal lives of patients, and in the minds of professionals. We have also tried to explain the value conflicts and value choices that confront patients and their families as well as policy makers. We have tried not to suggest that some values or some choices should be preferred. We have, however, suggested ways for patients and their families to think through such choices if they want to know not only what is going on but also how to influence what happens to them. We have provided general but practical guidance. Persons in the midst of an acute crisis or chronic distress must find out and work out the details germane to their own unique situations. Our goal is to assist patients to be more informed, thoughtful, and in control of their lives and deaths.

We have included a bibliography for readers who want more comprehensive information about modern health care and topics in bioethics. The journals listed are a useful source of technical information about current controversies in health care. The books cited also contain additional bibliographic materials.

In recent years, a number of books have appeared in which authors have detailed their personal difficulties with the health system. Many of these writers have felt that they or their friends or family members were steam-rollered by a system that is authoritative and disease- or doctor-centered. A few, like Norman Cousins, have triumphed over illness and gotten what they needed from the health care system. Some have suggested that only the powerful can prevail against the authority of hospitals and physicians. It is our belief, however, that ordinary patients can also maintain a considerable degree of dignity and control, even in crisis, if (1) they understand how the system works and (2) they know clearly what they want for themselves. We hope that this book helps them on both counts.

Acknowledgments

We thank our colleagues at UCLA with whom we worked closely for several years. They include Bernard Towers, Judy Schneider, Aviva Bergman, Donna Gregory, Carol Hartzog, Judy Weinstein, Jan Almquist, Mary Dewire, Paul von Blum, Mike Green, Alan Steinberg, Mary Hagman, Sue Formaker, Jean Smith, Jim Hornstein, Dave Shapiro, Kathy North, David McBride, Ray Lyons, Joan McDowell, and Pat Anaya. We are grateful to the National Endowment for the Humanities for financial support that enabled us to experiment in our teaching about the topics discussed in this book. Chuck Ries, while he was Vice-Chancellor for Undergraduate Instruction, and members of the UCLA Council on Educational Development provided academic and administrative support. Many friends and colleagues in the health care and legal communities, especially those who participated in the Medicine and Society Forum, courses, and seminars, helped us to understand and teach about medical problems and to find our way within hospital and legal bureaucracies. Several patients and families made us aware of the powerful emotions that arise and flourish in health care settings, particularly at times of crisis. A number of people carefully read all or part of the text, and we have profited from, though not always heeded, their suggestions. Joan Lang, John Arras, and Peter Williams read the entire manuscript and made many comments that helped us clarify our thinking and improve the text. Others who made helpful comments include Corrine Bayley, Nancy Rhoden,

Lillian Key, Jack Winslade, David Barnard, Chester Burns, Ronald Carson, Susan Cayleff, Thomas Cole, Anne Jones, Thomas Murray, and Harold Vanderpool. We want also to thank Beverly DeVries for proofreading the entire manuscript.

We owe special thanks to Kitty Moore, who, while senior editor at The Free Press, helped us develop the idea for this book and Laura Wolff, our subsequent senior editor, and Edith Lewis, editing supervisor, who made many helpful suggestions.

CHAPTER 1

The Context of Choice

Nearly all of us have been medical patients since birth. Some of our vivid early childhood memories may involve visits to doctors or hospitals—getting shots, examinations, stitches, antibiotics, or minor surgery. Or, we may recall being on the fringes while mysterious medical things were done to our grandparents, parents, or siblings. As patients, our images of physicians are shaped by our own experiences, by the reports of others, by popular portrayals of physicians in the media, by social attitudes toward physicians as a professional group, and by many other psychological and social factors. Despite all of this, few people understand much about how health care is provided.

Health care—a basic human need for all of us—is an important component of American life. Yet, most people are inclined not to think much about physicians, health care, or the health care system until they or someone close to them becomes ill. At that point, they deal with the immediate situation—a birth, an illness, a death—as well as they can, often with little time for reflection.

Every grandmother and great-grandmother has probably cautioned her grandchildren that life is wonderful, "so long as you have your health." The trouble is, we can't always have our health. Sometimes we have poor health and sometime we are going to die. In sickness and in dying, we are likely to need and to want very much the focused attention of the health care system. Yet, at a time of crisis we may find it most difficult to deal with a system on which we

1

are suddenly so dependent. While everyone agrees on the importance of patients having a voice in determining the kind of care they
receive, all too often they do not speak out or their voices are not
heard.

For all the talk about patients' rights, the reality is that patients
are unequal and thus are at a serious disadvantage in the health care
system. First, they are or fear that they are seriously ill. Thus, they
are psychologically vulnerable and have difficulty acting authorita-
tively. Second, they know very little about the technical aspects of
medicine and have many incorrect perceptions about how scientific
medical care really is and how much certainty doctors have when
they make their recommendations. Thus, they are in a poor position
to judge the wisdom of what health care providers are proposing to
do or are actually doing to them. Third, and perhaps most important, they seldom know much about how health care *as a system* or
the hospital *as an institution* actually works. This basic inequality
between patient and doctor, patient and health care team, and patient and hospital means that patients typically have little control
over what happens to them. Patients have rights (both legal and
moral ones), but in order to exercise those rights, patients must
know the strengths, weaknesses, and structures of the health care
system and how the patient fits into that system. If they do not learn
this *before* they need medical attention, they are likely to find that
all their decisions have been made for them. Only after the fact will
they realize that their interests, their preferences, their values, and
their health were not necessarily everyone's primary concern.

American medicine is facing a difficult period in which the old
ways of doing business (as well as some that are not very old) are being reevaluated, reformed, or rejected. Therefore, it is an ideal time
for patients to begin to regain some authority in health care. Many
medical and hospital practices are being seriously questioned, from
both inside and outside the hospital. In order for patients to affect
health care, however, they must understand how it has changed in
the past fifty years, what external and internal pressures the system
currently faces, how doctors' and nurses' training and responsibilities shape their perspectives, and how the fields of law and ethics
view the patient.

Patients are the center of the health care system but they are typically its most passive members. As a practical matter, the patient
may be the least important person in the health care system when it

comes to decision making. Often patients become active only after the fact, in law courts or in their living rooms, when they sue or wish they could sue those who provided their care. Although Americans are a litigious lot, litigation cannot change what has already happened. If patients want to be effective agents in the system (as opposed to criticizing it afterwards), they must understand the system as well as the roles of the other players.

✓When patients enter the health care system, they often feel poorly, both physically and mentally. They are afraid of a serious or fatal illness; they hope it will be nothing or that it will be easily cured. The dreadful ambiguities of unexplained symptoms make them uncertain about how to behave with their physicians. Should they be stoic and minimize whatever ails them? Should they detail every possible symptom and risk sounding like a nonstop complainer? Should they simply be *good*, answering only what they are asked, speaking only when they are spoken to? To ask these questions is to begin to construct a persona that will alter the patient's role. Medical responses to patients may encourage false identities. To be a patient is, in many ways, to lose one's ordinary identity. Medical care is a great equalizer in the sense that all patients tend to be rendered equal (and smaller than they are in their daily lives, be they children, teamsters, teachers, executives, physician-patients, scholars, merchants, or thieves). The naive man who enters the hospital for gall bladder removal and who accidentally overhears himself referred to as "the gall bladder in Room 23" may be furious, but he cannot help being diminished. To be turned into a "case" or a "disease" is to be made to feel less fully oneself and rendered less powerful. This makes control harder for the patient.

Patients who believe that they are the center of the health care system are likely to trust everyone with whom they come into contact. Because they assume that everyone's goals are the same (to do what is "best" for the patient), such patients tend to agree with whatever is proposed, even if they have internal reservations or don't really understand what is being offered or why it is needed. The diminution of personal identity experienced in health care makes patients even more amenable to following whatever orders or suggestions they receive. If all goes well, there is never any reason to question the assumptions about trust and common goals and interests. When things do not go right (and that happens frequently), it may be too late for the patient or family to take control. All the critical decisions have already been made, and it is psychologically far more difficult to stop what has been started (whether it is an intravenous tube, a respirator, a pregnancy, or an experimental therapy) than it is not to start it in the first place. At this point, the patient's previous uncritical trust is easily replaced by suspicion or bitterness. In many instances, however, that bitterness is primarily the result of unrealistic expectations, not of bad faith or bad actions on the part of the health care providers.

Modern health care generates complex moral dilemmas with few obvious answers. If there were easy answers, they would not be dilemmas. Americans—and perhaps all humans—don't like dilemmas; we tend to translate dilemmas into simpler problems with single, unified answers. The recent Baby Doe controversy is a good example. Problems tend to be posed as if there were only two competing considerations: is it better for treatment decisions about handicapped newborns to be made by their parents and physicians or by the government? The American ethic clearly prefers parental decisions to government-imposed choices. In fact, when the citizenry was polled, as in the Oregon Health Decisions Project, that was their preference. On the other hand, when members of the U.S. Congress considered the Baby Doe issue, they voted overwhelmingly for government-regulated decisions. Both the Congress and the Oregon citizenry seemed to have overlooked the basic question raised by the Baby Doe case: are there some handicapped infants whose lives should absolutely be saved and some whose lives should not be prolonged? The Oregon citizenry would give too much discretion to the families; the U.S. Congress gave too little discretion to anyone. It is not an either/or question, but it has received, on both sides, an either/or answer.

The cases we present and the medical, legal, ethical, and public policy perspectives we outline in each chapter are intended to help the reader understand the multiple factors affecting treatment choices. This applies to handicapped newborns as well as to the other issues we discuss. We attempt to identify and explain relevant factors and essential perspectives. We try to resist oversimplified as well as overly complex formulations.

As background for this discussion, it is important first to have a general understanding of the four primary factors in the health care encounter: the physician, the patient, the role of finance, and the rise of bioethics. All contribute to shaping individual choices.

The Role of the Physician

Although it is difficult to think of it as a recent achievement, contemporary scientific/technological medicine is of very recent origin. Scientific medicine began just before 1900, and the complex dynamics of modern health care emerged only after the mid-1940s. Medical practice changed dramatically during those postwar years as a result of scientific discovery and a new concept of the physician's role. Lewis Thomas, perhaps contemporary medicine's most articulate spokesman, described in his recent autobiography, *The Youngest Science: Notes of A Medicine Watcher*, an incident that aptly captures this radical change in medical practice. Thomas reports being invited to speak at a county medical society dinner during which the society's new president was to be inaugurated. As dinner was served, the president-elect received a phone call and immediately left, returning only much later, just as the event was concluding. He had missed his own inauguration. He apologetically explained to Thomas that the phone call had informed him that a patient near death for some days had in fact just expired. The physician left the dinner immediately upon receiving the news because "he knew the family was in distress and needed him." Thomas concludes the story: "This was in the early 1950s when medicine was turning into a science, but the old art was still in place." The old art: doctors practicing the art of medicine treated the patient in the context of the family. The new science: doctors practicing medical science concerned themselves with disease processes, and only secondarily with the person who had custody of the disease. Many physicians, of course, tried to do both, but the two roles were and are frequently incompatible. Modern medical education has chosen to make sure that its students learn science. It provides casual opportunities for learning the caring aspects of healing, but such matters are, as the medical students themselves would phrase it, only electives, not required: they will not be on the exam. It is assumed that the medical students will learn humane treatment methods at the bedside: but if these methods are not valued and consciously practiced by their teachers, from whom will these student doctors learn them?

It took many years to turn physicians from comforters and caregivers into scientists and technologists, of course. The process was under way in 1908 when the Carnegie Foundation commissioned

Abraham Flexner to study American medical education. The Flexner Report, which was very critical of most medical education, has-
tened rapid and radical change. Medical schools, most of which
were free-standing trade or vocational schools with low standards
of admission, changed their ways or closed down. Apprentice-
ship training—the primary method of handing down professional
knowledge—was cut back and a new and much more uniform cur-
riculum was devised for doctors-in-training throughout the United
States. They were to be schooled uniformly in standardized courses
in the natural sciences, and they were not to practice some intuitive
art of medicine but instead to pursue the objective and true *science*
of medicine.

When Flexner issued his report, physicians still had precious little science to practice, but by 1940, two decades of scientific training had produced a body of physicians who accepted their roles as
scientists. Many had been hard at work in research laboratories lay-
ing the groundwork for the scientific medicine that would characterize medical practice in the second half of the twentieth century.
In 1950, when Lewis Thomas attended that medical society inauguration, a physician who would leave an important professional occasion to comfort the family of a dead patient was already noteworthy, an anachronism, a symbol of medicine's past, strangely foreign
to the stainless steel laboratory image of the new academic and scientific medicine. These sublimely confident, new and improved
doctor-scientists were marching off to cure diseases, while the old-
time doctors, who had cared for their patients but been able to cure
very few, slowly died off. Their legacy was the art of caring and the
gift of service to their communities, often with little reward other
than the respect of their townspeople. That inheritance seemed pal-
try and even unnecessary compared to the prize that physicians believed was now within their reach: the conquest of disease and the
pursuit of immortality.

This shift in medical training and medical goals deeply affected
physicians' self-perceptions. Old-style medicine might indeed be
learned by anyone and practiced by almost any method. Homeo-
paths, herbalists, chiropractors, astrologers, and Christian Scientists
might be equally equipped to care for the sick when there was virtually nothing that could be done to treat or cure their illnesses other
than to provide them with emotional support and questionable nos-
trums. Scientific medicine was something quite different. To be a
doctor in the scientific age of medicine was to be educated in com-

plex and abstruse matters beyond the reach of the ordinary person. To control the very processes of life demanded superior skills and superior knowledge. Patients, yearning for reassurance, were as willing to assign authority to doctors in general as they were to place their unquestioning trust in their personal physicians. With scientific authority and public confidence and respect, physicians began to regard themselves as an elite, as holders of special capacities and responsibilities, perhaps entitled to superior status and power. The authority of science and the actual power of life and death that science gave to physicians sometimes led to authoritarian attitudes.

This change in the physician's role strained the reciprocity of the doctor-patient relationship. The doctor was interested less in the patient than in the disease that the patient brought. The physician's focus on disease brought with it a kind of war mentality in which disease was the enemy to be defeated. The physician led the attack and, as in any military situation, the questioning of orders was not tolerated. In a just war (and the war on disease was surely a just one), almost any means were legitimate, including deceiving the patient or submitting him or her to considerable risks. The patient became the battlefield upon which the war against disease was fought, and if the battlefield was considerably the worse for the experience, it was only what one had to expect in war. It was not desirable to destroy patients in order to save them, but sometimes it was necessary to risk destroying them to win the larger war, farther down the road. As a result, patients were unknowingly subjected to risky experiments and willingly agreed to questionable treatment on the assumption that "Doctor knows best!" The doctor-patient relationship scarcely had room for the patient as participant, only as subject.

Whereas the patients' respect for old-time doctors was based on the physicians' "bedside manner," the new basis on which physicians received their patients' respect tended to be trust in their *scientific* authority. Physicians had become the dispensers of life and death. Their power was reinforced by the widespread faith in science as well as by medicine's demonstrated ability to save lives where once they had been lost, to cure diseases that once would have left death or disability in their wake, and to halt diseases before they even began. A few physician-researchers even began to talk of eternal life, of curing death itself. No greater power could be imagined in a Judeo-Christian civilization than possessing the keys to immortality. The fruits of a scientific medical education, buttressed by a

vast government investment in scientific research, changed the face
of American medicine. And it changed the role of doctors. No longer
hand-holders, wise friends, or practical psychologists, they put on
their white lab coats in order to challenge destiny itself. They were
in control.

The Role of Patients

The civil rights movement that began in the late 1950s in the United
States changed the face of our society. Although we are still debating
how much it changed opportunities for most black Americans, the
ideological force of that movement made real changes in many
other areas, including health care. The civil rights movement
broadly declared that all who were oppressed and subject to authoritarian control should rise up and demand their human rights to
equal consideration and to equal participation. The Constitution
embodied America's commitment to individual rights, but that
commitment had frequently been subordinated to conform to the
values of the dominant culture, especially educated, white males
who held positions of power (a group that included most physicians). In the 1960s, individualism and individual rights achieved a
new prominence. The U.S. Supreme Court announced a constitutional "right of privacy," which had not been identified as a constitutional right prior to 1965. This right of privacy began to appear
more frequently both in legal decisions and in philosophical discussions during that decade, usually in the context of the importance of
individual autonomy. Privacy, it was argued, was what made it possible for a person to become an individual, to act as an individual, to
emerge from the mass of people. Only the realized individual, in
control of his or her life, could effectively fight against authoritarianism, the great enemy of the 1960s.

   In health care, this passion for individualism and the individual
struggle against authoritarianism found one target in the very unequal doctor-patient relationship. Critics claimed that patients had
the right to make their own decisions about treatment and hospital-
izations, and should not be made to submit blindly to the preferences of physicians, no matter how well-intentioned the doctors
were. Angry patients pointed out potential conflicts between their
interests and the doctor's interests, between their values and the doctor's values. Both federal and state courts reinforced the claims for

patients' rights when they insisted that physicians gain informed consent for all significant medical procedures or risk malpractice suits if matters went awry. The federal government acknowledged the legitimacy of these claims when it established the National Commission for the Protection of Human Subjects of Biomedical and Behavioral Research. The 1976 medical malpractice crisis, which resulted from the growing number of malpractice suits filed against doctors and the increasingly large settlements that were being awarded, suggested a public dissatisfaction with medicine. It was clear that the people who brought suit did not believe that the doctor either knew best or had done right. And their fellow citizens who sat on the juries and decided the size of monetary awards often agreed with them.

The civil rights movement focused on two themes: individualism (equal power) and equality (equal opportunity). When individualism emerged as one of the primary values in health care reform, the doctor-patient relationship was dealt another severe blow. The physician's claim to scientific authority was met with the patient's claim to individualism. It led directly to conflicts about *who shall decide?* These conflicts continue with us today and make the ethical dilemmas of biotechnology even more complex. Had authority continued in the hands of the physicians, it would have been relatively simple for the physicians' professional associations to establish ethical norms that would have controlled health care practices. The continuing high status of physicians (despite public distrust of them as a group) would probably have enabled them to insist upon their professional norms being used as social norms. Because physician authority has been so disputed, however, and because the doctor-patient relationship is now so strained, society must not only consider *what* should be decided about medical care in complex issues (such as treatment of handicapped newborns, withdrawal of treatment in terminal cases, and treatment of incompetent patients) but also *who* should make those decisions. In addition, physicians, patients, and policy makers gradually realized that these decisions were not exclusively medical but also had a significant ethical dimension.

The civil rights movement's emphasis on equality of opportunity has also left us with another important result: that of equal rights to health care itself. Twenty-five years ago, the primary national debate over health care centered on the serious inequities between the rich and the poor. The rich—and even the moderately well-off—

could expect to live longer than the poor, and their infants were substantially more likely to survive than the poor's. Hard political work since 1960 has been directed at equalizing health care for Americans. Many thought that national health insurance, following the British model, could achieve that goal, but national health insurance was crushed by a coalition that included the American Medical Association. The AMA demanded the preservation of fee-for-service medicine in order to maintain the physician's status as an independent, individual entrepreneur working on behalf of the individual patient's needs. Thus, the battle against national health insurance endorsed individualism and individual rights on two fronts: the physicians' right to practice as they saw fit and patients' right to receive medical care from the physician of their preference. AMA opponents, who urged national health care on behalf of the poor, could only point out that a family's right to do business with the doctor of its choice was valueless for the poor and for rural Americans. If the family could not pay for the services it wanted, then physicians would not provide the services. And where no physicians served the community, no choices could be made.

National health insurance was first urged in the 1930s, long before the significant scientific breakthroughs that led to high-technology medical care. It was pursued on the philosophical grounds that every American citizen had the right to necessary health care. The language suggests an egalitarian approach, although in fact it probably was a demand only for a minimum standard of health care. During the late 1950s and early 1960s when these appeals began to have an effect, the demand was for basic services, including prenatal care, treatment of chronic illness in the elderly, and treatment of infections among children and of ordinary illnesses such as pneumonia, tuberculosis, and the like among adults. There was no thought of heart transplants, test-tube babies, or respirators.

The civil rights movement in health care reform led not to national health insurance but to Medicare and Medicaid. These federally instituted programs were intended to ensure health care for the elderly and the poor, those groups that had not yet fully shared in the benefits of modern medicine. At the same time, private medical insurance, customarily paid for by employers as part of workers' benefits, was ensuring access to health care for the great majority of the public. This three-way system appeared to solve the problem of equal access to health care, although many Americans are covered by none of these programs even today. However, the legacy of that political movement for national health insurance has been a public belief in equal access to *all* health care, not merely in equal access to *basic* health care. Neither the public nor the policy makers took into account the effects that scientific research and technological discovery would have on medicine. At a time when *basic health care* and *health care* were practically synonymous terms, we failed to understand that the increasing supply of medical technology would meet with an unceasing individual demand for medical care. This union of supply and demand would create a crisis in health care financing, exacerbated by the medical establishment's disregard of accountability for costs and grievously threatening the trend toward equality of access that had been so recently initiated.

Public attitudes thus changed in two ways during this twenty-five-year period between 1960 and the present: patients demanded an equal and participatory role in the doctor-patient relationship, and the public believed that everyone had a fundamental right to receive necessary health care. Because of the increasing value placed upon individualism and autonomy, *necessary* frequently came to be defined not merely as lifesaving but also as life-enhancing. Necessary health care was thus felt to include services provided by physicians that were desired by patients, ranging from kidney dialysis to abortions to sex-change operations to infertility treatment. Necessary health care in the public mind also included any treatment available that might give the patient a chance at extended life, no matter how small the chance, how considerable the risk, or how poor the quality of life. Again and again, persons desiring services have been heard to say, "It's his [or her or my] only chance." The public's desire to defeat illness and death in order to extend their own individual lives joined with the doctors' desire to conquer disease and control life processes. To the extent that both doctors and patients wanted to extend life, the doctor-patient relationship managed to operate rather smoothly, despite the internal conflicts about decision-making control. When there was disagreement, however, the doctor-patient relationship became very rocky. For example, this occurred when medical research made life extension possible, but patients of their families were disturbed by the methods used to extend their lives. As doctors and patients and families fought, frequently in the courts, to assert their own views of what health care was necessary, the policy makers began to exhibit concern, especially over costs. Health care expenditures were increasing dramatically, but health outcomes were not improving. For all that was being spent, it was not easy to prove that people were much better off as a result of more health care.

The Role of Finance

In 1960, Americans spent about $129 per person on health care. By 1984, that amount had increased to $1500 per person. Although two-thirds of the expenditures are now paid by government or by insurance companies, individuals themselves pay more now for health care than they did in 1960, even when inflation is taken into account. The rapid inflation since 1975 accounts for some of these increased costs, but most of the rise results from increases in use of health care services and in the kind of services that are available. In 1960, for example, no dollars, either private or public, were expended on long-term kidney dialysis treatment because it was not available. By 1984, $1.2 billion was expended for kidney dialysis treatment. New services resulting from recently developed and very expensive technology like dialysis drove expenditures up rapidly.

In addition, many more people had access to the health care system. Both Medicare and Medicaid brought previously excluded people into doctors' offices and hospitals. The care they received increased expenditures. In addition, the increased practice of employer-paid private health insurance for American workers made consumers less sensitive to the cost of health care since, for the most part, they paid neither for the insurance nor for the health care they were receiving. As a result, people with private insurance also used more health care services.

The new technology was directly related to the change in the role of the physician and was underwritten by the government. Scientific medicine required scientific research. After World War II, the U.S. government became the major financial backer of medical research. The annual budget for the National Institutes of Health, which had been a miniscule agency before World War II, went from $180,000 in 1945 to $4 million in 1947 and then $46 million only three years later. The dramatic increase in research funding quickly produced progress in basic scientific knowledge. This led to profitable new technologies for health care, and once they existed, physicians wanted to use them in their war to conquer disease. The public, too, demanded access to these new possibilities, expecting third parties, either public or private, to pay the bills. When payment was not forthcoming, as it frequently was not for procedures that were still deemed experimental, citizens created lobbying groups that pressured legislators to ensure reimbursement for "potentially lifesaving treatment." The government was primarily interested in health care research in such areas as cancer or heart disease treatment that would affect large numbers of people. Those who suffered from ailments that affected smaller numbers of citizens then mounted campaigns to have their illnesses recognized for research funds as well. In time, virtually every disease had its lobby and its congressional spokesperson, urging increased funding. The lobbying eventually succeeded and Congress began to provide additional funds for research, one disease at a time, including those that affected relatively few people.

The third factor that significantly affects health care expenditures is aging. As life expectancy increased, a greater percentage of the population lived beyond the age of 65, suffering more of the illnesses that accompany old age. According to a 1984 survey in *The Economist*, the American of age 65 or over receives, on average, three times as much health care as does any other American other than the newborn, and that care is expensive. The technologies that led to the development of the hospital intensive care unit may have permitted extended life for the older patient, but they have dramatically increased costs.

Clearly, policy makers were aware that investing in research and new technologies, expanding government and private health insurance programs, and extending population life expectancies would result in increased health costs. No one appreciated how great the increase would be, however. Health care expenditures are now pressing toward 11 percent of the gross national product, far more than is spent per capita by other countries in the world. The major concern at the moment is that the government cannot afford its share of this 11 percent, but in the long run, it may be more important to consider whether the country as a whole can afford to spend that much of its resources on health care, regardless of who specifically is paying the bill. There are those who will argue (like the fabled old man who tells youth that you can't put a price on health) that we should spend whatever it takes to regain health and to prolong life. The unfortunate truth appears to be, however, that the 1000 percent increase in health expenditures between 1960 and 1984 has not improved our health or prolonged our life in any way commensurate with the size of the expenditure. A decade-long study conducted by the Rand Corporation shows that families that had free health care consumed 50 percent more than families that had to pay for initial levels of care. The health of both groups of families was pretty much the same despite the difference in care. Similarly, a recent University of California Institute for Health Policy study (National Health Insurance Survey) found that the health of the poor had improved very little despite vast increases in governmental spending on health care for the past twenty years. On a larger scale, the United States, despite its enormous outlay for health care, still ranks relatively low among developed countries in critical measures of health care. According to 1983 *World Health Statistics Annual*, the United States' overall mortality rate is above the average for all developed nations, our life expectancy is exceeded by fifteen other developed countries, and our infant mortality is worse than eighteen other developed countries'. In some of our inner cities the infant mortality rate approaches that of the Third World. The question of whether all our health care is doing us enough good cannot be ignored.

The changing roles for doctors and patients and the burgeoning costs of health care join to make the ethical dilemmas created by high-technology scientific medicine even more difficult. It is society's response to these ethical dilemmas to which we turn next.

The Development of Bioethics

Many ethical dilemmas in contemporary health care stem from the development of high-technology medical care. These developments affect medical care in two ways: first, they create or intensify head-on conflicts between the rights of different individuals, frequently because they make our traditional definitions of life and death useless or at least seriously flawed; and second, they are so expensive that not everyone may realistically have access to them, at least not indefinitely. Sometimes these aspects appear equally important in bioethics cases; sometimes one of them predominates.

High Technology

Some years ago, Lewis Thomas pointed out that medical research was increasingly committed to what he called "halfway technology." Halfway technology included things like transplants, artificial organs, and coronary bypass operations. These were the kinds of procedures that were pursued when the doctors didn't really understand what was going on and, in the absence of real understanding, they provided temporary, halfway measures. *Real* technology (that is, decisive technology), he claimed, demonstrated breakthroughs, permitting physicians both to prevent and reverse disease processes. Immunizations, antibiotics, hormone treatments for endocrine disorders, and treatment for nutritional disorders represented the kind of decisive technology that he thought was vital to genuine medical progress. The trend has not shifted since Thomas drew attention to this distinction in 1974. In fact, halfway technology (which is usually called high technology because it is complex and expensive) has flourished.

The average life expectancy for Americans has increased dramatically since the beginning of the twentieth century, but that increase has resulted almost exclusively from decisive technology, including improved hygiene, sanitation, and environmental conditions. These changes have led to an increased average life expectancy because they reduced the infant mortality rate. The principal discoveries of the mid-century period, which have decreased morbidity and mortality, were also decisive technology solutions. Salk's and Sabin's discoveries of polio vaccines, Fleming's discovery of penicillin, and its subsequent elaboration to numerous broad-spectrum antibiotics typify these technologies, which involve substantial basic research costs but can then be made available quickly to many people at relatively low cost. Since 1960, the emphasis has been on high technology, which emphasizes both basic research and engineering. The results, such as kidney dialysis machines, respirators and ventilators, the artificial heart, CAT (computerized axial tomography) scans, and the like, are expensive to develop, expensive to produce, and expensive to use; they are unlikely to decrease mortality on a large scale because they are useful only to a relatively small number of people and because they are not curative by nature. They might have a greater effect upon morbidity and mortality were it not that they themselves often have significant side effects that create other problems. High-technology medicine tends, to a significant degree, to be *iatrogenic*; that is, the treatment itself causes problems. For example, premature infants were given an increased chance of survival with respirators but they were often blinded by the same high oxygen concentrations that saved their lives. Recent studies have suggested that as many as 30 percent of hospital admissions are a result of iatrogenic disease.

Decisive technology involves relatively few ethical dilemmas, although many policy decisions still must be made that take into account the cost/benefit ratios involved in implementing their use. The use of flu vaccines for elderly patients, the practice of yearly physical exams for all patients, annual Pap tests for cervical cancer—all examples of low-cost procedures—have been extensively discussed in recent years with respect to whether their cost is justified by reductions in mortality or morbidity. High technology, on the other hand, is almost never evaluated with respect to whether *its* benefits justify the cost. High-technology medicine is aimed at "saving" (or, more accurately, prolonging) individual lives. Americans appear to believe as an article of faith that there is no way to put a price on an individual human life. Yet policy makers quite routinely do make such valuations with respect to low-level medical procedures (as well as in other areas, such as building and highway design and safety regulations). However, the development of high-technology medicine has not been accompanied by cost/benefit analyses that are required in other areas.

High-technology medical care is our culture's commitment to magic. (People who receive heart transplants, for example, often refer to the procedure as "a miracle.") It is our search for the Holy Grail and our attempt to pass through the eye of the needle. Through high-technology medicine, we soar to new and amazing heights, we seek out immortality, we strive to control the very processes of life itself. It represents both our finest desires and our tendency to overreach ourselves and to become victims of our own human pride. High-technology medicine creates our most troubling ethical problems because we fail to consider its implications carefully before we develop it. It has become, with exquisite irony, *our* century's Pandora's box, containing all the medical treatments instead of all the illnesses and diseases that the original Pandora let loose on the world.

High-technology medicine gives us the opportunity to create human life outside the normal reproductive processes, to reclaim some kind of life for those infants born with serious physical defects who would have otherwise have inevitably died, and to deny life to infants with abnormal genetic makeups. It makes it possible for us to extend life for people whose organs have worn out or given up, to ensure continued life for those whose spirits have waned as their bodies have grown less useful, to value a life of bondage to machines as a superior alternative to death, and to tempt those near death with the hope of just one more miracle through one more experiment. High-technology medicine requires decisions that are cogent, lucid, deeply thought through, and resolute. These paragon decisions must be made by human beings who, at best, are frightened, ill, depressed, and deeply ambivalent.

The field of bioethics came into existence because there was a need to talk about how those decisions should be made, who should make them, and the long-term social implications of the decisions. In the late 1960s, philosophers and theologians, physicians and lawyers, policy makers and legislators began to write about these questions, to hold conferences, and ultimately to establish institutes and publish journals for the study of legal and ethical issues in health care. The philosophers first wrote about the moral status of the fetus in relation to abortion while the lawyers and doctors described how death might be redefined to include brain death as well as cessation of heartbeat and breathing. Policy makers were considering whether high-technology dialysis machines should be guaranteed to all who had need of them. Legislators were writing new statutes that would make it easier for citizens to donate organs for transplants by signing simple consent statements on their drivers' licenses.

In 1973, the first edition of *The Hastings Center Studies* pointed out that

> Remarkable advances are being made in organ transplantation, human experimentation, prenatal diagnosis of genetic disease, the prolongation of life and control of human behavior—and each advance has posed difficult problems requiring that scientific knowledge be matched by ethical insight.

The Center's intention was to spur that ethical investigation. The federal government, universities, private philanthropists and foundations, and committed professionals quickly expanded their investigations in the 1970s. Physicians, attorneys, theologians, philosophers, and other academicians banded together in national and local organizations to create a network for the new field.

Most of those interested in bioethics did not believe they were expected to solve the problems they were talking about. Many saw themselves as latter-day Paul Reveres, writing along, proclaiming "The problems are coming! The problems are coming!" Many of the problems were already there but few people were aware of them. From the very first, there was no paucity of issues: the questions of abortion, transplantation, definitions of death, use of behavior-modifying drugs without patient consent, involuntary commitment of mental patients, experimentation by physicians and social scientists on unsuspecting subjects, and prenatal diagnosis lay immediately at hand.

In January of 1974, at the first meeting of the UCLA Medicine and Society Forum, a transdisciplinary panel discussed the ethical problems involved in deciding whether to treat infants with spina bifida. Almost ten years later, in the fall of 1983, American newspapers and television stations were carrying daily stories about the saga of Baby Jane Doe, who was born with spina bifida and whose parents chose not to consent to aggressive treatment. The problem was no different in 1983 than it had been in 1974, the solutions no easier. What had changed was that for a decade, professionals and academics interested in bioethics had been learning about the medical facts, analyzing the social consequences of various choices, and debating about the primary values. The bioethics community's response to the Baby Jane Doe crisis was far more sophisticated than it would have been in 1974. But it was not unified, for even among those who specialize in the ethics of the treatment of newborns, there are fundamental disagreements about what values are most important. What the bioethics community sought to do was analyze these problems and educate the public and the professions about their importance. The decision about which values should take precedence is not only a question for experts. It is a question for all individuals, but it is vital that everyone understand the complexity of these questions and the implications of different value choices.

Although the ethical dilemmas of contemporary medicine present problems that are extremely difficult to resolve, many of these dilemmas are the luxuries of an affluent society. In developing countries, no one worries about whether an infant with spina bifida will receive immediate surgery, because there is no surgeon, no hospital, and perhaps no antibiotics to treat the child. Such children will die, as they would have in the United States prior to 1958. Even in developed but less affluent countries, these questions may not be so pressing. A country like Great Britain, faced with an extended recession and a shrinking economy, does not even consider guaranteeing access to kidney dialysis machines or kidney transplants to all its citizens who need them. In the United States, ethical dilemmas have flourished because we could afford them. That is no longer the case. We now face a serious problem because our health care costs too much. In the next ten years, the public, legislators, and policy makers will be making ethical choices even more harrowing than those that have characterized the past decade. Bioethicists are only now beginning to address the moral conflicts involved in resource allocation in health care; that is, in rationing medical treatment.

Allocation of Resources

The federal government's decision to underwrite massive amounts of scientific research and biomedical technology has not only created financial problems by driving up the costs of health care but, in combination with other cost increases, has now led to significant problems in allocation of resources. Government funding of research led to free and unpatented use of all the technology that research created. If the costs of the research had to be recovered, as private industry would need to do, the financial situation in medicine would look very different, for the high costs would be more apparent beforehand. Industry might take a very jaundiced view of processes that were expensive to develop and had either an uncertain audience or a small audience. Joseph Newhouse, a Rand Corporation economist and expert on health insurance, has suggested that eliminating the National Institutes of Health would put an immediate stop to continued technological expansion, but that is only partly true. Some technologies *would* wither but others would continue to develop, especially those that had obvious commercial applicability with large numbers of people wanting the service. For example, although the government has refused to become involved in research that includes in vitro fertilization and embryo transfer to treat infertility among Americans, the private sector has funded the research just because it looked to be a profit maker.

Even if the government reduced (as it has) or eliminated (which it will not) its commitment to funding medical research, it would be left with the effects of all the technology that currently exists. Some scientists argue that further research and technological development will solve the current problems. Thus, some argue that the burdensome costs of kidney dialysis will be resolved not by more judicious use of dialysis but by increased success with kidney transplants. On the other side, the demand for heart transplants far exceeds any possible supply of usable cadaver hearts. Here, the technologists argue that the development of the artificial heart will eliminate the need to turn away patients and thus ensure greater justice. Justice will, of course, be purchased only at great price. Justice may improve momentarily. Increased costs will then make fairness less possible in practice, exacerbating the ethical problems even further.

Health care can be rationed in obvious or less obvious ways. Current attempts by the federal and state governments to reduce Medicare and Medicaid costs by changing methods of reimbursement may well result in a form of rationing that is unannounced and difficult to track down. Premature infants with indigent or underinsured parents may not be given the acute and intensive care that is currently routine simply because the hospitals cannot afford to pick up the extra costs themselves. Newspapers are now reporting that seriously ill elderly patients are being moved on to nursing homes—moves that result in earlier deaths—when the costs of their treatment exceed what will be reimbursed through Medicare. Hospitals may cut back on services to those people without political power as a form of cost-saving. This kind of rationing threatens much of the equity that has been achieved in American health care in the past twenty-five years.

The biggest problem with unannounced rationing is that it demeans us as humans. By permitting "unconscious" rationing, we avoid making the hard choices directly and instead make them blindly, without admitting to ourselves what we are actually doing. It is "line-of-least-resistance" rationing and supremely lacking in ethical sensitivity. It may be that as a society we would choose not to subsidize treatment of very premature newborns because we would prefer to put our health dollars into better prenatal care. Or we might choose not to automatically provide heroic care to elderly, frail, and demented or permanently unconscious patients because we prefer to put those health care dollars into improving nutrition or medical-social services for the elderly while they can still appreciate their lives. These, however, are conscious ethical choices that include assessments of different social values. They are also forms of rationing health care. The rationing that is currently being attempted is the worst kind, for it is chaotic and hidden and probably reaches most quickly to those who are most vulnerable and least powerful. It elevates the preferences of the wealthy and affluent to moral values and reduces the very lives and well-being of the less af-

fluent and the poor to matters of indifference. And it permits us to
deny what we are doing.

Conclusion

Health care does not exist in the abstract. It is not merely a series of
policies laid down from on high. Health care starts with a single
person, with particular feelings, thoughts, and desires, who lives in
relationship to other people. In the health care setting, that person
meets with a physician who also has individual beliefs and feelings
about the role of the physician and about his or her own humanness.
Because health care always starts with the meeting of those individuals, we have chosen to include extensive case studies. The cool distance of rational decision making is not always (and perhaps never)
possible in the face of the heated closeness of people's lives in crisis.
We can hope that rational decisions will result, but rationality must
be distilled from the deeply felt emotions that can be grasped only in
the immediacy of the individual case.

Physicians have often claimed that no external authority can
make decisions in health care because every case is different and
only the doctor and patient understand the nuances of the individual case. It is our belief that although every case surely is different in
its entirety, there are certain kinds of fundamental similarities that
can be conveyed to those who are not on the scene. What is important is that those who are to make decisions or to formulate policies
appreciate the intensity and importance of human concerns, even if
they do not observe them at first hand. There is an inevitable tension
between the individual case and the public policy. One cannot make
public policies on the basis of only an individual case. For example,
in 1982, an Indiana court allowed a baby with Down's syndrome to
die because the parents did not want to keep it alive. This case resulted in government regulations requiring posters in every hospital
in the country announcing a hot-line number that was to be called if
anyone thought an infant was being improperly treated. The posters
were abrasive and insulting and inappropriate, even though the purpose was a good one. The regulations did not result from stupidity
or thoughtlessness. Rather, an extreme set of regulations was developed in response to a single case. Regulations must apply to many
variants of a single case, and policy makers must also understand

how a regulation will affect the individuals whose lives are touched by those cases. It is only when we take human lives rather than numbers into account that we can understand where our values actually lie. An analysis that attempts to quantify all the factors inevitably distorts our aspirations to be more human and to be more humane. Conversely, focusing only on individual cases leads us to try to be everything to everyone, to deny that life must inevitably have pain and sorrow and that it must sometime end. An exclusive focus on individual cases does not deny values, but leaves us confused, undefined, and ultimately unable to accept our inevitable human limitations and the fact of death.

The challenge of decision making in health care is to combine our concern for individual patients with our concern for the entire society in which we live. In choosing for ourselves, we may also have to ask questions about our entire society:

What kind of people do we want to be? What kind of people do we want to live among? In order to be that kind of society, what must we give up? Inevitably, something must be lost, must be sacrificed.

Do we wish to be a society that welcomes and values its children, regardless of their condition or of whether their parents want them? Or do we wish to be a society in which no one has to operate at a significant disadvantage because of severe physical or mental handicaps when we have no way of remedying those handicaps?

Do we want to be a society in which everyone is entitled to children with genetic backgrounds of the parent's choice, even at the risk of children being viewed as property? Or do we want to be a society that protects all the children that currently are among us before we commit resources to creating new ones?

Do we want to be a society that preserves all life as long as possible, even at great cost, in order to demonstrate our respect for human life? Or do we want to be a society that gently lets go of those near death, even at the risk of also turning away from the severely ill or aged who are a burden and bring no apparent benefits?

These are the kinds of questions that we must begin to address now that we have the power to choose life or death.

CHAPTER 2

Kidney Dialysis
Catastrophic Illness
or National Catastrophe?

In 1960, Dr. Belding Scribner invented a medical device called a shunt. It revolutionized the treatment of chronic kidney disease, which is also known as end-stage renal failure. Before the shunt, patients with nonfunctioning kidneys died. After the shunt, they lived. The shunt cured no disease, but it provided physicians with reliable access to the patient's veins, and in this way it saved thousands and thousands of lives. It is the prototypical success story of modern medicine: where there had been certain death, now there was continued life, although of reduced quality.

Normally, the kidneys remove toxic substances from the blood. If the kidneys fail, the patient is slowly poisoned and dies. Research had earlier provided a dialysis machine that could cleanse the patient's blood, but the purification had to be performed several times each week. Every time, entry had to be made through the patient's veins. A vein will stand up to such treatment only so long; then it collapses and another vein must be used. Unfortunately the body has a limited number of veins that are large enough to accommodate the dialysis needles. When the veins are used up, dialysis is no longer possible and death follows. Belding Scribner changed all this by developing a plastic shunt that could be more or less permanently implanted in the patient's vein. Since the tubes of the dialysis unit could enter the patient's veins over and over again through the shunt, dialysis could be performed repeatedly as long as the patient

23

needed it. And the patient would need it, eight hours a day, three times a week, for as long as he lived.

Who benefited from this advance? Anyone. Kidney failure is not, for example, a disease of old age. It is the product of many other diseases, most frequently of hypertension, but the young, middle-aged, and the old are all susceptible. Early estimates were that perhaps 2000 to 3000 lives could be saved each year. Scribner's shunt and the existing short-term kidney dialysis joined to provide one of the first high-technology treatments that did not cure and yet extended life for those who would otherwise have died quickly.

The shunt was an important breakthrough, but some problems remained. There were very few machines—and many more patients than the equipment could handle. Furthermore, the treatment was extremely expensive—more than most patients could pay, especially when they would have to incur that expense every week for the rest of their lives. And finally, the patient's life-style with dialysis was very restricted—totally dependent upon the dialysis machine, the patient would be hard pressed ever again to conceive of himself or herself as an independent individual. If a person could find a machine, the emotional and financial cost of staying alive was extremely high. On the other hand, life was life.

The new hopes generated by Scribner's shunt were muted, however, when hospitals were faced with the problem of deciding which patients were to receive dialysis—and live—and which ones were to be rejected—and die.

Case Study

Joseph Wiler never met Carol Anne Cartwright, and it is probably just as well. He was a 25-year-old sculptor and she was a 35-year-old school teacher when, in 1965, they both suffered complete kidney failure. For Joseph, the failure was no surprise. He expected it, had known for several years that his kidneys were slowly losing their ability to cleanse his blood. Several other members of his extended family, including his father and one of his uncles, had died while still in the prime of life from the same disease. Because he felt he was being stalked by death, he had focused all his energies on his work, and had created a remarkable kind of sculpture. Its form bristled with the anger of a doomed man, but it conveyed as well a sense of the eternal connectedness of natural forms. Joseph was young and untaught and his work held a rough, electric energy that was not of much interest to the art world. He was not a world-famous artist, not even a well-known local artist. He lived with his mother in the family home, used the family garage as a studio, occasionally held part-time jobs that required no particular skills and made no significant demands upon him other than to take some of his precious time. In exchange, the work provided him with enough money to finance his sculpture.

His passion for his work, his family's disapproval of his life choices, and the knowledge that his physical condition might deteriorate rapidly (his father had died before reaching the age of 30) combined to isolate him from the world. Family members constantly worried about his behavior and urged him to be more careful about his health. He was advised to get more rest, to see his doctor more frequently or to get a new doctor he liked more, to drink and smoke less, to lead a steady life, to get a girl friend, to dress better, to get a steady job (preferably a good job), and please-please-please to be someone more acceptable to them. Joseph brushed away their concerns with the intolerance of youth and with the indifference of a man who already knows how the story will end.

On a regularly scheduled visit to his doctor, Joseph appeared undismayed by the news that the long-expected deterioration of kidney function was almost complete. His doctor had previously urged him to think about the new dialysis techniques there were proving so successful, but when Joseph heard that he would be required to stay in the hospital for three or four days out of every week, he had been unwilling even to discuss the matter further. Now, with no alternative but death, the doctor reintroduced the topic of dialysis. Joseph agreed at least to explore it and with that encouragement, the physician submitted his name to the hospital as a suitable candidate for long-term dialysis treatment.

Carol Anne Cartwright was unbelieving when she first heard her doctor tell her that she was seriously ill. She had no sense of herself as a sick person. Recently she had found herself growing tired and out of breath after very little exertion, but she had assumed that it was simply a result of end-of-the-school-year exhaustion. After twelve years of teaching third-graders, she had no illusions about the stamina that was required to keep up with thirty 8-year-olds for five days a week. It didn't surprise her that she no longer had as much energy as she had once had. The swelling in her ankles was surely just a matter of being on her feet all day long. With age, that could happen to anyone. When her physician explained to her and her husband that she was now facing total loss of kidney function, she began to formulate questions about what she had done wrong and what she could now do to correct those errors. Carol Anne faced her illness with the same spirit that she daily conveyed to her students: after finding out what is expected, work with neatness, quietness, and precision.

Her doctor explained that there were two possible treatments: first, a kidney transplant with a donation from a relative or a cadaver; second, the new long-term dialysis treatments. Transplants were still chancy, especially if there was no family donor whose tissue type closely matched the patient's. On the other hand, dialysis was low-risk but high-cost. Even if the money problem could be solved, Carol Anne would have to apply to be accepted for treatment. She might be chosen; she might not be. It was possible, however, that some of the costs would be taken on by the hospital if she were accepted into the program. The physician strongly recommended that she try dialysis. Within twenty-four hours, Carol Anne had considered the options and had decided to apply for the dialysis program. Her doctor immediately began preparing the necessary medical documents and arranging for a social worker to interview the patient, her husband, and children.

The Treatment Committee of St. Anne's Community Hospital met only when there was an opening in the kidney dialysis program. The members felt there was no point in making purely academic decisions about who should receive treatment when there were no available dialysis machines. The program was heavily subsidized both by federal and state funds, but there was not sufficient money to buy enough machines for everyone who needed treatment. Fortunately, the committee had had to turn away very few people. With good scheduling, the hospital's three dialysis machines could serve fifteen patients a week. Of course, when all fifteen slots were filled, the committee didn't consider any requests, so there were people who wanted and needed treatment but weren't getting it. But the committee wasn't actually turning them away. In any case, as one of the members pointed out, just a few years ago, everybody with kidney failure was dying, so the fact that some people were still dying wasn't nearly as critical as the fact that some people were now living.

New openings in the treatment program occurred when a patient left the hospital because he or she had been accepted in a dialysis program closer to home; when a patient received a cadaver kidney transplant and no longer needed dialysis; when a patient died of some cause unrelated to the kidney problem; or when a patient died from the kidney disease or from failing to comply with the medically prescribed regimen, a failure that many suspected was nothing more nor less than suicide. The committee was meeting now because a cadaver transplant had been successfully performed on one of the dialysis patients and a slot for a new patient had opened up. Two medically acceptable candidates were now before the committee: Carol Anne Cartwright and Joseph Wiler.

The committee included six members, two doctors (one a psychiatrist), one hospital administrator, one nurse, and a clergyman and a lawyer from the community. Except for the committee members themselves, only the hospital director knew who was on the committee. The decision to form the committee had been handled quietly and there had been no reason to identify the prospective members publicly. Then, after the first meeting, they had requested that their identities be kept secret because they feared that prospective patients would seek them out to argue for their lives. It had seemed a sensible request to the director for other reasons as well: if the hospital were going to ask the members to decide who was to live and who to die, it did not need to burden them additionally by making them publicly accountable for their choices.

In addition, the committee decided never to see the actual patients nor their physicians, first, so that they themselves would not be identified, but second, and more important, so that their decisions would not be inappropriately or emotionally biased. All information was to be submitted to the committee in writing, and for those purposes, special interview forms were developed in order to provide relevant information about the prospective patient's character, family background, employment history, economic situation, psychological stability, and community status.

Hospital social workers interviewed the family, friends, and colleagues of the patient as well as the patient him- or herself. In addition, the patient's doctor was asked to provide an extensive written assessment of the patient's ability to tolerate the rigors of treatment, to comply with the strict medical and dietary regimen, and to return to independent functioning. At bottom, that was the committee's standard for the best dialysis patients: those who were strong enough to handle a lifetime of complex and demanding treatment, who were intelligent enough to understand and follow intricate directions, and who would work hard to regain for themselves the life of productive, independent citizens, in the face of a continuing need for medical care that made normal life impossible.

When the committee met to consider the cases of Carol Anne Cartwright and Joseph Wiler, they had a great deal of information about the two. Carol Anne, according to her doctor, was a responsible patient, willing to adhere to strict medical and dietary requirements and able to do so. Her prospects of surviving with dialysis were excellent. The physician's judgment of her character glowed; he clearly found her a particularly worthy patient. She had a sympathetic and supportive husband, was respected by her fellow teachers, and had a temperate disposition. She was a devoted wife and mother of two charming young children. She had no debts and possessed a substantial savings account. She was realistic in her understanding of the implications of dialysis and accepted the necessity for giving up her career in order to undergo treatment. As the committee moved through its checklist of positive factors for selection, Carol Anne received the highest marks.

The members then moved on to assess their information about Joseph. His physician pointed out that this energetic young man's prognosis was good to excellent with dialysis. He characterized Joseph as a difficult though appealing patient. Intellectually he was perfectly capable of understanding what was expected of him, but he did not comply automatically. He was not a docile patient. On the other hand, if a relationship of trust could be established, Joseph would do what was needed, although perhaps in his own way. As the committee members heard the long letter from the physician read aloud, several members began to grow uncomfortable with what they were hearing. Mr. Wiler was beginning to sound uncomfortably individualistic. It was all well and good for individual physicians to enjoy the challenge of a demanding relationship with an unusual patient, but in the high-pressure atmosphere of the dialysis unit, there was no room for prima donnas. Mr. Wiler sounded like a patient who would take too much of everyone's time.

The final assessments of the two social workers who had interviewed Wiler and his friends, family, and associates were not in agreement. One report strongly intimated that he would be a good candidate; the other implied that he would not be. The disapproving report focused on the fact that he had no close friends and suggested that this was evidence of psychological imbalance. His lack of a steady job or of genuine career aspirations seemed problematic.

The interview with the patient himself had left the social worker with the feeling that he perhaps did not really want to undergo treatment as he had expressed considerable reservation—even resentment—about being "trapped" in the hospital all the time. He even seemed indifferent about whether the hospital would accept him into the treatment program.

The approving social worker, on the other hand, emphasized Joseph's artistic inclinations, pointing out his resourcefulness in being willing to make a living doing nondemanding work in order to reserve his energies for his creative work. She found him full of plans for the future and the creation of new sculptures. When Joseph's mother had expressed her willingness to provide as much financial help as she could (which would probably be very little) as well as to provide whatever other support might be needed, the social worker applauded Joseph's reaction. He had bristled at the idea of his mother's having to take care of him as if he were an incompetent child. The social worker pointed out that Joseph's strong desire for independence would keep him from sinking into the kind of dependent lethargy that was so common among dialysis patients, who were almost literally chained to their machines and their doctors. Furthermore, the fact that he was unmarried and had no children meant that there were no people dependent upon him and that he would not have to be emotionally drained by family problems during the difficult adjustment period at the beginning of dialysis.

Neither candidate could be disqualified by any of the standard factors: they were both residents of the state; neither had a criminal record; neither was mentally defective. They were not under the age of 18 nor over the age of 45. They were not indigent nor did they come from a poor family environment. Wiler's employment record was spotty, but it could not really be characterized as poor. They were both intelligent and they had no other disabling diseases. Clearly, if there were space for two additional dialysis patients, both were acceptable. But there was only one space.

The two final categories on the committee's general checklist were willingness to cooperate with treatment and ability to be vocationally rehabilitated. Here the committee members began to find some grounds for distinguishing the two applicants. There was no question but that Carol Anne would be a cooperative patient. Everyone had attested to her willingness and her sense of responsibility in such matters. With Joseph there was a question. He was clearly an unconventional person. Several committee members voiced their feeling that unconventionality was all right in its place, but was the hospital dialysis ward the right place? The nurse on the committee spoke of her experiences with dialysis patients and described how difficult it was for everyone if any of the patients became disruptive. Everyone was so bound together in dialysis that one patient's emotions always flowed over into everyone else's life. She thought that the committee ought to recruit only those patients who would contribute good feelings, not bring bad ones. She pointed out that the unit was very much like a family, with everyone dependent upon each other, and she didn't think that Mr. Wiler would be very happy in that kind of situation.

There was a general murmur of agreement from the committee members who were affiliated with the hospital. They had all spent time with patients who resented their illness and took it out on everyone around them. That kind of patient wanted to argue about every single blood test and what time of day blood could be drawn from their veins. They knew far better than the doctors and nurses which medicine would help and which wouldn't. They were always showing up with some tattered newspaper clipping or demanding that they be given the new treatment touted by the *Reader's Digest*, all the while suggesting that if they had a really good doctor he or she would be doing this research instead of leaving it to them. They were seldom grateful for all that was being done for them, which would be all right if they weren't so unrelentingly unpleasant to boot. They spoiled the work. With such patients, medicine hardly seemed a caring profession.

Still, Mr. Wiler did have his good points. The lawyer on the committee steered the group onto the question of vocational rehabilitation. Did it seem likely that that would be possible for either patient? He himself was of the opinion that Mrs. Cartwright might be such a good patient that she would give up everything else to become a good patient. She appeared almost anxious to give up her job, whereas Wiler sounded like somebody who would do everything he could to get back to being a productive member of society. He wasn't so sure that his view of productive work was shared by Mr. Wiler, but still, perhaps artists contribute something even if they are not successful. The committee physician thought that it would be impossible for Mrs. Cartwright to continue her teaching career under the present conditions of hospital dialysis, but that in any case, she was a wife and the mother of two children and she would be fully able to contribute to society in that role. He gently pointed out to the lawyer that she would have to be dependent upon medical care for the rest of her life and that it was unrealistic to require that she not accept those limitations.

The clergyman sensed the committee's growing agreement that Carol Anne Cartwright was the better candidate for the program but was also aware that some members could not comfortably reject Joseph Wiler unless they could find an acceptable reason for doing so. In an attempt to find some kind of reason, he asked the committee's psychiatrist member what he thought about Wiler's chances. Did Wiler seem to have difficulty in dealing with authority figures? And would that increase the natural stress of being in the dialysis program so much that Wiler might abandon dialysis after he began it?

The psychiatrist acknowledged the possibility, pointing out that there was some evidence of an unusually high rate of either direct or indirect suicide among dialysis patients who couldn't cope with the burdens of such a restricted life. She thought that Wiler was the type who would be capable of taking that kind of action because he apparently had such strong ideas about how things should be. Faced with the disparity between how things ought to be and how they were under dialysis, the psychiatrist thought that Wiler might decide that no life was better than a life in bondage. Certainly it would not surprise her if that were to be the case.

The members' questions and comments began to dwindle and the clergyman now proposed a formal vote. Carol Anne Cartwright was to be accepted immediately for kidney dialysis. But the lawyer suggested a compromise for Joseph Wiler. He would not be rejected but would be deferred for judgment and considered again for the next opening.

Carol Anne began dialysis almost immediately. She was an excellent patient and, the next year, when home dialysis units were introduced, she and her husband were among the first to be trained. She has cared for her children and husband and lived a surprisingly normal life, considering the burden of her illness. She has coped well with the demands upon both her and her husband to orient much of their life around her illness. They hesitate to travel far, because complex and time-consuming arrangements must be made with other dialysis facilities if they are away from home for more than a day or two.

She has learned to abide within the strict diet of the dialysis patient. Not for her the casual cup of coffee or the tall, cold glass of ice water on a sultry day. She must calculate every ounce of fluid that her body takes in, and very little is too much. No salt, as little potassium as possible, tiny portions of water-rich fruits and vegetables, and tiny amounts of protein are her daily commandments. She has learned what it is like to gain six to ten pounds through fluid retention every few days and then to lose it in a few hours through dialysis, leaving her weak and dizzy. She has lived through the muscle spasms and cramps, the dizziness, the nausea, the piles of pills every day, and the ceaseless medical routine of a person who must regularly attend to and observe the washing of her own blood. For Carol Anne, the alternative was death and she cannot imagine that the hardships she has endured are not justified by the fact that she continues to see each new day.

Joseph Wiler did not survive long enough to be reconsidered for the dialysis program. He became sicker and sicker and finally was admitted to the hospital only when he was too weak to protest the action any longer. Almost immediately after admission, he lapsed into a coma and died.

───────────

These painful selection processes were repeated in hospitals throughout the United States during the years between 1962 and 1972. Kidney dialysis became a uniquely frustrating problem. Having discovered a way to keep patients alive, physicians were unable to use the method either because there were no dialysis machines available or because the patient had no way to pay for the extremely expensive treatment. As a result, doctors had to tell patients that although treatment existed that would certainly extend their lives, they could not receive it. When doctors and patients and their families looked for funding sources for additional machines and hospital space, the suppliers of funds—insurance companies and government agencies—were unwilling to be wooed. Although the number of patients needing treatment appeared to be fairly small, some people feared that dialysis funding could prove to be a very expensive and problematic choice. They were right.

In 1962, *Life* magazine published an article by Shana Alexander describing how the selection committee chose patients for Belding Scribner's dialysis unit in Seattle, Washington. The story provoked widespread comment, and considerable disapproval was expressed about anonymous committees playing God. The story did not produce a significant public demand for change, however. The number of people who yearly suffered from kidney failure was small—surely not more than 3000 throughout the United States. Thus, the number of people directly affected by the availability of dialysis (these 3000 plus their families) was too small to create any kind of political force, especially since they were not concentrated in any single geographical area.

It is not hard to see why there was so little government response in the early 1960s. Dialysis was very new—the first four patients to receive long-term dialysis had begun treatment in Scribner's experimental program only in 1960. It was experimental and few statistics demonstrated its success. Perhaps it would provide only a brief life-extension. Perhaps if it were effective, it would be so only for a very small group of patients who met strict medical criteria. It would take at least five years to collect enough data to find out how good the treatment was. Many policy makers believed it would be foolish to pursue this very expensive treatment when there was still so little evidence that it would prove the miracle that some doctors believed it to be. As Dr. Scribner himself pointed out, no other treatment was as expensive as dialysis and the expense would continue every year for the rest of the patient's life. The government might have taken a chance on underwriting a cheap treatment, but not such an expensive one.

As a result of conclusions like these, those few hospitals in the country that were using dialysis on an experimental basis in the early 1960s were obliged to keep their programs small and to screen their patients very carefully. Either the physicians on the unit, their hospital colleagues, or committees of doctors and lay persons were stuck with the unhappy job of deciding who should live and who should die. It was not a situation that could last. Either dialysis would prove ineffective and would be abandoned or used only as a treatment of last resort, or dialysis would prove effective and it would have to be dealt with as an accepted, standard treatment for end-stage renal disease.

In 1963, the first change in the official mask of disinterest came. The Veterans' Administration began providing dialysis at V.A. hospitals to all veterans who needed it. Then, in 1964, dialysis machines that could be used in the home at a much lower cost than in-hospital dialysis were made available. By 1965, the statistics on patient survival were beginning to look very good. After an average of two years on dialysis machines, 87 percent of the patients were still alive. Most had returned to productive lives.

The government could no longer ignore the issue. The U.S. Public Health Service established a research program and funded several kidney dialysis demonstration programs. Public Health was to provide initial three-year funding; then the centers were to find other moneys. If lives were to be saved, the government intended that, in the long run, someone else would pay for the saving.

The search for financial support for dialysis had always been directed at the federal government because only at that level could equity be provided. If each state had to be convinced, then inevitably some states would fail to provide funds. Nor could each person in need be expected to take to the streets or the newspapers and television, pleading for donations for his or her life, although many did. The federal government's slow response, of course, made the problem an intensely personal one for those who needed treatment and for their families. The government was involved in expanding a war in Vietnam, however, and Lyndon Johnson was certain that guns and butter were both possible. Others felt that, at least in the abstract, guns, butter, and kidney dialysis were not all possible or even necessary.

Between 1965 and 1972, over one hundred bills were introduced by individual members of the U.S. Congress as their constituents reached out to them, urging them to provide some kind of extensive federal support for kidney disease. Yet, according to Richard Rettig (perhaps the longest surviving chronicler of the dialysis drama) not one single hearing was ever scheduled until *after* the passage of the 1972 amendment that extended Medicare coverage to all victims of end-stage renal disease under the age of 65. The passage of this amendment, which was discussed on the floor of the Senate for a full ten minutes before the members voted overwhelmingly in its favor, is somewhat puzzling. The tenor of the senators' limited discussion suggests something about why it passed. Senator Vance Hartke berated his colleagues for the primitive ethics that preferred the deaths of American citizens to expenditures of mere public dollars. Senator Henry "Scoop" Jackson, a senator who was particularly familiar with Dr. Belding Scribner's work in Seattle, told his colleagues that it was "a great tragedy, in a nation as affluent as ours, that we have to consciously make a decision all over America as to the people who will live and the people who will die."

Prior to the introduction of this amendment, dialysis patients personally told congressional committees that without financial support they were dead people. One patient was dialyzed before a congressional committee. The newspapers, radio, and television also recounted the stories of people who faced death because they could not afford dialysis. A government that had permitted far too many unjustified deaths in an undeclared war in Vietnam had this chance to save someone. Although the 1972 amendment excluded those citizens who were ineligible for Social Security protection, it did extend coverage to over 90 percent of American citizens. To those in Congress who voted in favor of this extension of Medicare benefits, it seemed the only decent thing to do.

Like the treatment committees in the hospitals, the Congress was being given the responsibility for deciding who should live and who must die. The resounding passage of the amendment affirmed the view that, in this country, life is precious and everyone has the right to receive all the medical care he or she needs at government expense. Or, at least they had the right to all the medical care they needed if they had end-stage renal disease, for no other catastrophic disease was or has ever been given total financial coverage by the federal government. Congress thought they were providing life-saving treatment for a maximum of approximately 20,000 patients. In 1974, Belding Scribner was still predicting that the number of people needing kidney dialysis would stabilize at about 20,000. But Scribner was wrong this time. In 1980, 60,000—not 20,000—people were on the Medicare rolls as beneficiaries of the End-Stage Renal Disease Program, a number made possible by the 1972 Social Security Act amendments.

Now the expected $75 million outlay has mushroomed to nearly $2 billion and contributes significantly to the weak financial structure of Social Security's Medicare program. When the experts made their predictions, they did not anticipate that guaranteeing payment, even when the patients themselves had to cover some costs, would encourage much more widespread use of dialysis, in many more questionable cases. The terrible days of choosing between patients who desired, needed, and could benefit from treatment were over. Within a very few years, dialysis centers were relatively common and anyone in kidney failure was promptly placed on dialysis, regardless of medical prognosis. Families began to beg that patients *not* be given dialysis, though these requests were seldom honored, whether they came from the family or the patients themselves. The human impulse to provide treatment for everyone led to a new era of problems with dialysis: the 1960s problem of scarce resources gave way to the very different problems of excess resources in the 1980s, whereby individual patients were unable to choose *not* to receive dialysis.

Case Study

In 1978, an 80-year-old man named Ned Thomas was hospitalized with end-stage renal disease. Ned had been a patient in a nursing home for the past eight years as a result of advanced senility. His children had placed him in the nursing home when his wife, Rebecca, became too ill to care for him. When she died, three years later, Ned's senility had advanced to the point that he no longer recognized her or their children. By the time he was transferred to the hospital, Ned's ability to relate to anyone was minimal. He frequently went without speaking at all for many days, and seldom uttered more than a few words at a time when he did talk. The attendants at the nursing home occasionally observed him weeping, but no one had been able to engage him in coherent conversation during those times.

When Ned Thomas became ill, the nursing home director informed Thomas's two children, Fred and Lila, that Ned would have to be transferred to the local hospital for treatment. Both Fred and Lila were so distressed by their father's condition that they were anxious to do anything that would help him to feel better. At the hospital, Ned was immediately placed on dialysis. The attending physician explained to Fred and Lila that without regular dialysis treatments their father would die. Ned would be kept in the hospital for a week or two, but after that, he could be transferred from the nursing home to the hospital three times each week in order to continue the dialysis treatments. Concerned about the cost of the treatments, on top of the nursing home charges they were paying, Fred and Lila were assured by the young doctor that the treatment would involve very little hardship to them since Social Security paid almost all the costs.

For two months, Ned was transferred back and forth each Monday, Wednesday, and Friday. The nursing home staff dreaded those days because the old man became so truculent when they prepared him for the trip. The dialysis staff, too, were unhappy to see Ned arrive. He occasionally kicked a nurse who came too close, and he regularly ripped the dialysis needle out of his arm. He was an old and frail man, but all his strength seemed to gather together to express his anger at the treatment he was receiving. In order to transfer and treat him successfully, the physician prescribed heavy sedatives. When Ned came out from under the medication's influence, he frequently was very dizzy, once falling down a staircase. After that, he was kept more closely confined to his room except when someone could keep a watch on him.

At the beginning of the third month, Lila asked her father's physician to stop the treatments. He lectured her sternly about her request, pointing out that she was asking for her father's death, in the face of treatment that could keep him alive. He reminded her that only five years earlier, people died because dialysis was not available for everyone who could benefit from it. She was lucky, he concluded, that her father had not developed the condition earlier. Lila hesitantly reported her discussion with the doctor to Fred but was comforted to find that he shared her uncertainty about their father's treatment. They decided to wait a few more weeks to see whether their father would adjust before they spoke to the doctor again.

In the following weeks, Ned began to develop severe leg cramps, causing him to cry out in pain. His periods of weeping began to increase and each time his children saw him, they felt worse about the anguished life he seemed to be living. Lila discussed the situation with a sympathetic nurse on the dialysis unit, and bolstered by her comments, she and Fred concluded that the physician must not understand the quality of her father's daily life. If only they could adequately explain the old man's agony to him, perhaps the doctor would permit the treatments to cease.

A second consultation with the doctor was no more successful than the first one, although the physician did not criticize them. He seemed moved by their compassion for their father, but explained that he could not possibly stop treatment because it would be tantamount to killing his patient. His obligation, he explained was to the patient and to keeping him alive. If a decision were to be made to stop treatment, it would have to be made by someone higher up in the hospital than he or by a court. He arranged for them to meet with the chief of the service and with a hospital administrator. Both expressed their understanding of Fred's and Lila's concerns but assured them treatment could not be stopped as long as it was lifesaving. The administrator explained the hospital's legal concerns and the service chief pointed out his own moral belief that it would be wrong to abandon the patient by stopping lifesaving treatment. He realized that Mr. Thomas was fretful about the discomforts caused by dialysis, but, he reiterated, it was his only access to life.

Realizing that the hospital was unmovable, Fred and Lila appealed to the legal system. Two months later, an appellate court judge gave final approval to Fred and Lila's request to end the dialysis treatment. The thrice-weekly transfers to the hospital came to an abrupt halt and Ned died in his sleep within a week. He had spoken no recognizable word for over six weeks and had made scarcely a sound in the last week of his life. The lawyer's bill was considerable, but Medicare paid for the dialysis.

The Decision Makers: Their Perspectives and Interests

Kidney dialysis has advanced in the last fifteen years from being a matter of too little treatment to one of too much treatment. In order to understand how these decisions are made and why there is so much disagreement about who decides and what they decide, it is necessary to look at the perspectives of the different institutions, groups, and individuals who have a direct or indirect interest in the results of health care decisions. With respect to kidney dialysis, we must look at the perspectives and the concerns of doctors, nurses, the legal system, ethical analysts, and policy makers, before we determine what patients can do to have their wishes seriously considered.

Medical Perspectives

American doctors are quick to use kidney dialysis because it is effective, because it is available, and because payment is guaranteed. Medical education continues to focus on the physician's duty to preserve life whenever possible. Physicians who recall the days when kidney failure was untreatable or when treatment existed but was unavailable to the patient because of scarcity of machines or inadequate finances are very likely to provide treatment without hesitation when it is available. If patients themselves were required to pay for dialysis, physicians might be more hesitant to urge the treatment in the case of comatose patients or patients who are near death.

Since the cost to the patient is minimal, especially when in-hospital dialysis is used, physicians are inclined to use it routinely as a standard form of treatment, even in those cases where its value to the patient is marginal or negative. In addition, it is a very profitable form of treatment which is provided, in great part, by free-standing dialysis clinics owned by doctors.

More recently, some physicians have begun to talk about considering the quality of the life that they are saving. Although there is much to be said for this point of view, quality-of-life considerations always run the risk of being judged from the perspective of the individual who has a normal life, rather than from the perspective of the patient whose life is in question. The illness-ridden life of the geriatric patient may look to be of low and even negligible quality to the active, healthy, young physician. It may appear very different to the geriatric patient: complex, frustrating, and painful, it still may be better than no life at all. When quality-of-life considerations are being made, it is vital that the decision be based on patients' views of their lives, rather than on physicians' views.

Even when quality of life appears low, physicians may hesitate to accept family wishes to terminate treatment because it implies that sick, elderly patients are not worth treating. Doctors may be damned if they do provide treatment and damned if they don't. Because of this uncertainty, they sometimes insist upon courts taking final responsibility for a decision not to treat if that decision will result in the patient's death. Of course there are also sensitive and caring physicians who want to respect the patient's preferences but are pressured by family members to keep the patient alive at all costs. Sometimes physicians and families are fearful of legal consequences, although they may be acting in ignorance of what the law permits or requires by continuing futile treatments and procedures.

Nursing Perspectives

Because nurses provide the day-to-day and even minute-to-minute care to their patients, they frequently develop very protective attitudes toward them. In addition, they are more sensitized to the patients' own responses to treatment, especially because they see responses across time, as opposed to responses that are generated during brief physician visits. As well, nurses are frequently the source of much of the family's psychological comfort.

Dialysis unit nurses bear the substantial burden of caring for dialysis patients who do not want dialysis. Whether the patients act out their anger with physical blows, as Ned Thomas did, or through psychological assaults as do patients who are disruptive, rude, and indifferent to unit rules, the nurses are on the receiving end of the anger, not the doctors. Many nurses express their discouragement with patients who refuse to comply with the medical regimen that dialysis requires and who repeatedly have to be brought back from death's door. Caring for those who want to live can be exciting, rewarding, hard work. When patients are ambivalent about or indifferent to life, it makes the nurses' work much harder and far less gratifying.

Legal Perspectives

The law is no more comfortable with these cases than physicians are, but when they reach the courts, judges are obliged to provide answers as well as offer their reasons. In some cases, courts base their decisions upon whether a specific form of treatment can be considered extraordinary/heroic or ordinary/necessary. The former is optional; the latter is required. This distinction has not been very useful, however, because it is not clear exactly what the terms *ordinary* and *extraordinary* mean. Although dialysis is extraordinary treatment, in the sense that it is complex and expensive, its wide availability and routine use make it appear to be ordinary and usual. Recently, some courts have introduced a new distinction: "proportionate and disproportionate treatment." This distinction attempts to compare the complexity, invasiveness, and discomforts of the treatment with the potential benefits of its use (burdens vs. benefits). It appears at first glance to be more productive than the older heroic-ordinary treatment distinction. It too, however, suffers from critical difficulties.

Unfortunately, we have no way to measure the proportions and thus to balance the likelihood of benefit with the degree of benefit. For example, one treatment might be relatively simple, not very invasive, and involve few discomforts, with an 80–90 percent chance of sustaining nonconscious life. Is such a treatment more or less proportionate than one that is difficult, invasive, and *moderately* uncomfortable, and that has only a 10 percent probability of sustaining conscious life? One does little good and little harm; the other may do a lot of harm but it may do a lot of good. How are we to judge? In the absence of patient preferences, such measurements are very uncertain.

In some cases in which the patient has been unable to express a preference, because he is either unconscious or mentally incompetent, courts have used the doctrine of substituted judgment, rather than the ordinary/extraordinary or proportionate/disproportionate distinction. In these cases, a guardian is appointed. The guardian, who may be a relative, must try to decide what the patient did want (if the patient ever expressed a preference) or would have wanted (if the patient didn't) if he were able to make the request. Judges have gone to considerable lengths to argue that these do not constitute quality-of-life decisions on the part of the court. The decision involves a quality-of-life judgment, but it is to be made (if only imaginatively) by the patient through his guardian. Fearful of opening the doors to legally sanctioned quality-of-life decisions made by third parties, the courts have had to provide very twisted reasonings for these decisions. Nevertheless, their insistence that the guardian attempt to determine what the patient would have wanted and then to explain that decision to the court makes the process more self-consciously rational than intuitive quantifications of benefits and burdens.

Courts have ordered that dialysis treatment be stopped when family members requested it and when treatment seemed to provide no benefit to the patient other than to continue physical existence. Courts accept stopping lifesaving treatment when patients are permanently unconscious. When they are still conscious, but senile, the legal climate is more uncertain. Courts are most impressed in these cases by evidence that stopping treatment is consistent with the patient's own wishes. Court decisions would establish procedures for withdrawing dialysis without prior court approval, but even if they did, hospitals might be reluctant to follow such procedures if there was disagreement among family members or if the medical staff involved did not believe that stopping treatment was appropriate.

Ethical Perspectives

Ethicists are likely to consider two major questions about the automatic use of dialysis with end-stage renal disease patients when the benefits are minimal—for example, when it would merely prolong the dying of an irreversibly comatose patient. (What counts as benefits so minimal that they do not justify treatment, however, is and is likely to remain controversial no matter who makes the decision.) The first is whether a decision not to begin treatment is morally different from a decision to stop treatment once it has been started. The second is whether dialysis in this situation fails to respect the patient's human dignity.

Doctors frequently say that it is much easier not to treat patients in the first place than to withdraw treatment once it has been initiated. Ethicists generally maintain that there is no moral difference between the two. There is also a psychological difference for doctors, in that the physician has developed psychological attachments to the patient and has invested skill and time in keeping the patient alive. The doctor then has an investment in the patient's continuing to live and a personal desire for the patient to live. A decision to withdraw treatment denies the value of the physician's investment; it declares it, in a sense, an error of judgment, even though an inevitable one. As well, and perhaps more important, a decision to withdraw treatment is psychologically perceived as killing whereas failing to institute treatment can be perceived in other ways (e.g., inability to help because the case was hopeless).

From an ethical perspective, a physician shows respect for the patient by acceding to the patient's preferences and by acting in the patient's best interests. When a patient is incompetent, it is hard to know how to judge expressed preferences. If preferences were expressed previously, when the patient was competent, then these should be determinative. If there is no specific previously expressed wish, then the immediate family's preferences ought to be given very great moral weight unless there is some reason to suppose that their judgment is faulty with respect to the patient's attitudes and values.

Policy Perspectives

Policy makers struggled with the dialysis problem for years before providing federal funding. The current policy means that care is provided aggressively and widely to all whose kidneys have failed regardless of the perceived benefit to the patient. It also means that patients who want to stop dialysis must be very aggressive in their refusal. Dialysis patients receive special consideration as a result of policy decisions to fund all treatment. Often, they are expected to be especially grateful for this consideration. When they are non-compliant or unable to adjust to or accept the altered quality of life that dialysis gives them, they may be viewed with hostility by health providers because they have, in effect, refused the gift of life that society has generously extended to them. They have failed to be sufficiently appreciative of what is given to them.

What's a Patient to Do?

In this section we first look at certain aspects of the Ned Thomas case presented earlier. Then we provide some general guidance for persons confronted with choices about treatment for kidney failure.

In Ned Thomas's case there appears to be a very limited consideration of his quality of life and a very perfunctory respect for Ned as a person. Because Thomas is incompetent and his preferences cannot obviously be determined, he is treated as if he had no other desire than to stay alive. Keeping Ned alive may be in his interests, but it may also be reflex behavior on the physician's part, enabling him to feel he is doing something. What is missing is a thoughtful analysis of Thomas's condition and prospects. The physician appears to have no concern for Ned as a person or with Ned's preferences. Although Ned cannot state his preferences directly, the physician seems to be unwilling to consider that Ned's behavior indicates anything at all. When Ned resists transfer, attacks the unit nurses, and rips the dialysis needle from his arm, these are not considered to be hints of Ned's preferences. Instead, the physician pursues the goal of extending life while eliminating Ned's responses to treatment by sedating him as much as necessary. The doctor's preferences about treatment seem to be more important than the patient's indirectly expressed preferences or the considered judgments of the patient's children.

The physician is, however, in a difficult position. He has no knowledge of Ned prior to the time he arrives at the hospital for the dialysis treatment. Ned is unable or unwilling to communicate in any direct verbal way with the health care staff about his preferences. Because of his senility, he may be cognitively incompetent to convey his wishes and his resistance may be generalized fear.

One might question whether Lila or Fred are justified in asking that the dialysis treatments be stopped because of the side effects. If Ned had not demonstrated his distress before and during the treatments, would that make a difference? Is it the overall quality of Ned's life that leads us to think that treatment is disproportionate, or the individual aspects of the situation, including costs of treatment, burden on the care-givers, probability of extending life, and possibility of the patient's attitudes changing? Although the burdens on others are considerable, that cannot justify a decision to stop treatment. Only the benefits and burdens to the patient can morally be considered in denying life-extending medical care.

The nurses are sympathetic both to Ned's distress with treatment and to his children's unhappiness at having the dialysis inflicted upon their father. Nurses cannot, of course, ignore physician's orders, whatever their degree of compassion for the patient. Even though nurses may want to act as the patient's advocate rather than the physician's helper, they are caught in an administrative structure that often makes action difficult. It is, however, always advisable for the family to ascertain the nurses' perception of how treatment benefits the patient and to encourage them to convey their impressions to physicians.

Ned Thomas's case is typical in that the family makes an initial attempt to change the course of care but when immediate agreement is not forthcoming, everyone backs off. Fred and Lila failed to present a united front to the physician from the very beginning. They did not present a reasoned argument about why continued treatment was not indicated. By failing to use their superior knowledge of what their father was like as a person, they reduced the issue to a matter of personal opinion. In such a conflict, the expert medical opinion of the physician is bound to dominate. Lila and Fred needed to assure their father's physician that stopping treatment was what Ned himself would have wanted and to pursue why the doctors or hospital thought there was a legal risk. They could have suggested guardianship proceedings, if necessary, in order obtain court authorization to legally refuse consent for treatment. They should also have known whether other members of the treatment team thought dialysis should have been stopped and then they might have suggested a meeting in which everyone discussed what would be best.

Ideally, the question of what Ned wanted, of what would be best for him, should have arisen earlier when his competence was not so impaired. Typically, these questions are left until it is too late to get answers because patients and their families do not think to ask them and the health care team is uncomfortable broaching the subject of what should be done if matters get a lot worse instead of a lot better. Even though Ned is incompetent, his behavior suggests that he is not pleased with what is happening. His judgment at this stage is not determinative, but Fred and Lila need to press the physician to find out what benefits Ned is now receiving or can be expected to receive in the future by continuing this treatment that imposes so many burdens upon the patient.

Just as a decision had to be made in the case of Ned Thomas, any patient (or his or her representative) with end-stage renal failure must choose dialysis, transplantation, or death. The effects of kidney failure often include mental disturbances such as depression and confusion. Thus patients seen in crisis may not be competent to make decisions about the kind of treatment they want. Patients understandably want to believe that treatment will restore them to their previous condition. Dialysis has little promise of doing this, but transplantation may not be available. Choosing either dialysis or transplantation is a compromise, but it is a choice for life. Some patients, after experiencing dialysis, choose death. For them, the compromise is too great.

Currently, virtually every patient whose kidneys fail will automatically be offered and probably given dialysis. There is no shortage of equipment, staff, or funds. Dialysis may be provided in the hospital or in free-standing dialysis clinics, or, if the family is able to provide space and technical assistance, home dialysis units are available. Recently, short-term portable dialysis units have been developed that make it easier for dialysis patients to travel.

The abundance of resources may be reduced in the future as the government continues to cut back on health funding. It is unlikely, however, that dialysis patients will ever face patient selection committees like those of the 1960s (though transplant patients may do so). If coverage is reduced, however, treatment decisions may be handled as they are in England. Although the British have no stated policy about denying dialysis to older patients, as a matter of fact, few older patients in need of dialysis receive it. Because of inadequate resources, aged patients with end-stage renal disease are simply not told about dialysis. Their families are counseled that "there is nothing further to be done" and Grandma or Grandpa is taken home to die. Aged patients who know about and want dialysis have been known to take themselves to specialists' offices and insist upon it. It is reported that if they do so they will receive it, but only because of their own persistance.

For the moment, however, no patient in America need fear being denied dialysis. What they do have to fear is being kept on dialysis long past the time when it provides them with any reasonable benefits.

Some patients are extraordinarily grateful for the opportunity to receive kidney dialysis. Others are not and either resist the treatments or refuse to accept the life-style demanded by dialysis and are repeatedly returned to the dialysis unit close to death, only to be revived once again by the technicians. Because the dietary regimen is so strict, noncompliant patients are routine events on most dialysis units. Life on dialysis requires a maturity and discipline that not every patient can manifest, and children can have special difficulties since they are not, almost by definition, mature or disciplined. Children who are on dialysis must learn discipline quickly and thoroughly or live chaotic and probably brief lives.

Competent patients whose medical condition includes or may lead to permanent kidney failure need to learn about the kind of benefits and burdens that dialysis offers and consider how they themselves value those aspects of life. These are highly personal choices and no general rules can be made. Competent patients will almost always initially consent to a treatment like dialysis because it is impossible for them to know whether its burdens are acceptable without actually experiencing them. Social workers are usually willing to put patients into contact with other people who have struggled with dialysis regimens. Since kidney transplant is sometimes a possibility, patients should also consider talking with those who have turned away from dialysis, accepting instead the risks and difficulties of transplant.

All too often, however, patients consider only the immediate benefits from dialysis and do not have a very good sense of what to expect over the long run. Understandably, they and their physicians are intent upon the lifesaving nature of the treatment rather than upon the severe alterations to the patient's quality of life or what may happen if the patient's condition deteriorates. Both patient and doctor may be content only to talk about what is happening now. Patients who want to make responsible decisions need to address the question of long-term care as well, and they may have to be very assertive in order to get the necessary information. Dialysis may be effective and its burdens tolerable in the present, but in the long run, their condition will deteriorate and the burdens may become intolerable. Dialysis patients need to think about the time when they will be unable to dress, feed, or care for themselves, or when they will no longer engage in meaningful relationships. And they need to think about it before they have reached that stage. Unfortunately, patients who are doing well on dialysis feel that they can postpone such decisions, but the fact is that their situation can change so gradually that they don't notice the change or it can change suddenly and dramatically.

Two kinds of situations are particularly relevant here. The first is the competent dialysis patient with severe medical problems who finds life increasingly unrewarding. The second is the incompetent patient who is kept alive by dialysis. In some cases, patients in the first category move into the second one.

Competent patients who wish to stop dialysis (and die) because they find the burdens greater than the benefits are likely to face great resistance from their personal physicians and the hospital treatment team. For many health care workers, permitting a patient to stop dialysis appears to be assisting a suicide. Everyone knows of those rare instances in which acutely handicapped individuals manage, apparently through force of will, to lead personally rewarding lives. With that in mind, the health care team is likely to feel that patients' desires to stop result only from temporary discouragement, failures of will. A little more support and encouragement, a little more time, it is believed, will change their minds. In some cases, treatment will be given without patient consent either under the cover of involuntary treatment (which may or may not be illegal, depending upon the state) or as emergency treatment. Patients who can anticipate difficult courses of treatment should try to talk openly to their physicians about what quality of life is important to them. Physicians may not share their patients' values, but if they know what those preferences are, they can become more accepting over time. A physician who has heard a patient's preferences expressed over a long period of time will be more likely to act in accordance with those preferences than one who hears about them for the first time in a crisis. The blind, diabetic patient will probably not find a sympathetic audience for refusal of dialysis (e.g., when leg or foot amputation becomes necessary, as is not uncommon in advanced end-stage renal disease) if he or she has not earlier made clear that any further reduction in quality of life is unacceptable. The patient who has made it consistently clear that any further handicap cannot be accepted will probably find more understanding.

Even when competent patients have the support of physicians, nurses, dialysis technicians, and so on, they may find that their wishes are not respected if their families disagree with them. Hospitals are very fearful that families will sue for malpractice if necessary treatment is not provided. Thus, patients must also make sure that their families also understand why they wish to refuse treatment. Although it may seem unfair to patients that they have to *persuade* others to respect their autonomy, the legal and psychological factors are such that persuasion is necessary. In some situations, when a patient disagrees with family and physician, it may make sense to propose a time-limited "contract" as a compromise measure. The patient might agree to continue or accept treatment for a specific period of time and then if he or she still feels that the burdens of continued life are unacceptable, treatment would be discontinued. This may give those who feel continued treatment is desirable a period of time in which they help to improve the patient's psychological view of life, if such change is possible. It also gives them time to adjust to the implications of the patient's desires, if they last.

Competent patients must also be prepared to make their wishes known in writing. Because of legal fears, few physicians or hospitals will terminate lifesaving treatment without written directives from patients or their authorized guardians. In some states, there are legally recognized documents that patients can sign. Patients should inquire of their physicians whether their state has a statute governing durable power of attorney for health care that permits them to specify who should make decisions for them should they become incompetent and how those decisions should be made. Some hospitals have patient directives specifically designed for dialysis patients that are similar to living wills. These are intended to make sure that patients think about what they might want done in the future should they become incompetent, and to make sure that the treating team is informed with the patient. Even if the state or hospital has no such form, the patient could write one and ask that it be included in his or her medical record. A statement of preferences signed when the patient is competent can be very helpful to those who are trying to make treatment decisions later on, especially if the family or physician feels that treatment should be stopped but hesitates to do so for fear of legal repercussions or psychological guilt. It cannot be too thoroughly emphasized, however, that patients will have to take the initiative in these matters. Doctors and hospitals are, for the most part, too psychologically invested in saving lives to have much interest in planning deaths.

If patient, family, and primary physician cannot agree about stopping dialysis, the opinions of other doctors familiar with dialysis can be solicited. Sometimes, experienced dialysis physicians have developed a sensitivity to the difficulties of dialysis and understand that it is not always medically indicated just because it is available. The treating physician's decision may change if other doctors are willing to say that further dialysis is not medically indicated; that is to say, if someone else will accept responsibility for the decision or if responsibility can be diffused.

If consultants cannot resolve the issue, then the patient or family may wish to consult the hospital ethics committee. (For extended discussion of ethics committees, see Chapter 6, "Treating Handicapped Newborns.") If the hospital has no ethics committee, it may have an ethics advisor who can help to negotiate a solution to the problem. Sometimes, hospital chaplains or pastoral counselors can be helpful. The role of clergy varies in hospitals and it may be hard to determine whether any clergy are involved in ethical decision making. Patients or family can always request a clerical visit and then inquire from the visitor whether any help is possible. In some cases, religiously oriented persons will claim that they can do nothing to help because lifesaving treatment should always be provided. Catholic, Jewish, and major Protestant faiths do not hold this view, however. The Catholic Church, for example, has clear teachings that heroic, extraordinary, or disproportionate treatment need not be provided, even if a failure to treat results in death. Disproportionate treatment is defined as treatment whose costs outweigh its benefits. Life, even though it is life, may not always be worth living.

If all else fails, it may be necessary to resort to the courts. The law is likely to support patients' wishes if they are clearly stated, if they were made when the patient was clearly competent, if they were consistently stated over time, and if they were not made in the midst of some kind of crisis. Legal resolution may be necessary even if physicians agree that foregoing treatment is desirable, in order to convince the hospital that there will be no legal liability.

Patients are best protected by their own willingness to state clearly, in writing, what they want and when they want it. These statements should make clear that the patient's request is based on a sound understanding of the implications of and alternatives to refusing treatment. There is usually time for the patient to make these decisions and to make them known, but it is not usually done because no one—patient, doctor, or family member—wants to think about such unhappy prospects as incompetence and death. Patients have a right to refuse dialysis if the refusal is based on careful thought and reflection. Too often, no one is sure what is the actual basis of the patient's or family's refusal. Where there is uncertainty, it is not surprising that treatment is continued.

Conclusion

Between 1972 and 1982, an expected 20,000 dialysis patients turned into 60,000 dialysis patients, and an expected $75 million per year in costs grew to exceed $1.2 billion per year. The apparent fairness and equality of Social Security's End-Stage Renal Disease Program, which provides almost everything for almost everyone, masks another inequality: those who have kidney disease are treated far more generously than those with other catastrophic and treatable diseases, and are sometimes treated excessively. Despite all this care, end-stage renal disease continues unabated, for all the dialysis in the world neither cures nor prevents kidney failure, and all the money that goes into sustaining lives does not go into preventing illness in the first place.

Medicare's End-Stage Renal Disease Program is also our first national experience in choosing life or death, and if we are to learn anything from it, the first lesson must be that when faced with such a choice, our primary inclination is to save lives without questioning why. The hospital treatment selection committees, dialysis physicians, and Congress all learned how hard it is to say *no* to any patient with the smallest chance of being helped by medical technology.

√ The cost of using those machines appears to be more than we can afford. Now we are questioning the personal or social benefit in keeping some patients alive with dialysis. In contrast to the early days of dialysis when almost all surviving patients were brought back to active and productive lives, by 1981 approximately 44 percent of those receiving dialysis were still too sick to work and 35 percent were receiving disability payments as well as Medicare payments. The active suicide rate of patients on long-term dialysis continues to be high. Indirect suicide—the death rate for patients who simply refuse to live within the limits that their illness and its treatment requires—is also very high. After twenty years, we know a great deal more about the kind of problems that a high-technology treatment like kidney dialysis creates. We still know very little about how to decide who shall live and who shall die.

CHAPTER 3

The Newly Dead, the Nearly Dead, and the Living Dead
Societal Ambivalence Toward Death and Dying

In 1976, when the *Karen Ann Quinlan* case began first to nag at the consciences of physicians, lawyers, philosophers, and theologians, and then to filter into the general public's awareness, death was still generally perceived to be the enemy, to be fought resolutely. The history of Western medicine has been, for the most part, the history of human inability to master death. The doctor's charge was to help patients pass on to the darkness and to comfort the family in the aftermath. Scientific medicine, the child of the mid-twentieth century, changed all that. For the first time, doctors could put death off and they (as well as the public that so generously supported their enthusiasm for defying the grim reaper) began to talk about permanent defeats of death, about freezing the barely and even the nearly dead, so that they could be thawed out at some later date when cures for their ills had been perfected. In the golden age of America, it was suggested that immortality, the real thing, was just around the corner.

In that climate, doctors treated aggressively, generally with public approval. In addition, doctors treated aggressively because they believed that the public did not understand the subtle aspects of technological capabilities; that they could, for example, keep the patient nearly dead, nearly indefinitely. If families and lawyers did not understand the complexity of technological medicine—and there was ample evidence that they did not—then keeping a patient alive, however marginally, avoided the possibility of litigation. Both these reasons—staving off death in the pursuit of immortality and staving off lawsuits in the pursuit of personal peace—strongly influenced physicians' choices about treatment.

Doubts about these practices had been expressed in the 1960s when discussions about death and technology began to heat up. Physicians, as well as lawyers and philosophers, argued that total cessation of brain function should be made a new criterion for declaring death. Using total brain function as a legal definition for death meant that, at least in some cases, the patient's death would be declared earlier. This seemed a clear violation of the attempts to push death farther away, and the ensuing discussion set the scene for the *Quinlan* puzzle.

When the Harvard Medical School's Ad Hoc Committee published its guidelines for determining brain death in 1968, they, too, were primarily concerned with the threat of civil or criminal lawsuits, in this case against physicians who were removing organs for purposes of transplantation. The Committee acknowledged in its document that there was also a problem about the status of patients being maintained on respirators who presumably were not suitable candidates for organ donation. Nevertheless, their intent was to make transplant organs available more rapidly than would be the case if the physicians had to wait until breathing and heartbeat stopped. The hearts and lungs of patients on respirators could be spurred on by the machine, long after the brain had given out.

There was never any suggestion that Karen Ann Quinlan was brain dead or that she might provide donor organs for transplant. The *Quinlan* case moved the discussion about the *newly dead* one step further. Quinlan was *nearly dead*. Should she be advanced, by turning off the respirator, to *newly dead*? When her physicians decided that she would never recover consciousness, the concerns that had been raised earlier by the brain-death issue provided the background for the *Quinlan* decision. The doctors and the Quinlans disagreed right through the trials about who had first suggested that the ventilator be removed. Even if the physicians did first suggest it, as Mr. Quinlan insisted, they quickly backed off. *In the Matter of Karen Ann Quinlan* reached the New Jersey courts precisely because the physicians refused to turn off the respirator when the parents, with the support of their parish priest, requested it.

The first court hearing resulted in a "victory" for the doctors. At the trial, the physicians all agreed that turning off the respirator for a patient like Karen Ann was not standard medical practice. When the New Jersey Supreme Court heard the case, they ruled otherwise. Their decision was courageous, for all too often when courts are asked to rule on these very difficult questions, they simply throw up their hands and say, "Well, these are really medical questions, so don't ask us; doctors will just have to decide."

The New Jersey Supreme Court chose not to use standard medical practice and asserted that Karen Ann, even though comatose, retained a right of privacy that could be exercised on her behalf if physicians, family, guardians, and a hospital "ethics" committee (actually a prognosis committee) agreed that she had no chance of regaining a "cognitive or sapient" life; that is, she would never again be conscious and aware of her surroundings. Further, the justices explained that the physicians, too, would consider such decisions standard medical practice if only they were not so afraid of being hauled into court on a criminal charge or subjected to a civil suit. This was a reasonable fear in the case since both the local district attorney and the state attorney general had indicated that homicide charges would be filed if the patient died when the respirator was turned off. The New Jersey Supreme Court stated unequivocally that if the decision were made as they prescribed—doctors, family, guardians, and hospital ethics committee in agreement—then the participants could not be held criminally liable. Two months passed before the doctors finally did turn off the respirator. Had it been turned off immediately, Karen Ann probably would have died quickly. The physicians, curiously unwilling to let the patient go, instead weaned her slowly and successfully from the machine. Against expectations, Karen Ann Quinlan lived for more than nine years. Her vegetative coma indeed proved persistent.

Three questions were addressed by this case: Was Quinlan dead? Was she still a person? Were the doctors required to do everything possible to continue her life? The court replied that she was definitely not dead; she met neither the criterion for cardio-respiratory death nor that for brain death. One of the primary justifications for declaring brain-dead patients legally dead was that even with maximum medical support, their hearts and lungs would continue functioning only for a limited time, usually a few weeks at most. In declaring them *newly dead* (as opposed to *nearly dead*), the Harvard Committee and the states that adopted brain-death statutes were acknowledging that inevitability. The death of a merely comatose patient such as Karen Ann was neither imminent nor inevitable. Comatose patients may continue to exist in their comatose state for

many years, with or without respirator assistance
this latter category of patients whose cortical fur
or totally destroyed but whose brain stem (control
tions like breathing and heartbeat) is operating v
quately.

The court concluded not only that she was ali
was still a person with interests and rights, including the right or
privacy and the right to refuse treatment. And last, the court decided that for patients like Karen Ann, doctors did not have to do
everything possible: respirators could be turned off. Their decision
was, however, the beginning of a continuum whose shape and char-
acteristics are still being determined. The *Quinlan* court decided
only that the respirator was not necessary. That is only one aspect of
the care of patients in persistent coma. What of food, water, antibiotics, and decent care to ensure the patient's comfort (even if the patient isn't aware of discomfort)? Neither the court, the Quinlans,
nor the doctors discussed or even considered these matters. Sufficient unto the day was the giant step made by the justices when they
authorized physicians to turn off respirators for patients in irrevers-
ible comas as long as that appeared to be what the patient would
want and the surviving family requested it.

Eight years later, in 1983, another case arose in which a very different question was asked. In California, the case of Clarence Herbert filled the newspapers for many months when his doctors, Nejdl
and Barber, were charged with murder in Herbert's death. Clarence
Herbert had entered the hospital for elective surgery. The surgery
was uneventful, but problems arose in the postoperative period and
Mr. Herbert became comatose. Three days later, after consulting
the family, the physicians turned the respirator off. Like Karen Ann
Quinlan, Mr. Herbert was expected to die. Like Karen Ann, he lingered, he breathed, and he failed to meet medical expectations.

Once Quinlan demonstrated her ability to live without ventilator support, she was no longer a patient in need of a doctor's treatment; hers was a chronic condition in need only of nursing care. She
was promptly shipped off to a nursing home. When Clarence Herbert continued breathing, his physicians decided not to prolong his
life in a coma. With family consent, they removed the naso-gastric
tubes used for feeding and they removed the intravenous lines used
to provide fluids and medication. Mr. Herbert finally died.

This case was different from the *Quinlan* case, however, for a
substantial step had been taken during those eight years. The step

as controversial, but inevitable. When the Los Angeles District Attorney's office filed first-degree murder charges against the two doctors and the case went to preliminary hearing, the question was not "Must doctors do *everything* possible to keep a permanently unconscious patient alive?" The question had become "Must doctors do *anything* to keep a permanently unconscious patient alive?" Those who supported the doctors' actions, including the state appellate court, argued that fluids, food, and antibiotics were logically no different from respirators and that this was merely an elaboration of *Quinlan*, not an advance beyond it. Others, however, less certain of the wisdom of the "logical'" step, thought it looked like an advance and wondered whether the next question would be "May doctors actively terminate the lives of permanently unconscious patients to prevent possible further harm, either to the patients, to their families, or to society who must pay for their care?" And then, "May doctors allow elderly, senile patients to starve to death if their lives appear to benefit neither themselves nor others?"

Quinlan and Herbert had not, of course, been the only cases to raise these kinds of questions. In between, cases had arisen about the rights of all kinds of patients. Could, for example, a conscious, intelligent man who had suffered severe burns and who would doubtless endure significant handicaps (such as blindness) if treatment were successful refuse treatment, even if his mother disagreed? (He could, said the courts, but it was many months before he was able to get the question into the court and by then the worst of the treatment was over.) Could, for example, a fully mentally alert quadriplegic, paralyzed from the neck down, demand that the ventilator be turned off, even when his family disagreed? (He could, said the courts, but by the time the court decided, the man was already dead of natural causes.) Could the guardian of a severely retarded man refuse cancer treatment that would considerably extend the patient's life but not cure his disease? (The guardian could refuse the standard treatment, said the court, but by that time, the patient had died from untreated leukemia.) Could a senile man's family refuse kidney dialysis, when dialysis was keeping him alive? (They could, said the court, and the man died promptly.) May physicians force feed a competent, elderly, terminally ill woman who refuses to eat in order to end her life? (They may not, said the courts, and the woman expired.) May a previously active, eccentric, elderly woman refuse to have her leg amputated, when she may die of gangrene without the surgery? (She may, said the court, for she may determine what quality of life is acceptable to her.) May parents refuse treatment for a handicapped infant with additional life-threatening disorders because the child's quality of life will be inadequate? (Yes, said the court, as long as a physician recommends nontreatment.)

In addition to these cases that reached the courts, many more cases were quietly handled by doctors alone, or by doctors in consultation with patients, family members, or both. Doctors, especially those in trauma centers, who believe that they should spare patients' families, are known to have turned off the respirators of temporarily unconscious patients who have been acutely injured in car accidents, for example, because they will never return to more than a state of conscious quadriplegia. Physicians caring for terminal stage cancer patients may suggest to family members that the next time the patient dislodges the naso-gastric tube, it not be replaced, or that the next time the patient goes into cardiac arrest, cardiopulmonary resuscitation (CPR) not be performed. Doctors sometimes indicate to terminally ill patients with pneumonia or to their families that they may wish to refuse antibiotics. Pneumonia, which used to be called the "old man's friend," is still friendly in some settings. In eight years, the law, the medical profession, and many members of the public have come to accept that there are instances in which we ought not to fight death, and may even court it. Not yet, however, have we decided that we may *impose* it, although many argue that that, too, should be the patient's right.

Attempts to provide public policy guidance about these questions have been sporadic and ineffectual. The courts have, on a case by case basis, given some guidelines that have been effective. Some hospitals have attempted to establish clear and specific policies about how and when No Code orders—orders not to perform CPR for patients who go into cardiac arrest—can be put into effect. Private organizations have conducted extensive public education campaigns to encourage individuals to sign "living wills." Although these living wills are not always legally binding, they do provide family and physicians with some idea about patients' preferences. Finally, state legislatures have made occasional attempts to provide statutory protection for citizens facing the overwhelming power of medical technology. Many states have passed laws like California's Natural Death Act, which permits patients who are terminally ill to refuse further lifesaving treatment when death is imminent. These statutes have, however, been very ineffective both because people do not know about them and because they are legally binding only upon a small category of people. Some states are now experimenting with durable powers of attorney for health care. Durable power statutes will enable any competent adult to appoint another adult to make health care decisions should the person giving the power become incompetent to make those decisions. Although durable powers will be useful in some cases, they, too, are very limited in that lifesaving treatment cannot ever be refused by the person holding the power unless the patient's death is imminent. Legislators have been (and will probably continue to be) unable to write effective legislation because (1) many people insist that life should always be saved and (2) others greatly fear abuses in which lifesaving treatment will be refused for patients who are poor, handicapped, socially unproductive or undesirable, or alienated, without friends or family to care about whether they live or die. In addition, they worry that the power to refuse potentially lifesaving or life-extending treatment will be abused by family members who can financially or emotionally profit by the patient's death. By attempting both to appease the pro-life faction and to prevent potential abuse, legislators have left little room for the patients themselves or their families to exercise power over these decisions in nonterminal situations or when death is not imminent.

In the eight years between *Quinlan* and *Herbert*, the situation has changed significantly. The courts have provided some leeway for patients' preferences about refusing treatment; many physicians have grown somewhat more apprehensive about acting where there is no promise of judicial immunity; other physicians, especially younger ones, have grown more accustomed to the idea that someone—courts or family members—should make these decisions; the public has become more insistent upon its right to make these decisions individually and more distrustful of the doctors' involvement; some legislatures have devoted enormous time and effort to the problems but have been unable to find reasonable statutory solutions. In the meantime, while these changes were taking place, the costs of care have inexorably increased. In the long run (a period that may last only five or ten years), the problem may be solved not by settling on rights to life, rights to death, patients' rights, or doctors' responsibilities but by economic imperatives. Termination of treatment may become the desired option because treatment is too expensive. Economic analysis does not come with built-in ethical concerns. Before we are bludgeoned into policies determined by costs, we need to try to find the path with a heart. Unfortunately, there isn't much time.

Brain-dead patients became the newly dead; permanently unconscious patients became the nearly dead. The next problem we are facing is that of patients perceived to be the living dead: the conscious or semiconscious, elderly, demented patient, who no longer shares fully in common human experience but who has no terminal illness. Some writers have referred to these patients as "biologically tenacious." Such language suggests that these people have worn out their welcome, and in such language lies the ethical dilemma that discontinuing treatment brings.

Case Study

May Reynolds slumped listlessly in the wheel chair where the nurses had placed her early in the morning. The room opened onto the main hallway and nurses, aides, patients, and families could regularly be seen passing by. Since the room had no window, the nurses always placed the chair so that May could benefit from whatever diversion the passing parade offered her. At 84, she was small—almost shrunken—and frail, but in surprisingly good health except for the recent hip injury that had placed her in the hospital. Her mental state, however, was not good. Her understanding of who she was, where she was, and why she was there was diminishing, almost perceptibly, from day to day. She seldom spoke when spoken to, but occasionally carried on one-sided conversations when alone in the room.

She was to be transferred from the hospital to a nursing home as soon as the orthopedist signed her off and the social worker and her granddaughter found a suitable placement. The nurses on the day shift were glad that it would be only a matter of days before May moved on. She was not a difficult patient in most ways; in fact she was an extraordinarily easy patient. What unsettled the nurses was May's lack of response to the ordinary offerings of care that they could provide. Whatever they did for her, even the simplest matters, like helping her into the chair, straightening the bed, bringing her food and drinks, brought no response. On a busy ward, it made it easier to attend to her least or even to skip her entirely whenever the routine called for care that the nurses judged was not really essential to her physical health. A back rub, a few minutes of talk, changing the television channel, or helping her to alter her position in the chair seemed more trouble than it was worth when the patient never acknowledged that the nurses' efforts made any difference. Only one nurse, Jill Carter, who was young and new on the ward, seemed to connect with May (even though May didn't connect with her). Jill would take the extra time to talk to May, to hold her hands and brush her hair, to show her things or look for television programs that might capture her nonexistent interest. Jill seemed unaffected by May's lack of interest. She believed that patients needed kindness and caring, even if they could not or would not respond to it. The need was basic and human; it was not eliminated by sickness or weakness or senility. So Jill took the time to make an effort for May even though nothing was returned.

One evening, just before dinnertime, Jill went to May's room to get her ready to eat and help her back into her bed. When she walked into the room, May was absently waving her hands in the air, humming quietly to herself. Jill explained to her that it was time to get ready for dinner, but May did not respond except to turn her head away from Jill. She began to croon something like "I'm going away, today, today, I'm going away today." Her hands waved faster, making it difficult for Jill to make any headway in moving her toward the bed. Jill tried to coax her into standing up, but May would have none of it, continuing to look away from Jill and keeping her hands moving in front of her body as if they were a shield that could keep away all interference with her being. Finally, Jill called another nurse and together they moved May into the bed. She stiffened rigidly as they moved her and once in the bed, she turned her expressionless face into the pillow. When the evening meal arrived, Jill returned hoping to make some amends, but May lay in bed, her eyes fixed on the wall, even less responsive than usual. Jill took a spoonful of food and held it close to May's mouth, but May only turned her face farther into the pillow. When Jill persisted, May again began to wave her hands erratically, as if the hands themselves could erase Jill's presence. Jill moved to the other side of the bed, hoping to force May into some eye contact, but May, determinedly gathering all her strength together, rose up in bed and pushed the tray of food on the floor. As the silverware and dishes scattered across the floor, a harsh moaning sound escaped from May's throat. The guttural "NO" only accented the silent struggle in which the two women had been engaged. Jill called out for assistance and as she began to pick up the pieces, May sank back into bed and pulled the sheet up over her head.

Next morning, May refused both to eat and to get out of bed. The morning shift nurses, busy with an emergency on the ward, simply left her alone in her irritated and irritating state. She lay with her eyes closed, almost unmoving throughout the day. When her physician came to check her out in the late afternoon, the head nurse was given a quick but thorough tongue lashing for failing to keep the patient as active as was possible in order to make sure the hip healed properly. The patient's failure to eat was not discussed. As Jill came back on the ward, the departing nurse told her of the problem and of the nurses' inability to make any headway with the demented old lady.

Jill went directly to May's room, noting that over twenty-four hours had passed since May had last eaten. A tiny, frail, elderly lady who barely moved had a very low calorie requirement, of course, but even tiny old ladies must eat something to stay alive. When she entered May's room, she was immediately assaulted by a dank and decaying odor. May lay in bed, eyes closed, apparently asleep. At the table beside her head stood a vase of dead flowers whose stems were rotting in their water. As she cleared away the flowers, Jill talked to May in a calm and easy tone, describing what she was doing and why she was doing it, then moving to what May was doing and why she must not do it. Jill expected no answer, but hoped that May would respond with actions, rather than with words. She offered no threat to the old woman, no comments about what the doctors would do if she didn't eat. That could be saved for later. First, reason and kindness. Second, the family would be called in to convince the patient. Only third would come the announcement of the unhappy alternative of forced feeding.

Neither reason nor kindness worked. May failed to acknowledge even the presence, let alone the desires, of the nurses who tried to get her to eat. She closed her eyes; she shielded her face with her hands; she turned into the pillow. To questions and comments, she was mute, and Jill was not entirely sure that she even heard what they said to her. Often, when she turned away, it was as if she were listening to something else, something other than the tense and angry person who stood before her. Her eyes would open and an expectant look would appear on her face, as if she were straining to catch messages too faint for easy listening.

Jill called Mrs. Reynolds's granddaughter, Melissa, as soon as it became apparent that the nurses would make no headway. Melissa, a 30-year-old woman, was the old woman's only close relative, for May had outlived her husband, her siblings, and her two children. Prior to her hip injury, May had lived alone in a small apartment in a senior citizens complex. Her mild dementia had not caused any great problems as long as there were people in the building who looked out for her and whom she could call upon for help. Melissa visited her regularly and helped to support her financially, but her involvement in her grandmother's life was a matter of family ties and the obligations of blood rather than one of emotional closeness. Jill doubted if Melissa would be any more successful than she had been in persuading May to eat, but perhaps Melissa could trigger some ancient embedded sense of family loyalty and obedience.

When Melissa arrived, she listened quietly to Jill's detailing of her grandmother's withdrawal and refusal of food. Her intuitive response was that her grandmother no longer wanted to live; this behavior was her way of refusing treatment. She agreed to talk with the old woman, but Jill saw that her heart was not in it and that through her offices, May would not be persuaded to do anything. When Melissa entered the room, May did not look away from her. There seemed to be a sense of recognition, but she did not speak. When Melissa began to talk of food, however, May grew restless, began to hum tunelessly to herself, and then closed her eyes. Melissa stayed a half hour with the woman, but once May broke the contact between them, it was not restored.

Jill explained to Melissa that if May continued to refuse to eat, it would be necessary to force feed her. Otherwise, she would quickly die from starvation. She explained the manner in which the feeding would be conducted: a naso-gastric tube would be inserted through the patient's nose and a high-calorie preparation would then be pumped directly to the stomach where the body could then convert it into necessary energy in the normal way. She assured Melissa that it was not painful, though there was some degree of discomfort when the tube was being inserted. This was especially so if the patient were resisting. Mrs. Reynolds, however, was already very weak, and she would doubtless be very unlikely to provide much resistance. If she did, however, they would have to keep her arms tied down. Once they got some food into her, she would very probably be willing to eat again in the normal way. As soon as Melissa left, Jill put in a call to Dr. Collins, Mrs. Reynolds' physician, to tell him of Melissa's inability to get the patient to respond.

Melissa had somehow accepted the idea of forced feeding as Jill
had explained it to her, but by the next morning the prospect disturbed her considerably. As she thought of the grandmother she had
known before this hospitalization—the feisty, independent soul who
had insisted on taking care of herself even though she knew that she
had lost some of her powers—she knew that her grandmother would
want no such treatment. Gathering her courage, she called Dr. Collins, explaining her visit of the night before. Hesitantly, she inquired
whether he might not leave her grandmother alone, let her refuse
food and, if she were to weaken and die, which she obviously would
if she continued, so be it.

Dr. Collins replied, without hesitation, that such a course would
be impossible. He counseled Melissa confidently, explaining that, in
his experience, elderly patients in hospitals often become depressed
and irritable, but they soon come round to their former attitudes
when they are able to return to their homes or to other, perhaps
more cheerful, surroundings. Melissa pointed out, first, that her
grandmother was not simply an elderly patient but an elderly demented patient whose dementia seemed to be progressing very rapidly, and second, that she was not going to be returning to her home
but would go to a nursing home which she would probably never
leave. Dr. Collins acknowledged that both of these were true, but
maintained that the current situation was sufficiently unusual that
even strong minds were affected; weak minds even more so. His
duty, after all, was to help his patients get better, not to help them
kill themselves. When Melissa appeared to be persisting in her suggestion that Mrs. Reynolds be allowed to decide for herself whether
she wanted to eat, Dr. Collins cut her off sharply. He pointed out
that she could always take her grandmother home against medical
advice and fail to feed her there. Then, when the old woman died,
she could think about what to tell the coroner, the police, and the
newspaper reporters when they inquired as to the circumstances of
her untimely death.

Dr. Collins immediately visited Mrs. Reynolds, explaining to her
unhearing ears that if she did not eat, she would be fed by tube. May
failed to respond to him visually or verbally. She made no sound, appeared not to be aware that he was there. Only her body seemed to
be in this world; the rest of her seemed to be elsewhere where discussions of feeding and nursing homes and life in a wheel chair were
not on the agenda. The doctor started to speak in a soft and persua-
sive tone, but her lack of response began to provoke him and, like an

angry parent who demands a response from a wayward child, he began to bully her. The tone of voice became more aggressive; the tube feeding became a threat; feeding itself became not a means of life but a means of punishment. Whether this approach genuinely expressed Dr. Collins's feelings or was instead merely an actor's calculated attempt to provoke response, it failed. May Reynonds's narrow little fine-boned face lay unmoving on the plump hospital-issue pillow. Her pale, watery blue eyes looked about the room without recognition. When he grasped her hand, it lay limply in his own vibrant palm like a lifeless object. When he left the room, he ordered the nurse to make arrangements to have her fed immediately.

May did not resist the placement of the tube for, as Jill had predicted, she was too weak to offer much struggle. When it was in place, however, she would frequently, and sometimes successfully, try to dislodge it. When the evening feeding took place, Jill would remove the restraints and sit with Mrs. Reynolds, holding her hands gently, both offering the comfort of human touch and preventing her from interfering with the equipment.

May's transfer to the nursing home was postponed because of the feeding problem, but it was still on the schedule. She could be fed there as well as in the hospital. Melissa did not come to visit her grandmother during this intervening period. The evening before the transfer was to be made, however, she came to sign papers and ensure that the arrangements were all made. She spoke with Jill and then they sat together during the evening feeding.

Jill tried to convey to Melissa her feelings of hope and of helplessness about May. She explained why she could not have sat by and watched May starve to death; what it would have done to her as a nurse, feeling that she had allowed a person to die who did not need to. It was not the legal issues that bothered her. If she thought May should be allowed to die, then she would do what she could to that end and worry about explaining it to outsiders when they asked. She would not do it if she didn't believe that she could explain her actions. She was worried that letting May die would make it not only easier but necessary to let other patients die. Once she had embarked on such an uncertain course, then the next time the question arose, she would be inclined to take the same action in order to prove that the first decision had been correct. As well, she acknowledge that sometimes she felt that May was already dead; that the feeding process was like a child taking care of a doll, pretending that the doll was a live, real person and that the food was needed. She really did not know whether they fed May for her sake, for their own sakes, or for the sake of other patients. But she knew that feed her they must.

Late that evening, as Jill prepared to leave the ward, she made one last trip back to May's room. The faint yellow night-light in the room softened everything: the sharp lines, the sterile colors, the hard textures. Even May looked softer, less fragile as she lay asleep. Jill did not approach the bed, but only stood in the doorway and whispered a soft goodbye. She had disturbed the woman enough. As she went to her car, the image of death in life lingered in her mind's eye.

The ambulance arrived promptly at ten o'clock the next morning and May made her journey to the nursing home. Melissa attended to the paper work and then came to her grandmother's room to see if anything remained between them. Her grandmother had slipped to a lopsided position in her wheel chair and when Melissa tried to straighten her out, May's little body stiffened, rejecting the touch. May's eyes wandered about, but never fastened on Melissa, and Melissa felt the avoidance was a direct rebuke. They sat together silently for awhile; as Melissa rose to leave, she whispered—as much to herself as to May—"It's not my fault, grandma. I tried." She left the room and May did not blink.

The days in the nursing home moved by inexorably. May spoke to no one, responded to nothing. Five months passed and May continued to be fed by tube. As before, she did not resist it, although she often tried to pull it out when it was in place. She grew perceptibly weaker and could no longer sit up in the wheel chair without being tied in place. Then, one evening, her temperature began to rise sharply. When the doctor arrived, he listened briefly to her heartbeat, then to her lungs. He noted to the attendant that it looked like pneumonia, but suggested that they wait till the next day to see how she was doing. He did not prescribe antibiotics. The next day, May was dead.

The Decision Makers: Their Perspectives and Interests

Medical Perspectives

When there was little that physicians could do to postpone the patient's death, they cultivated the *art* of medicine: of comforting and

caring for both the dying patient and the patient's family. When effective intervention became possible, they prolonged life and did not
always worry about the kind of life the patient had. Other factors,
too, have encouraged a tendency to overtreat. The ability to keep
patients alive (to "keep them going") tended to prove medicine's success as a science, and *to be scientific* has been the highest accolade
offered in our time. In addition, the institutionalization of medicine, whereby health care is provided not in the doctor's office nor
in the patient's home but in hospitals, has made aggressive treatment more likely because the setting is more public.

In the past forty years, research medicine has become much
more prestigious than clinical practice. Similarly, specialists have
more prestige than general practitioners. The medical-research
model and the specialist-care model are both disease-oriented. That
is, they focus on the diseases that attack patients. The general practitioner, on the other hand, has traditionally been more oriented to
caring for the patient who had a disease. Between 1940 and 1970,
the general practitioners' approach was replaced by the scientific
approach. Disease was treated; death was postponed. It was at this
time that the first disturbing results of this change in American
medicine began to reach the public. It appeared that patients were
being kept alive but that no further therapeutic benefits were anticipated.

When patients died at home (up until World War II, home
deaths were very common), decisions about whether to provide
some kind of care that might extend life, if only for a short time,
were made by physicians who knew the family, knew their circumstances and personalities and what they would prefer, even if they
had not specifically expressed their preferences. When a physician
decided not to try to prolong a patient's life, the decision was made
with knowledge and was made privately. No nurses, no specialists,
no other doctors were around to observe what was or was not being
done. Once the patients entered the hospital, however, there was a
full audience to observe omissions and commissions. Actions freely
performed in private with compassion, knowledge, and a belief in
common values could not be performed in public where observers
with different values might disagree. As a result, decisions became
more conservative, more clearly within the letter of the law. Although hospital-based physicians still talked as if they had total discretion in these matters, as a matter of fact, they exercised their discretion much less frequently, choosing, for the most part, to

accommodate their actions to what they perceived to be the mainstream of medical values. Thus they avoided their colleagues' potential criticisms and the threat of lawsuits. Thus did the band of choices narrow.

Until very recently, no doctor had been brought into court for continuing treatment, for *keeping* a patient alive. In Ohio, a family recently sued a physician for putting an unconscious patient on a ventilator without family consent and against the patient's previously expressed wishes. The court held that the family could prevail if they could show that the ventilator support was not part of emergency treatment. (Emergency treatment does not require consent: there is implied consent for saving lives in an emergency.) In California, a competent, fully conscious patient who wanted treatment stopped took the physician and hospital to court to honor his wishes. The court agreed that the patient was entitled to refuse lifesaving treatment and that the hospital's and physicians' beliefs were less important than the patient's. Despite these cases, physicians and hospitals are likely to continue treatment in most cases, especially when the patient is incompetent and has not previously made his or her preferences clear.

Nursing Perspectives

In casual writing and in after-dinner speeches, physicians occasionally acknowledge the vital role played by nurses, but in practice medicine has been, and still tends to be, rigidly hierarchical despite attempts to democratize it. In an era of women's liberation, nurses have vigorously tried to renegotiate their positions within the hospital hierarchy. They have been most successful, perhaps, around questions that involve termination of treatment, not least because they are potential threats to physicians who choose courses that are neither amenable to the nurses nor clearly consistent with legal standards. Nurses have been known to go to prosecuting attorneys, as one did in the *Herbert* case discussed previously, in which two physicians were charged with murder for terminating all treatment.

Nurses have been very vociferous about terminating treatment because doctors make the decisions and then sometimes leave the nurses to unplug ventilators and to stay by the patient during that dying period. In addition, because nurses are much more likely than doctors to have developed personal relationships with the patients under their care and their families, they frequently have an emotional (as well as professional) investment in the patient's recovery. Finally, and perhaps most important, just as doctors tend to believe that their power to defeat illness lies in their ability to be scientific, so do nurses believe that their power to defeat illness lies in their ability to provide emotional support. When the physician withdraws from the patient, thus reducing his or her own sense of frustration, he or she has concluded that none of the tools of scientific medicine will help. The patient, however, is not dead. He or she continues to need and sometimes to want the supportive care that nurses offer. Thus, nursing skills continue to be effective long after the doctor has left the field.

On the other hand, nurses may be much more sensitive to the ravages that a drawn-out, terminal illness brings to the patient and to the family. Because of their emotional identification with patient and family, they are sometimes more willing to terminate treatment than physicians are. In addition, nurses tend to be the medium through which patients, families, and doctors talk to one another. In that role, they have enormous power to shape the communication that they transmit. The nurse knows how much hope the doctor has and how much distress and discouragement the patient and family have. He or she may transfer that information or not, depending upon the nurse's own assessment of the situation.

Legal Perspectives

There are at least five kinds of cases in which termination of treatment might be considered and which will most probably result in prompt death. First is patients who are permanently unconscious; second is patients with severe dementia or severe mental defect; third is patients with chronic disease whose deaths from the disease are imminent but postponable; fourth is handicapped newborns with life-threatening conditions; and fifth is patients who are presumably competent and do not have terminal illnesses but who believe that their quality of life is so low that they wish to refuse treatment. Courts in different states have dealt with each of these, but their responses have been quite varied both with respect to their analyses of the questions and their conclusions.

In cases of permanently unconsciousness patients, if the patient previously expressed desires not to receive such treatment *or* if the family wishes treatment to be stopped, the law generally permits doctors to withhold or withdraw treatment like respirators. It is less clear whether it is legally permissible to stop fluids, food, or medications like antibiotics. Hygienic care must always be provided as long as the patient is alive. Although the law has created living wills, natural death acts, and durable powers of attorney, it has structured them very narrowly. Furthermore, in most instances, they apply only in extreme cases and to "heroic" or "extraordinary" treatment, often (but not always) referring to high-technology treatment like respirators. An assumption that a signed document of any sort extends to withholding ordinary forms of care, such a antibiotics or food, would be very questionable and dangerous from a legal perspective.

√The possibility of withholding lifesaving or life-prolonging treatment from patients with severe dementia or with severe mental defects has raised enormous problems because of the implications of discrimination. When physicians or family members withhold treatment from such individuals, the possibility that the decision is based on the best interests of society or of the family rather than of the patient is of great concern. Some have argued that these individuals ought always to be treated if only to avoid the appearance of improper acts. Others have urged that mentally deficient patients ought to have the same rights to refuse treatment as do competent patients, even though someone else must exercise the right for them.

In one noteworthy case (*Saikewicz* v. *Supt. of Belchertown State Hospital*), the Massachusetts courts did directly address this issue. Mr. Saikewicz was a 67-year-old profoundly retarded man who suffered from leukemia. Although it was generally agreed that in most instances, a 67-year-old person with such a diagnosis would enter chemotherapy, the court permitted a guardian to refuse treatment on Mr. Saikewicz's behalf, stating that, because of the patient's retardation, he would not be able to understand the reason for the pain inflicted upon him by the treatment, whereas death from leukemia would be relatively painless.

One specific form of withholding treatment that can be applied to any patient is called a Do Not Resuscitate or a No Code order. The term "No Code" is used in contrast to "Code Blue." A Code Blue means that a patient who has experienced cardiac arrest should be resuscitated. A few years ago, No Code orders were being discussed in furtive whispers among doctors and nurses. In recent years, however, No Code has come out of the closet and is not infrequently a matter of frank discussion between doctor, patient, and family. A decision to No Code a patient means that, should the patient go into cardiac arrest ("should he arrest," in doctor parlance), no cardiopulmonary resuscitation (CPR) will be provided. Hospitals frequently have very specific policies about the circumstances under which a No Code order is permitted, how frequently it must be reviewed, and who is to be consulted prior to the writing of an order. Customarily, the order is written on the patient's chart and, if the patient is conscious and competent, he or she must consent to it. Hospitals that have official policies about No Code orders often have unofficial practices about slow codes or partial codes. These are seldom written in the charts and are generally regarded as improper medical practice. "Slow codes" are verbal orders for the medical staff to respond slowly when the patient has a cardiac arrest. A slow code is sometimes used to give the appearance (usually to the family) that the staff is trying to resuscitate the patient. Hence, slow codes are sometimes called "show codes." "Partial codes" involve the use of some aspects of CPR, but not all that would normally be used in a full-scale attempt to resuscitate the patient. A partial code might be limited to the use of chemical stimulants, in which case it is often called a "chemical code."

Although physicians often resist competent patients' wishes to refuse available life-prolonging treatment, the courts have ruled that competent patients have the right to refuse treatment even when it will prolong life. Physicians often assume that patients who want to stop life-prolonging treatment are incompetent. Competency determinations can be made legally only by courts, but competency assessments are extremely difficult to make because people who are facing death are usually under such strong emotional stress.

In practice, informal determinations of competency are made every day in the hospital. Only rarely do competency cases go to court. Current practices in hospitals and among physicians vary widely in terms of how this issue is handled. Some physicians presume that all patients are incompetent to decide for themselves. Others go to great lengths to respect patient preferences. Some are unsure about how to proceed when their own preferences do not match the patient's wishes. Patients are almost always treated as competent if they accept what the physician recommends. When the patient refuses the physician's recommendation, then his or her competency is likely to be questioned.

Patients may have difficulty demonstrating their "rationality" to others. If a patient demonstrates any ambivalence, it will be seized upon as evidence of either incompetence or indecision. On the other hand, because patients are often very depressed in such circumstances, one must be careful to sort out clear desires from fleeting despair. When acceding to a patient's preferences will lead to certain and rapid death, the law demands a very high degree of proof about the certainty of those preferences, since the action is not reversible.

The law is inclined to move slowly in hastening death. The critical factors are the patient's competency and his or her ability to benefit in any way from continued treatment. If death is likely in a matter of weeks regardless of treatment, the law is likely to approve withdrawal of treatment as long as patients give some kind of competent indication that they prefer that course of action. Because American law is based upon a theory of individual rights, competent patient preferences will ultimately be honored in most cases. Unfortunately, patients near death are seldom at their peak of competency.

Courts are reluctant, however, to authorize withdrawal of treatment for incompetent patients. When they do make such authorizations, they typically insist that they are not endorsing quality-of-life judgments, even though critics often point out that a decision to withdraw treatment (e.g., stopping artificial feeding) or to withhold treatment (e.g., not providing chemotherapy for leukemia) *is* a quality-of-life judgment. The semantic concern reflects the courts' awareness that quality-of-life judgments are controversial and difficult to justify because they are so open to abuse. Still, some courts have overcome their reluctance to authorize withdrawal of treatment even in the absence of previously expressed patient wishes. This is an area of law that will certainly see further development in the near future.

Ethical Perspectives

Philosophers have focused primarily on two areas: society's duty to care for the ill and the individual's right to die. Some writers have argued that as long as a patient is conscious or will probably return to a conscious state, society has a duty to provide all care necessary to preserve his or her life. Others have suggested that society has a duty to preserve life in all cases, conscious or not, unless the individual has made a competent refusal of care. Still others argue that individuals, unconscious or otherwise, who are unable to make competent decisions about life-preserving treatment should not be kept alive indefinitely simply because they are unable to express preferences. Instead, they also should be permitted to refuse treatment through the authority of proxy decision makers who should base their judgments either on the best interests of the patient or on what they believe the patient would have preferred.

Public Policy Perspectives

Policy makers have two major concerns when treatment refusal leads to death. First, they want to maximize individual rights. Doing this probably means encouraging less end-of-life care and permitting doctors to withdraw high-technology care when the patient or family refuse them. Second, policy makers need to reduce health care costs, especially the specific increase in costs surrounding treatment in terminal illness. In 1983, Medicare spent $15 billion on the last six months of Medicare patients' lives, an astounding figure for care that apparently did not offer much additional lifespan to the patients. These two goals place health care policy makers in the unusual (for them) position of having two concerns that support one another instead of conflicting with one another. Less high-technology medicine could lead to lower costs.

If the news media are to be believed, Americans are not currently demanding that they receive more medical care at the end of their lives; they are complaining about receiving too much and not being permitted to *refuse* care. Thus, if policy makers can respond to popular demands and make it easier for patients to refuse care, their other concern, reducing health care costs, would also be met. Although this dovetailing of objectives for policy makers appears to be a blessing, it has its dark side. Responding to public demand and cutting costs may also lead to increased opportunities for abuse of procedures, so that treatment is refused too easily for those people who are an inconvenience or a burden to their families, friends, and to society in general. Although policy makers have good reasons to pursue this topic very aggressively, the implications of their actions are very problematic. If making refusal of treatment easier also devalues human lives in general, then a policy of citizen accommodation and reduced costs will have been very shortsighted indeed.

Permitting thousands of May Reynoldses to starve to death simply because their deaths are, at best, a matter of indifference to themselves and to others would save money. As the aged population increases, increasing numbers of people will find themselves isolated within the society, without family or friends to care for them or to care about them. A public policy that made it easier for these persons to end their lives by withdrawing medical care, whether food, medications, or machines, would be efficient, but may not be compassionate. On the other hand, a public policy that insisted on keeping these persons alive in dismal and degrading conditions cannot be said to be any kinder.

What's a Patient to Do?

May Reynold's case illustrates the problems of providing life-extending treatment for incompetent patients. Mrs. Reynolds has no terminal illness; she may live for a very long time if the full force of medicine is directed upon her. Her state of mind makes it impossible to know her wishes and she has left no prior record of what she might want. Her only family, a granddaughter, has had only a limited relationship and is not able to speak effectively to her grandmother's character and attitudes.

On the other hand, her quality of life is severely diminished and it might be doing her a kindness to let her die by going along with her refusal to eat. Yet, we do not know that she is refusing to eat because she wants to die. Furthermore, it may be wrong to let her die when her behavior only gives evidence of the fact that she is alone, frightened, and aged. Her hip injury and hospital stay have surely created increased stress for her and the rapid increase in her incommunicativeness may be response to stress rather than natural development of senility. If she continues to receive compassionate care and human attention, she may well be again willing to eat. Certainly without testing this hypothesis, it would be wrong to let her die.

The case demonstrates other matters that also generate conflict. The physician, for example, is not willing to accommodate uncertain patient preferences and clear-cut family wishes because of the possibility of legal complications. Were May at home, rather than in a hospital, it is possible that a compassionate family physician might not insist on forcing food into her, even at the cost of keeping her in restraints. It is also possible that at home she might feel less alienated, less burdensome and less burdened, and thus might have continued to eat.

It is hard to know whether her apparent preferences not to eat *are* rational. Such wishes may be transitory, given the difficult aspects of May's life. Since she is destined to leave the hospital soon for a nursing home, her physician would prefer to export the problem to someone else (an understandable if not particularly commendable attitude). He may perceive his job as one of keeping her alive until she becomes someone else's problem. On the other hand, he may believe that not feeding her would violate his own moral obligation to save life whenever there is a possibility of the patient's being able to enjoy some aspects of life. In fact, Mrs. Reynolds may respond differently in other surroundings; her dementia may level off. Merely to be demented does not necessarily destroy all of an individual's quality of life, although it does radically change that life. It may only be radically awful from the point of view of those who still lead a mentally active life.

The law says that patients have a right to refuse treatment, even if it means they will die, but social ethics also proclaim that medicine has a duty to help those who need help. Medical situations like May's are on the edge of current medical ethics problems. Even if her medical condition does not worsen, she is a candidate for Do Not Resuscitate orders. But she may not have a cardiac arrest. As it is, she may be living and dying in a society that values her symbolic life far more than she values her actual life. Or, she may live not because *anyone* values her life, but because medicine must accommodate society's basic uncertainty about whether we *should* value her life.

The patient caught in the grip of modern medicine may indeed feel trapped and powerless.* In the contemporary Temple of Aesculapius, patients may feel as insignificant in the face of the powerful god of modern medicine as did Greek petitioners in ancient times. Furthermore, they are usually unsure of what rights they have and

*In this section, advice that is given to the patient is usually also appropriate advice for the family member. Sometimes patients can and are able to do their own negotiating in the hospital. In most cases of terminal illness, however, they need help from family members who are free to move about in the world and have the energy to do so.

fearful that if they overstep the bounds, they will suffer for it. As a result, they submit to the choices of physicians, nurses, and administrators despite their own desires to do otherwise. If they rebel against the system, their rebellion is often indirect (e.g., generalized complaints about care, failure to report changes in symptoms or to take medication), unnoticed as rebellion, and thus ineffectual. Or, at worst, their noncompliant, uncooperative behavior encourages hospital staff to pay as little attention to them as possible.

⸬ Patients who have strong feelings about how their lives—or deaths—should be ordered need to express themselves clearly, forcefully, and, if humanly possible, without hostility. They must understand beforehand that the entire health care system prefers that they simply do as they are told, agree to what is recommended, and either get well or die with a modicum of efficiency. If the patient or family asserts preferences that are not consistent with those of the physicians, nurses, or administrators, they will meet resistance.

Physicians and other staff may also experience conflicting feelings. They are likely to feel considerable compassion for their patients' sufferings, even if at the same time they feel a duty to save and preserve their lives. Compassion pulls them toward relieving suffering by reducing or withdrawing treatment, while duty presses them to keep a patient alive. Concerns about publicity as well as potential legal conflicts promote a conservative attitude toward limiting treatment and shortening life, even if the physician recognizes that suffering could be relieved by curtailing life. When patients are indifferent, incompetent, or ambivalent, this makes physicians' decision making more difficult and increases the likelihood that treatment will be continued. Patients and families who know what they want and why they want it can help physicians plan a course of treatment.

Conflict at such a time is unfortunate, but probably inevitable. It is the price of modern technological medicine, of health care in a giant-sized institution, and of living in a pluralistic society that settles its disagreements in very damaging lawsuits. Nevertheless, an increasing number of patients and their families do not want to stand by passively in the face of terminal illness and suffering, but they may not know what to do or how to proceed. To control decisions over health care, it is essential that patients and their families get the facts about their medical condition, prognosis, and treatment. In addition, they must find out how hospital policies can help or make harder their decision making, enlist supporters within and without the hospital to aid them in determining their medical course, and know clearly what they want, both in the present and in the future, with respect to quality of life and death. This may seem like a lot of work, but the process itself helps to defuse the feeling of helplessness that illness creates for patients and family. Although the occasion may be a crisis, patients remain consumers of health care services and they can be either active or passive consumers. The following suggestions apply not only to questions of terminating treatment, but to any situation in which patients or families must make difficult choices about medical care.

Getting the Facts

Before any action is taken, it is essential to obtain clear, accurate, and complete information about the patient's condition. Patients should know the diagnosis, the prognosis, the probability that each is accurate, and alternative treatments to those recommended by the physician, including no treatment at all. Physicians are not accustomed and sometimes not inclined to explain medical facts in detail to patients and families and even if they are, they sometimes don't give explanations in language that ordinary people can understand. One reason they don't give explanations is that they may be themselves uncertain about diagnoses, treatment, and outcome. They have been taught that patients will do better if they have confidence in their physicians, and few doctors believe that admissions of ignorance will build confidence. Beyond that, they may be disinclined to go into lengthy explanations because they believe that patients can't or won't understand. When courts began to insist that patients give informed consent to treatment, physicians repeatedly complained that the courts were expecting them to give "mini-medical educations" to patients, an expectation that they clearly believed could not be reasonably met. Finally, they often give explanations in medical jargon because that's how they are used to talking and thinking about their work.

Patients must persevere in asking questions. Frequently, patients who get up their courage to ask a question quickly lose steam when they don't understand the answer the doctor gives. Patients need to think about the conversation they want to have ahead of time, realizing that they are likely to be easily intimidated. Patients should talk over their uncertainties with someone else (friends, nurses, clergy, social workers) to clarify what aspects of treatment concern them. They should make lists of the questions they want to ask. Patients should think about what information they really want to know and make sure that the discussion isn't over until they either know the answers to their questions or know why there isn't an answer to some of their questions. Patients need to remember that it is their lives, their treatment, their pain and suffering, and often some of their money that is involved. A hospital is not a hotel: patients didn't come because they want to. They and their families deserve to know what is going on. In the long run, it is they who will live with the care that is received, not the physician or hospital staff.

The burden of asking and even pressing for information falls on the patient or a family member. They cannot expect that it will be provided. Many people feel that although they would like more information, it is inappropriate to bother physicians with their questions because doctors are too busy and have other, more important things to do. Also, they do not want to offend the physician by asking too many questions, by "being a bother." Physicians cultivate their image as authority figures for many reasons, some personal, some professional; some legitimate, some illegitimate. They are authorities; but they are also doctors to individual patients, and as such have information that those patients need to know. It is unwise to depend too strongly on the nurses for this information as many patients are inclined to do. Nurses know a great deal about medicine and frequently provide superb ordinary-language interpretations of what doctors tell patients, but they may be very reluctant—because of interprofessional codes of conduct—to provide information if the doctor has not already done so. A patient should first try to get the information that is needed from the doctor. If that is not successful, the patient can ask the nurse how to do better. The nurse probably knows the doctor better than the patient does and may have some advice.

Patients need to find out whether there are alternative forms of treatment available. When the physician recommends a particular form of treatment, that is his or her judgment of what is best in the circumstances, but other forms of treatment with different risks and benefits may also be available. The patient or family may well have a different view of what best fits their circumstances. This is especially true when the physician does not know the patient well.

In medicine there is a rule: surgeons recommend surgery. That is, doctors who are asked for treatment recommendations are likely to recommend that whatever *they* do is what needs to be done. A patient who has talked with a surgeon should also be sure to ask an internist if there is treatment less aggressive than surgery that might be helpful. Likewise, the patient who first talks with an internist should be sure to ask a surgeon if there is a possibility of more aggressive treatment.

If the patients or family do not find the treating physician's recommendations consonant with their own values, they should obtain second opinions about treatment and management options. It may be awkward or unwise to ask primary physicians to suggest colleagues for second opinions. Those they recommend may share their values and in any case are likely to feel some tension between personal/professional loyalty to a colleague and duties to a patient. Ask friends or the local medical association for the name of a board-certified specialist who can serve as an independent consultant. Second opinions are especially important when the diagnosis is difficult or confusing, when the prognosis is uncertain, and when several forms of treatment are possible. Insurance companies usually encourage second opinions. If the attending physician seems offended, patients can point out that second opinions dramatically reduce medical costs, a cause that everyone needs to support.

Patients should know about drugs that have been prescribed and their side effects, common as well as uncommon. Many elderly people who are thought to be senile are, in fact, suffering from inappropriately prescribed medication or needed medication that is prescribed in dosages that are too high. If the physician does not provide thorough enough information, it can be obtained by consulting the PDR (the *Physician's Desk Reference*), which includes all the commonly prescribed drugs and gives thorough descriptions of their side effects. Medical school libraries always have copies in their reference departments, and large public libraries also may have copies. One might do even better by consulting a reputable pharmacist who can explain the drugs, how they work, and what side effects might occur.

Patients need to consider whether their care can be managed in a different environment that will make them more comfortable. It may be appropriate to explore the possibility of nursing homes, of changing physicians, or of investigating home health care (which the hospital may be willing to subsidize for Medicare or Medicaid patients since it will lose less money if the patient is not kept in the hospital). For terminally ill patients, family should inquire about the existence of hospices in the vicinity. The hospice movement has grown significantly in recent years and some hospices provide help both in the home and in a hospice facility for dying patients. Maximum attention to reduced suffering rather than aggressive prolonging of life for the sake of prolonging it marks the difference between hospice care and (at least some and perhaps most) hospital care.

Patients who are suffering a great deal from pain frequently feel that they are not getting enough medical assistance. Pain has both a psychological and a physiological component and both need to be treated. Patients who are in pain should find out why the medication they are receiving does not diminish the pain and whether more careful prescription of pain medication can keep the terminally ill patient relatively mentally aware and pain-free. In addition, some hospitals may have psychologists or psychiatrists on staff who can help the patient cope better with the psychological dimension of pain.

Finding Out About Hospital Policies

Different doctors and different institutions have different policies about patient care. Since the doctors and hospitals are not likely to propose these alternatives, patients and families must take the initiative to find out what options they have, even if they don't choose to exercise them. Does the patient know the hospital's policy about Do Not Resuscitate orders? About living wills? About family consent to treatment if the patient becomes unconscious? About treatment for permanently unconscious patients? About competent patients refusing treatment? Hospital policies are ordinarily open to the public and patients should be able to see copies of them if they exist in written form. Policies that are not written are not policies. They are hospital customs, habits, and preferences, but they can be gotten around.

All hospitals treat patients without consent in emergencies. When patients come into the hospital in cardiac arrest or otherwise in desperate need of treatment, physicians will provide a full course of treatment, even if the patients appear with "I do not want to be treated" tattooed on their chests. Refusing lifesaving treatment is possible, but hospital and humane policies require that the patient's decision be made carefully and that the hospital have some time to make sure that the patient does actually and sincerely not want to be treated. If patients make unusual requests to refuse life-prolonging treatment, they should not expect the hospital personnel to respond quickly. They are professionally committed to saving lives and it may take them some time to be certain about the patient's true wishes and to adjust themselves to the idea that further life may not be in the patient's best interests, even from their own viewpoint.

Hospitals, like all bureaucratic institutions, operate most efficiently when friction of any kind is minimized. If a patient challenges an institutional rule or procedure, balks at treatment, or demands special attention (such as additional information, or outside consultants), then friction is generated. When a patient does disrupt the bureaucratic flow, it is likely that pressure will be applied to minimize the conflict. The patient is likely to be told, "You can't do it." Variations of this are "That isn't done here" and "We have a policy against that." This is a blockade strategy that requires the patient or family members to go higher. They may have to talk with key administrators (hospital directors or attorneys, for example) who allegedly prohibit the conduct. Often patients do not deal with administrators because they never get past physicians or nurses (who may not even know for sure what hospital policies are). When going to higher authorities, try not to find fault with those staff members who were simply trying to minimize friction. Present the problem as a matter involving some confusion. The patient will still be in the hospital, still dealing with those same people after the problem is resolved, and it helps to remember that as irrational as some actions seem, people do have reasons for their behavior.

Enlisting Support

To balance the power of hospital bureaucracies, patients and their families may need to enlist support from one or more of several sources. Patients and families may be helped by patient advocates, hospital chaplains, bioethics consultants, hospital ombudsmen, social workers, ethics committees, attorneys, insurance companies, or personnel from the bureaucracy itself, such as a hospital administrator. Hospitals usually will not tell patients as a routine matter whether they have people on staff to assist with patient care problems. Patients should be specific about the type of assistance they need.

Ethics consultants and ethics committees are the newest form of in-hospital help for patients. Many medium-to-large sized hospitals have one or the other. Ethics committees differ in their policies about who can bring a case before them, and if patients do not have access to the ethics committee itself, they should try to find out who the committee members are. It might be possible to speak individually with one of them. The ethics committee is very likely to have a member of the clergy as a member, usually one who is regularly in the hospital as a chaplain or member of the pastoral care staff. He or she may also be a local member of the clergy who regularly visits the hospital.

Outside the hospital, there are likely to be attorneys or other professionals who have a special interest in patient care problems. Some psychologists, social workers, philosophers, and theologians who have a special interest in bioethics *might* be identified through other patients, professional organizations, or the local grapevine. Inquiring of local colleges whether someone in the philosophy department specializes in bioethics could turn up an appropriate consultant. The local bar association or American Civil Liberties Union chapter also may have a committee whose members are versed in bioethics issues. Seeking an attorney should be a matter of last resort as matters are very likely to get worse once an lawyer is introduced into the problem. Although lawyers may be very effective and indeed devoted to protecting patients' rights, the hostility level between doctors and lawyers tends to be very high. As a result, the hospital is likely to perceive the patient's involving a lawyer as a threat of a malpractice suit. Lawyers who specialize in medical malpractice are not ideal choices for situations that involve patients' rights to choose treatment.

Knowing What You Want

Patients have a right to have their preferences respected, but that cannot happen if the patients themselves are uncertain about what they want. Once caught up in serious illness, it may be difficult to know preferences unambiguously. For this reason, it is important that people reflect on their personal values and preferences prior to entering a hospital. Only persons who have articulated values for themselves can preserve them when external pressures are designed to treat everyone alike, rather than to encourage individual choices.

Patients need to find out what resources are available within the hospital, and if nothing—or not enough—is found, then to look outside for help. Frequently, communication that has broken down or never gotten flowing can be helped by a neutral third party who can command the respect or attention of both patient and health care provider. As well, knowledgeable third parties may know about other resources to help the patient understand and achieve his or her own goals.

Patients should find out what legal directives are appropriate in their own state. Is there a statutory living will, natural death act, or durable power of attorney for health care? If so, patients should obtain these forms (if the physician does not know how to get them, a hospital administrator can assist). Patients need to read the forms, think about them, and discuss the possibilities with close friends and with a family physician if they have one. Then they should decide what they want and fill the forms out appropriately. Some forms need to be witnessed or notarized; others do not. Individuals should take care to ensure that they have completed the forms properly since hospitals will be very unwilling to honor documents that may not be legally sound. Once the document is completed, the signer should give a copy to his or her physician and another to a trusted family member or friend. If a durable power of attorney is signed, the signatory should discuss it with the person who is named to hold the power of attorney and should also give that person a copy of the form, appropriately signed and witnessed or notarized. These forms will be of no value if the patient is admitted to the hospital in a coma and no one knows that the form exists.

If the individual's state of residence has a legal document that permits people to specify kinds of care and kinds of situations, the individual should talk about his or her feelings and preferences with someone else before filling out the form. Statements such as "I don't want to be a vegetable" should be avoided because no one is sure what that means. Does that mean no ventilators but antibiotics? Antibiotics but no food? Food but no fluids? Nothing? All the hospital knows for sure is that it means "don't do everything."

If the state has no legally approved document to indicate treatment desires should the patient become incompetent, then the patient needs to sit down and write out his or her own preferences. Such a document may not have any legal force, but it will make it clear that the person has thought about what he or she wants and will give family members and physicians moral support if they decide to terminate care before the patient is dead. Again, however, generalized statements about "vegetables" and machines will not be very useful to the health care providers. What specifically are the conditions under which the patient no longer wants treatment? If he or she is no longer able to relate to other humans? No longer recognizes family members? Is unable to feed and dress him or herself? What specific treatment should be withheld? Cardiopulmonary resuscitation? Dialysis? Antibiotics or other medications? Food? Fluids? All food and fluids, or only artificially provided ones?

Patients and family members need to communicate clearly with one another. If patients and families disagree about what should be done, cannot reach consensus, give conflicting advice to the physician, or have no spokesperson, then physicians are likely to do what they themselves think is best. They will bear the legal brunt of the decision, and to ask them to go along with nonstandard treatment in the face of disagreement, uncertainty, or ambivalence is unrealistic. If the patient and family speak with one voice, they have much more power.

Conclusion

Deciding to forego lifesaving or life-prolonging treatment is the most common ethical dilemma in modern medical practice. The medical profession is geared to saving life and American culture is oriented toward clinging to life. Both deny death. The patient who wants to die sooner than absolutely necessary goes against the grain.

There are increasing numbers of family members who speak bitterly of the unwanted, aggressive treatment given to a parent, a sibling, a child, or a friend: treatment that did not defeat death but merely prolonged dying. All too often it was the patient who was defeated. It seems obvious that such treatment ought not to be given and yet it is. The problem is, in part, a difference between the perspectives of those who treat and of those who receive treatment. Beyond that, however, there is a great fear that if we accept individual requests to withhold or withdraw life-prolonging treatment, health care workers will eventually find it easier to withhold treatment from others who have not expressed such wishes.

If doctors always knew clearly what patients wanted, it might be easier. The fact that the preferences of incompetent patients are usually unknown will continue to make these end-of-life decisions difficult for everyone. The desire to reduce health costs may make these decisions more acceptable, but it will be sad if the ideology of patient autonomy is used to justify (and encourage) withholding treatment when the actual motivation is to save money. Aged, senile patients may need compassionate care more than they need artificial feeding. If withholding care becomes an easier choice, the risk is that patients will receive neither food nor care but, marked for death, will be set aside to exit this world truly alone. To avoid that risk it may be necessary, in the absence of knowing what specific patients want, to continue to feed them as well as give them all the care of which we are capable. Yet, this brings us full circle back to the problem of intervening perhaps only to prolong the dying process. The circle can best be broken by individuals having the foresight to plan for and document their own preferences about continuing or foregoing treatment before the issue arises and when they have the time to think about it carefully. It is easy to put off signing a durable power of attorney. It is a curious fact that many people who work in the field and believe in the importance of such documents have not themselves signed patient preference documents. It is uncomfortable to think about being so ill and so helpless. Yet, it is better to think about it now than to have one's family and friends bear the burden of feeling that they can do nothing to prevent treatment that they firmly believe the now-patient would not want.

CHAPTER 4

Genetic Screening and Counseling
Remodeling the Human Race

The belief that humans can and should control the processes of the universe drives Western civilization. So far, we have demonstrated remarkable ability to understand, to manipulate, and to alter those processes, but little indication that we are in control of anything. Our interest in control stems from honorable dreams of improvement: not content with the world as it is, we dream of making it better, even perfect. Our oldest myths sing of the invention of the world; they tempt us to equal and surpass the task, to invent again what already exists, but to invent it better. Mankind, for example, with its numerous imperfections has been something of a disappointment. Remodeling humans, eliminating some of the inborn errors, could reduce suffering, increase individual choices, lighten medical and welfare costs, and . . . well . . . provide a better product. Genetic technology will lead us to that improvement.

While the problems of defining life, creating life, extending life, and terminating life are making their daily demands upon us, the problems of *altering* life are lurking, just offstage, in the form of genetic technology. Genetic screening, genetic counseling, and genetic therapy all exist in some form already, but only screening and counseling are being actively pursued with human populations. Genetic therapy, in which scientists actually alter or replace individual genes or chromosomes, is very controversial, but this work remains experimental and, for the most part, involves only animal subjects. Genetic screening and counseling, on the other hand, are already active callings. Counseling and screening programs have provoked some controversy in the past, but the major difficulties still lie in the future, when we will be able to identify even more genetic defects but may not be able to do anything about curing them or changing them.

Genetic screening exists in three distinct forms: carrier screening, newborn screening, and fetal screening. The first two depend upon blood tests, while fetal screening may require a sample of amniotic fluid. The medical purpose of screening is to determine whether the adult, infant, or fetus either has a specific genetic disorder or carries genes that will leave his or her potential children at risk for genetic disease. Once that information is available, then either the law or the individual can make choices about what should be done. Choices might include the immediate treatment of the disorder (if treatment is available), sterilization, a voluntary choice not to reproduce, or fetal destruction by abortion.

Because technology develops at an uneven pace, the methods for carrier screening, newborn screening, and fetal screening have developed more quickly than treatment. If it were always possible to identify a genetic defect and follow diagnosis with treatment that had a reasonable expectation of success, then genetic screening would probably be questioned only on the basis of costs; but that is not the case now. With some defects, we can identify carriers but not fetuses; with others we can identify fetuses but not carriers. With some, we have treatment, occasionally curative but more frequently only palliative; for others we have nothing at all to offer beyond diagnosis. If genetic screening had nothing more to offer, then perhaps it would not have been pursued. It has had significant successes, however.

Detecting a disorder known as PKU (phenylketonuria) is the best example of the value of genetic screening. PKU is a metabolic disorder that can be diagnosed in the newborn but not in the fetus. If the PKU baby is left untreated, he or she will very quickly undergo irreparable mental damage and be severely retarded. Diagnosis is accurate and treatment is available, however. Because there is no specific population that is at particular risk for PKU, all newborn babies are screened for the disease. The screening is done with a small blood sample and the tests are highly reliable. In addition— and of great importance—they are quick and relatively inexpensive.

Babies with PKU are placed on special diets for the first six or seven years of life. Severe retardation is avoided and children who

would have existed with lives of very questionable quality have normal lives instead; children who would have drained their families
both financially and emotionally provide pleasure and become productive. The screening has entailed some problems, for if a baby is
erroneously diagnosed as having PKU and is then placed on the special diet, that baby can be severely harmed by the treatment. In
general, however, PKU newborn screening has been very successful.
Babies with PKU are born; they are diagnosed; they are successfully
treated. That is medicine at its best.

Our experiences with other forms of screening have not been
quite as successful, however. The presence of Tay-Sachs can be detected by fetal screening and a genetic tendency toward it by carrier
screening, but no treatment is available. Tay-Sachs is a genetic, inherited disease in which the infant is born, to all appearances, a normal child. Physical and mental deterioration quickly set in and the
child usually dies a lingering and difficult death between the ages of
2 and 4. An infant has Tay-Sachs because both mother and father
have recessive genes for the disorder. When both parents are carriers
of the recessive gene, one out of four of their children is statistically
predicted to have Tay-Sachs, two will be carriers but will not have
the disease, and one will neither be a carrier nor have the disease.

From a medical perspective, Tay-Sachs has the advantage of being largely confined to a small population: Ashkenazic Jews. Thus
the carrier population can be screened, through blood tests, so that
individuals will be informed whether they have the recessive gene.
They are at risk for giving birth to Tay-Sachs children only if each
partner in the marriage carries the recessive gene. If all members of
the population know whether they have the recessive gene, they can
take that into account when making marital choices. If two people
who both have recessive genes for Tay-Sachs marry and the wife becomes pregnant, fetal screening can be conducted during the pregnancy. Either amniocentesis or the newer chorionic villi testing can
be used to determine whether the fetus has Tay-Sachs. If the test is
positive, then the couple may choose to abort the defective fetus
since no treatment of the disease is possible and slow death is inevitable. In most instances, abortion is chosen.

Identifying a fetus with Tay-Sachs offers the potential child only
an earlier death and relief from a short life of suffering. Since diagnosis through amniocentesis is not available until late in the second
trimester, the family members have already developed significant
emotional attachments to the fetus and its destruction is emotion-

ally difficult, even though desired more for its own sake than for the family's or society's. Certainly a reasonable argument can be made that the life of a child with Tay-Sachs is so painful and burdensome to the child itself that no life would be preferable to such a harsh one.

Sickle cell anemia screening presents yet another level of genetic technology. Sickle cell anemia is an inherited disorder that displays great variance in its manifestations. It may be fatal, but it is not always or even usually so. It may be burdensome and debilitating with joint pains, fever, and anemia; it may be so minor that it escapes diagnosis. Sickle-cell, like Tay-Sachs, is found in a relatively circumscribed population, including blacks and individuals who come from Mediterranean areas. Carrier screening is available, but fetal screening enjoys only experimental status. Its accuracy remains under study. If both the mother and father of a child are carriers, they must wait until the child is born to find out if he or she has the disease. If they knew sooner, they might choose abortion since no cure is available for the condition. In most instances, palliative treatments make it much less problematic.

This is a situation very different from Tay-Sachs: with sickle-cell, individuals can be informed that they are carriers, but they cannot be reliably told when they have conceived a child with the disorder. Since there is no fetal screening, couples who are both carriers and who wish to avoid giving birth to a child with sickle-cell must have no children, even though three out of four of their children would be normal. In addition, unlike the Tay-Sachs child, a child with sickle-cell does not face a life that is inevitably short and painful. Thus it is much more difficult to argue that a child with sickle-cell anemia has a life that is not worth living.

When fetal screening is available for sickle-cell, the situation will probably parallel our experience with fetal screening for Down's syndrome. In the vast majority of cases, parents choose abortion for fetuses with Down's syndrome, even though many Down's children lead lives that appear to be rewarding to them. Many who argue that abortion is appropriate for Down's fetuses base their conclusions on the fact that the infant will be mentally retarded. When a society places enormous emphasis on mental skills and accomplishments, mentally defective children are seriously disadvantaged. Although they are able to sustain relationships and develop emotional aspects of their personalities, those qualities are not valued as much as intellectual capacities. Thus, many people perceive these children's lives to be a hardship not only to their families, but to them-selves as well because they are always shut out from the "real" life of the culture. Sickle-cell anemia, on the other hand, may include early death for the child, but does not include any degree of mental retardation. The same arguments that justify the abortion of Down's fetuses cannot be used to justify the abortion of sickle-cell fetuses. Genetic screening may be used to justify abortion, however. If the disorder is serious enough to merit screening, then the mere discovery of the disorder prior to birth may be used to justify de-struction of the fetus.

A new profession has recently arisen to implement genetic screening: the genetic counselor. Initially, physicians who were closely involved with genetic screening research acted as counselors to patients. As screening became more common, whether through mandated or voluntary programs, it quickly became apparent that there were insufficient numbers of doctors with adequate training. Even now, when genetic technology has advanced considerably, many medical schools do not include genetics courses in their cur-riculum. As a result, many—and perhaps most—physicians are not skilled enough to provide expert genetic counseling.

Nonphysician counselors usually have completed a graduate de-gree in genetic counseling, including training in both psychology and biology. Despite the degrees, however, there are substantial dis-agreements about the role of the counselor. Are counselors only to provide information about the screening procedures and the options available when positive tests are received, or do they have some obli-gation either to their clients or to society to urge those with positive tests to take particular forms of action? For example, when a preg-nant woman is advised that her fetus has Tay-Sachs, should she be informed that abortion is an available option or should she be ad-vised that abortion is the most common or the best solution? If she is opposed to abortion or is uncertain about her choices, should she be introduced to parents whose children died from Tay-Sachs?

The role of the genetic counselor is very controversial because counseling can be used to pursue eugenics policies. If the purpose of genetic screening is to maximize individuals' reproductive choices, then genetic counseling can only be informative, as all choices must be truly voluntary. No mandatory screening programs could exist. If, on the other hand, the purpose of genetic screening is to permit society to take a hand in human evolution by deciding whether cer-tain genes should be discouraged, then individual choices would be minimal. Screening programs would be mandatory, and sterilization for carriers of disapproved conditions and abortion for disapproved fetuses would be necessary. Eugenics theories have had a long history in the United States, but they are currently out of fashion, both in the courts and in the media. Nonetheless, an undercurrent of interest in eugenics continues to be felt in this country and its effect should not be underestimated.

Because of the recognition of individual rights and the still-fresh abhorrence of Nazi Germany's eugenics practices, it is extremely unlikely that any extensive eugenics policies could be officially established in the United States today. This does not, however, mean that genetic technology will be used only to further individual choice. Because the genetic counselor is in a position to influence significantly the kinds of choices that people make, there will always be the possibility that eugenics concerns will be indirectly pursued. Genetic counselors will have a point of view and it is unlikely that people who are drawn to the field as a profession will favor the birth of genetically defective children. Thus the profession itself is likely to have an active bias toward carrier restraint (through sterilization) and fetal abortion. In addition, other forms of societal pressure will doubtless be felt by couples who face these problems. The birth of a genetically defective child inevitably places a significant financial burden upon a family. Currently, whether a defective child's special needs are met largely depends on government funding for health care, special education, family assistance, and, in many cases, for residential or institutional placement. Public policies that reduce or eliminate this assistance to families will, in effect, indirectly further eugenics policies. These welfare programs are always susceptible to cutting since the handicapped are not a very powerful political force. At present, however, families can argue for these funds on the grounds that neither they nor their children are responsible for the position in which they find themselves. When carrier screening and prenatal screening for most handicaps are available, that argument will be more difficult to make. Thus, in a time when welfare funds are under attack, the family who *chooses* to give birth to a defective child will risk being told that they must accept the responsibilities— financial and psychological—that their choice entails.

By 1984, 190 defects including Down's syndrome, spina bifida, and Tay-Sachs could be detected prenatally, but nothing much could be done about them. Research is progressing on all fronts of genetic technology, but the closest advances will not include new treatments; instead, they will increase the number of defects that can be detected. Techniques for detecting both cystic fibrosis and Huntington's chorea are close at hand. When these tests are available, yet new problems will be upon us. The population at risk for cystic fibrosis is not a relatively small, discrete population; instead it is all Caucasians. Screening for cystic fibrosis will necessitate a substantial financial investment.

Huntington's chorea offers a different kind of problem. This disease, which leads to paralysis and debilitating mental destruction, does not usually manifest itself until the person reaches the age of 30 or even older. Because it is a disorder involving a dominant gene, only one member of a couple need have the single gene, and statistically half of their children will have the disease. Many have argued that, in the absence of carrier screening, anyone who might have the disorder should not have children. When the disorder can be detected prenatally, many will urge abortion. Yet, Huntington's is not like Tay-Sachs, a disease that leads quickly to a difficult death. The individual's life will proceed normally for thirty to forty years, though shadowed by the possibility of a dark death. Woody Guthrie, who made an immeasurable contribution to American folk music, was a victim of Huntington's chorea. His dying was harsh and hard for him and his family; yet, his life and the music that grew out of his life gave this country a touch of glory. Was his a life not worth living?

It is not clear whether genetic technology offers us a real frontier or an illusion of control in which destroying fetuses with genetic defects is our solution to genetic imperfection. The research has been inspired by a desire to provide treatments for newborns, but few treatments have been found. Instead, such knowledge as we have gained—the ability to identify those at risk of defect—has largely provided us with even more difficult choices. How much perfection do we require in a human being? Unless genetic technology provides treatments for genetic defects (and so far its record is very poor), that is the question we have to answer. That is the question that those who already know they are at risk ask themselves often. As for the rest of us, we may not yet know what risks we are running.

Case Study

Barbara Booth was 32, happily married, and a successful free-lance writer. An outsider would be inclined to say that, except for the fact that her parents had both died too young, Barbara's life was uncommonly happy. The outsider would be wrong, however, for although Barbara presented a calm and competent face to the world, she regularly suffered from shattering migraine headaches caused by extreme and unresolvable stress. A portion of the stress stemmed from the fact that Barbara and her husband Mark remained childless after eight years of marriage. Mark believed that Barbara's failure to become pregnant was a result of some medical problem, but Barbara knew that pregnancy was virtually impossible since she took birth control pills with rigid regularity. Mark was unaware of this fact and Barbara could not bring herself to explain the reasons to him. It was this hidden aspect of their relationship that accounted for the headaches more than the childlessness, although Barbara very much wanted to have children of their own.

The outsider would have been startled to discover the kind of turmoil that had marked Barbara's life from the time she was 14 and through her college years, but it would have led him or her to understand immediately the distress in which she now found herself. Mark, too, would probably understand Barbara's situation. Having failed to tell him about her family and herself from the beginning, however, she could now find neither the courage nor a decent explanation for her failure to tell him the truth.

Barbara and her younger sister Dorothy had grown up in a small town in Utah. Her father, Jack Simmons, had owned a hardware store that had been a gathering place for all the local farmers. Jack was himself a farmer's son who had moved into town and into business, but he continued to be close to the land, even after he had left it. Barbara's mother Amanda had been an elementary school teacher who had married Jack at the age of 30. In the 1940s, everyone still thought of a 30-year-old single teacher as an inevitable old maid, so the marriage had been a surprise to the townspeople and to Amanda herself. It had, however, turned out well and she and Jack produced two daughters within the first two years of their marriage. Dorothy and Barbara were their father's delight. When Amanda returned to teaching, their father insisted that they come to the store after school and wait there for their mother to pick them up. He liked having them around and taught them to wait on customers as soon as they were tall enough to see over the store counters. The girls liked being with their father whenever it was possible, for their mother retained too much of the schoolteacher's insistence on doing things the right way. Their father, on the other hand, simply reveled in their being and they were as anxious to please him as he was willing to be pleased. Their ordinary, pleasurable family life continued as if it were guaranteed by the American dream until Barbara was fourteen, when the dream suddenly turned into a nightmare that showed no signs of changing.

In the winter of Barbara's fourteenth year, her mother and sister were killed in a car accident when the car that Amanda was driving skidded out of control on an icy downhill stretch of the road and crashed head-on into a truck lumbering up the hill. Jack Simmons was devastated by the tragedy, but for the first week or so after the accident, he stayed very close to Barbara, both offering her the comfort of his presence and hoping for some solace in their shared sorrow. Although Barbara had always had a loving relationship with her father, in the face of her mother's and sister's deaths, she withdrew into herself, ignoring both his silent offers and spoken entreaties.

Totally engrossed in her own suffering, Barbara failed to notice much about her father's situation in the ensuing months. Neighbors and the farmers who gathered at the store, however, did notice that Jack had lost much of his quiet zest for life. They talked quietly among themselves with sympathetic noddings about the effects that personal tragedy had on a man, and awkwardly patted Jack on the shoulder when they left the store after making a purchase. They assumed, as farmers do and must, that time alone holds the changes needed for life's continuance. Jack did not return to his former ways, however. His distracted sorrowfulness slowly transformed itself into distracted irritability. Friends began to shake their heads at Jack's moodiness when, a year after Amanda's and Dorothy's deaths, time seemed to be making no inroads, seemed in fact to be losing. Barbara had made some adjustments during the year, but she still found herself estranged from her father. Her forays into adolescent life seemed to enrage him, forcing them even farther apart at a time when she very much needed him—not least because he was all the family she had.

Jack was bewildered by the changes in his being. He found himself angry, depressed, and dejected. He seemed unable to control his mood swings. Struggling to get a hold on his life, he continually failed and could not understand why he was so unsuccessful. He had avoided doctors, even though several friends had suggested that a doctor's visit might be in order, but when he began to experience jerky movements of his head, quite outside his control, he was concerned enough to schedule an appointment. This first visit was inconclusive, but the family doctor was not content with the idea that this was all the natural result of Amanda's death. Many visits to many doctors followed until, finally, the Salt Lake City specialist diagnosed Huntington's chorea. By the time that diagnosis was final, Jack's physical condition had begun to deteriorate even further, with increased facial tics and jerks. The specialist explained to Jack that the involuntary body movements would increase and that medicine would be able only to slow down the disabilities but not eliminate them. He did not give him a close or graphic account of the mental disabilities that would probably accompany the course of the disease, in part for fear of creating them sooner by suggestion. In any case, there would be time enough for further discussion and further education of the patient. The news that a patient, even someone else's patient, has an incurable disease with acute physical and mental suffering cannot be delivered too slowly.

Jack did not tell Barbara about the doctor's diagnosis for some months. He did not believe it entirely himself and he waited, in part, for some sign that the doctor was wrong. He began to pray at night and at odd moments during the day found himself talking to a God he had long ago lost interest in. He became acutely self-conscious about the uncontrollable facial tics and jerky hand and arm movements and hired a young man to do more of the counter work in the store. He retreated more and more to the rough office he had carved out of the store's storage area. He began to keep journals, attempting to track the effects of the disease, but over time, his attempts to discover whether he was changing became lost in his conviction that his doctor was trying to poison him with the constantly changing medications he urged upon him.

At age 17, Barbara was faced with the knowledge that her father would never be the same again. The disease was progressing. The separation that had grown between them during the three years since her mother had died was too great for her to cross, and Jack was not steady enough in his purpose to heal the rift. Barbara watched her father with despair and a kind of hatred, for he seemed to be inflicting his disaster upon her, abandoning her just as her mother had, even if neither had done so by intent. She could not come to terms with the dreadful disease he had taken on, so she acted as if no illness existed; her behavior suggested, instead, that her obstinate, angry, and irrational father had become her adversary.

He urged her to go away to college and she did so, with feelings both of guilt and of joy at escaping the doom-filled atmosphere of their daily life. She did not return home at Thanksgiving, going instead to her roommate's nearby family home, explaining by telephone to her angry father that there was not enough time to make the trip back to their home. She intended to return at Christmas, but the day before she was scheduled to leave, she received news that her father had shot himself with a rifle in the fields behind their house. He had died instantly. Being orphaned the second time was less painful for Barbara than the first. In part she was numbed to the loss; in part she had expected it, though not, of course, so quickly; in part she was grateful that her father had spared himself and her the continuing deterioration. She returned home for the funeral and the comforts of the friends and neighbors of her childhood.

When she saw Doctor Sloane, her father's doctor, at the funeral, he urged her to come by and see him before she left town. When she did, he told her of his last meetings with her father and of Jack's profound concern about her. He had asked the doctor to talk with Barbara sometime soon, perhaps at Christmas time, to make sure that she understood the medical facts about her father's disease. He had said that perhaps the worst of it all was thinking that he had passed this death sentence on to her as well. He could, he said, never forgive himself for that. Dr. Sloane assured Barbara that her father had chosen his path well and urged her to consider her father's experience. "God willing," he told her as she was leaving, "you will escape this. But if you don't, Barbara, then at least don't burden the end with the knowledge that you may have done this to your own child. That's what your father wanted me to tell you." His intentions were kindly, she knew, but when she left the office, she felt as if he had stamped the word DOOMED on her forehead for all to see. When she boarded the plane, she left with a resolve never again to return to the town; instead to create for herself a future that would have no room for the despair of her past.

Barbara completed her college degree promptly and moved east, putting even more distance between her and the cemetery that sheltered her family. She found a job at a pharmaceutical supply house where she edited research reports. A year after she began work, she met a young biochemist researcher named Mark Booth. Two years later they were married, rather to Barbara's surprise since during her last years in college she had convinced herself that the possibility that she too would develop Huntington's chorea was sufficient reason for her neither to marry nor to have children. Mark had broken through all her defenses with his engaging charm and his extraordinary zest for the possibilities of each day, and had lifted her neatly out of the brown study in which she had enshrouded herself for so many years. He reminded her of the possibility of lightness and laughter and she began to make tiny connections between the sunny 14-year-old she had been and the serious, reliable 22-year-old she had become. For over a year, Mark tried to persuade her to marry him. Barbara finally accepted not only because she was worn down by his unanswerable arguments but also because she could not, in the last analysis, resist holding onto the love he offered her and which she very much wanted to have and to return.

He wanted children someday but was in no rush to become a father. A dozen times, or maybe a hundred times, Barbara tried to tell Mark the truth about her father's death, but each time she faltered. Mark sensed her discomfort in talking about her deceased parents, but he attributed that to the deep loss she had experienced when (as he believed) her parents and sister had been killed in an automobile accident. As a result, he did not encourage her to talk about them and thus made it harder for her. When she began to bring up the subject of her parents, even in a very tentative way, he did not ask questions or help her to advance the topic. Instead, he left her alone, accepting her need to say only what was comfortable for her, only what she wanted. Since the topic could not possibly be comfortable for her and she wanted to say very little, very little was said.

They were married and they were happy at first, despite Barbara's occasional gloomy spells when the thought of her clouded future and of Mark's ignorance about her condition pressed too much upon her. Later, these periods of withdrawal began to drive a small wedge between them and Barbara realized that she had to do something. She spoke with her physician about the headaches and depressions and he referred her to a therapist, after a physical exam displayed no problems. When she confessed the truth of her father's death to the therapist, she urged her to talk with a genetic counselor and then to tell her husband the truth. Barbara met with the counselor, Mr. Purdy, but he was able to tell her nothing that she did not already know, had not already been told, or had not read. Like her father's doctor, he advised her to have no children. Unlike her therapist, he did not seem to care whether she told her husband. He focused on the agonizing prospects for the Huntington's victim and asked her straightforwardly if she were prepared to inflict yet another suffering person on the world. He understood that choosing not to have children would be a great personal sacrifice, but by having no children, the line of disease that stretched out from her father would be definitely, permanently stopped. His logic was impeccable and yet Barbara was not convinced that his advice was correct.

She had a 50 percent chance of having the Huntington's gene, and if she had it, the disease might begin to show itself by the time she was 35, three years hence. Or, it might wait longer as it had for her father. If she had it, any child she gave birth to would have a 50 percent chance of also having the disease. In fact, she sometimes thought, her statistical chances were not bad: if she didn't have the gene, none of her children would have the disorder, and if she did only half would. The statistics were on her side, really: a 75 percent chance of winning would surely make you gamble on a horse. But would it make you gamble on a baby or on a husband? Even if she had a child with the gene, it would have a life before the disease showed up. If it had been her mother rather than her father who had carried the defect, she would never have known it, for her life ended before then. Should *she* have never lived because she died young?

As Barbara repeatedly struggled through her thoughts and feelings about her own life and about the possibility of having children, she came again and again to the same question. Does the fact of a hard death and disease make all the life that precedes it worthless? She thought about whether her parents would have remained childless had they been able to foretell the future. She knew that, like her father, she would kill herself as soon as she realized that the disease was upon her, if that time came. Yet, was it worse to choose one's death rather than to be captured by it unaware? Was the possibility that she might die early a reason not to live at all? Didn't that possibility give more intensity to each day of her life?

Someday, probably very soon, science would arrive with help for those like her. They would tell her for sure that she was—or was not—a carrier. Those who were free of taint would breathe easier at the expense of those who were left behind. With accurate carrier screening, one group of people would be cursed with the certainty of their defect without any hope of treatment or cure. Or perhaps the scientists would also quickly learn to spot the defect through amniocentesis and the hopeful parents would be free to abort all those fetuses who, like themselves, were fated to die sooner. But would abortions for this reason be justified? She wasn't sure.

Barbara spent countless hours going over the arguments in her own head and with her therapist. Unlike the genetic counselor, the therapist urged her to no particular decision, suggesting only that as the child would be Mark's as well as hers, so ought the decision to be shared. When a year of weekly meetings with the therapist had passed, Barbara realized that both her headaches and her periods of depression were decreasing in intensity and frequency. Simply grappling with the question, regardless of how ineffectively, appeared to give her some relief and she found hope in that knowledge.

One day some months later, when the lingering grip of winter had briefly given way to the promise of spring sunshine, Barbara stood looking across a city park where tiny green leaf tips were edging up out of the sullen dirt. As she breathed in the smell of spring, she watched the people jostling by, clearly lightened by the indications that warmth and flowers and blue skies would return to them. As a rainbow promised an end to God's boundless wrath, so the return of spring promised the cycle of life would continue. Infused with that promise, Barbara at last went home, this time able to tell Mark of her father's death and of her own compromised future.

Fifteen months later, Barbara gave birth to a baby boy. She and Mark do not know what the future holds for their son any more than they know what the future holds for Barbara. It is possible that they will never have need of a cure or treatment for Huntington's, or if they do, one will become available. They take the days as they come. Everyone's future is a mystery; why not theirs?

The Decision Makers: Their Perspectives and Interests

Medical Perspectives

Medical perspectives in genetic technology, like medical perspectives in fertility programs, may differ depending upon whether physicians are primarily interested in research or in clinical care. Furthermore, the traditional doctor-patient relationship model does not function well in genetic screening because in many instances the person (or prospective person) with the disorder or defect is not the patient and because the disorder cannot usually be treated. The apparent "patient" is the individual whose carrier status is being determined, but the individuals who will be most affected by whatever decisions are made within the doctor-patient relationship are the unborn or as-yet unconceived children of that person.

The physician whose primary interest is research may have no involvement with patients. The pure research perspective is frequently committed to extending knowledge without attending to the effects of that knowledge on society. Individuals who argue that the search for knowledge needs no justification beyond itself will understandably reject claims that the benefit of genetic research may not outweigh harm caused to individuals. Other researchers are prepared to acknowledge that the currently available fragmentary knowledge about most genetic disorders can make individual choices more difficult and can lead to psychological harm. They contend, however, that this is only a short-term problem caused by insufficient knowledge. In the long run, more extensive research efforts will provide enough knowledge to enable individuals to make better choices about whether children should be conceived or born.

Other researchers are not particularly concerned about the value of individual choice or expanded knowledge. Instead they worry about the biological and societal effects of all reproductive choices involving genetic dysfunctions on the human genetic pool. Because of medical advances, they argue, more people with genetic defects are living to reproduce and pass on their defective genes. As a result (or so the argument goes), the human gene pool now contains a larger percentage of defective genes than it once held. Now that science has uncovered the role of heredity in many disorders, humans are obliged to reduce the possibility that people with defective genes will reproduce. Only in this way, they argue, can the species's deterioration be prevented.

Physicians actively involved with patients who risk genetic defects may have a perspective very different from those of the researchers. Because they work with individuals who are struggling with choices about reproduction or are coping with genetic disease itself, these doctors are much more likely to be interested in reducing their patients' pain, stress, anxiety, and discomfort in whatever ways are possible. However, they are likely to be strong supporters of research, expecting that it will eventually lead to genetic alterations, cures, or effective treatments of genetic diseases. In the absence of cure or treatment, clinicians are likely to encourage abortion when there is a strong possibility of genetic abnormality or to discourage reproduction when the couple's carrier status makes having children a risky business.

Furthermore, it is well known that patients are for the most part very responsive to physicians' recommendations and suggestions about treatment in serious situations. Thus, physicians may very well not be responding to parental requests as much as they are offering recommendations that will in fact determine the kinds of requests that parents make. As a result, physicians who are directly involved in either carrier or prenatal screening may actually discourage patients either from conceiving children or giving birth to children when there is a risk of genetic defect, even though they believe that they are only providing information so that parents can make their own choices.

Genetic Counselors

The role of genetic counselors is controversial because genetic technology can serve either individual interests or societal interests, either for increasing personal choices or furthering eugenics policies. Since there is no societal consensus on what interests genetic technology *should* serve, genetic counselors may be inclined to either (or to both). Physicians, as high-status professionals in American society, have considerable discretion with respect to their actions. When physicians were providing genetic counseling, there was less concern about what patients were being told. Now that genetic counseling is primarily in the hands of both medical and nonmedical professionals, numerous questions arise about what the genetic counselor should offer to the client and whose values are to prevail.

The genetic counselor's first duty is to provide accurate information about the genetic disorder and about the individual's risk. The complications arise with the counselor's role in decision making. Should the counselor offer advice to the client? The counselor is, like the physician in a doctor-patient relationship, in a superior position with respect to knowledge. Physicians are expected to make recommendations about appropriate measures for the patient to take, whether they be surgery, medication, diet, or exercise. The genetic counselor has in fact replaced the physician in this role, and as the physician was expected to make recommendations, then perhaps the counselor should also do so. If clients need only basic information, then there is perhaps little need for counselors: videotapes or information booklets will suffice. Counselors can also help clients clarify their values and their choices. But should counseling go on to provide individualized advice? The counselor's personal knowledge of the client makes this possible. Giving advice, however, may lead to a conflict between the counselor's values and the client's values.

Although the counselor-client relationship parallels the doctor-patient relationship, it also differs from it in that the client has not come for diagnosis and treatment. Clients come for information about possible reproductive problems in the future. Any advice (as opposed to information) that the counselor might offer would not be of a medical nature but would, instead, be a value judgment about whether the individual should have children or whether a fetus should be aborted. These are not medical questions. It is well known, of course, that physicians frequently offer value judgments under the guise of medical advice to their patients, but these judgments are at least intermingled with actual medical information and frequently are based upon value assumptions that both doctor and patient hold. For example, when a doctor tells a patient to quit smoking or stop drinking, these are value judgments in the form of medical advice. The underlying value assumption is that "you should want to live longer" or "you should want to retain your health," and thus should follow your doctor's advice. Do clients share assumptions with genetic counselors like "you should want to improve the human gene pool" or "people with genetic defects would be better off if they had never been born"? If clients ask for advice, should the counselor offer it or remain neutral? The question is difficult and professionals disagree about its answer.

Genetic counselors have additional problems with respect to confidentiality. When a counselor has information about genetic defects, does anyone but the client have a right to that information? Does a husband, for example, have a right to know that his wife has a genetic defect? Does a brother have the right to know that his sister carries a defective gene, if that indicates that he too may have the gene? Although many policies are guided by a general belief that everyone should have as much relevant information as possible when making important decisions, individual rights to privacy must also be considered. Some writers argue that the genetic counselor's obligations are only to the patient and thus the counselor may not reveal any information without the client's consent. That position assumes that genetic technology is intended to serve only individual interests as opposed to the interests of larger groups, including couples, families, or society as a whole. Certainly counselors may (and do) attempt to persuade clients to reveal information. Nevertheless, clients may remain unwilling to tell others who might benefit from the knowledge. Although it may appear wrong or even irrational to the counselor, the quality of the client's reasons are irrelevant if genetic technology is intended to serve the client's interests and preferences.

Legal Perspectives

Because genetic screening is, at least in part, a matter of eugenics policy, the law's perspectives include attitudes toward sterilization and abortion. It is only in recent years that the law has directly addressed genetic screening. The law has been concerned both with permitting and prohibiting abortion, with voluntary and involuntary sterilization, and with mandatory and voluntary screening. Currently, abortion laws are very permissive, voluntary sterilization is widely available (now the most common method of contraception, in fact), involuntary sterilization is almost totally prohibited, and although legally mandated genetic screening programs exist, most are voluntary.

The second primary legal interest in genetic technology involves confidentiality of genetic information. Here again individual privacy rights can come into conflict with public welfare claims. Mandatory premarital screening of specified populations means that the couple must be informed of one another's genetic status. Some have also argued that sperm donors for artificial insemination should be legally required to undergo genetic screening and that appropriate records should be kept on donors. Similarly, many have urged that public welfare claims justify maintaining available records on the genetic status of the parents of children who have been placed for adoption. In all these cases, adults' expectations of confidentiality would be overriden by claims that the public welfare would be better served by making genetic information available.

At present, the legal climate defers for the most part to individual choices. It is very unlikely that there will be any significant attempts to require abortions of defective fetuses or to require sterilization of individuals who carry genetic defects, or even to require participation in screening programs where no treatment is available. The undercurrent of approval for eugenics that exists in the United States, however, might eventually manifest itself again if it were coupled with strong economic arguments relating to public welfare. Because involuntary sterilization of the incompetent is now so severely circumscribed, any legal changes toward involuntary sterilization of the competent seem very remote and perhaps impossible. The possibility of public policies that use social and economic pressures to achieve those ends can easily be imagined. For example, welfare benefits for genetically defective children might be eliminated or reduced significantly if parents voluntarily choose to give birth to such children.

Ethical Perspectives

Philosophers' primary concerns with genetic screening and counseling have been the conflicts between autonomy, privacy, and the obligation not to harm others. Many philosophers have urged that all applications of genetic technology be voluntary in order to maximize personal autonomy and demonstrate respect for the individual. The argument has been that if individuals must bear the burden of either the prospective genetic disorder or the knowledge about their carrier status, then they have the right to choose to participate in tests and to decide whether to take on parenthood.

Such positions seem quite adequate as long as only the individual parent is considered. It is possible that the individual's desire to be a parent conflicts with the child's right not to have to live a life of considerable suffering. The autonomy rights of individuals thus come into conflict with the child's rights not to be subjected to future harm. The adult's "right" to become a parent cannot be reconciled with the duty not to bring children into the world knowing that they will suffer harm. Some philosophers have argued that the right to choose parenthood should fall before the child's right to a reasonable chance for a healthy life. Especially where parenthood can be pursued by other means (such as adoption, artificial insemination, or embryo transfer), they argue, a child should not be brought into the world when the parents know it will live only a short time and suffer considerably (as with Tay-Sachs). Similarly, it should not be conceived when there is a substantial probability that the child will suffer from a genetic disease that involves substantial suffering. This position argues that genetically defective children ought not to be conceived or born because being born violates the child's rights to a healthy life.

Others, however, have maintained that parents alone have the right to decide whether they should give birth to children and that their choice should be the dominant value. Here, the argument is that the mere fact of genetic defect or possibility of such a defect does not necessarily constitute a life that is not worth living, even though suffering may be a part of the life. Individuals then would be morally entitled to give birth to genetically defective children because those lives, even though imperfect in some biological way, are still human lives that have value, both to the child and to the parents. The simplest (and also perhaps most extreme) form of this position is that, for the child, any life is better than no life. This argument is also closely connected with the sanctity-of-life argument that would prohibit aborting of fetuses simply because of a genetic defect on the grounds that all lives must be shown equal respect. This position concludes that parents have the right to give birth to genetically defective children because all life has value and because parents are best able to decide whether being born will serve their children's interests.

A third conflicting position between autonomy rights and the duty not to harm others focuses on the individual's right to procreate versus the *society's* right not to be harmed (as opposed to the child's right not to be harmed). Some philosophers have argued that both the individuals' rights to be parents and the prospective child's "right" to be born are less compelling than society's right not to be harmed. In these instances, society is harmed by increasing the number of defects in the genetic pool and by burdening society with the extra care and extra costs required by the genetically defective. This position underlies public policy arguments suggesting that those who have knowingly given birth to defective children have no right to expect society to provide additional financial assistance or other aid not received by families with normal children.

Public Policy Perspective

The basic public policy question is whether genetic screening and counseling should serve public interests or private/individual interests. At present, policy makers have concluded that individual and private interests are the most vital. Although some mandatory screening programs for defects without cures still exist, the trend is toward increased public education and voluntary screening. The federal government provides funds to assist the states in this effort, but has backed education and voluntary screening rather than mandatory screening.

Public policy questions still remain, however, with respect to the social costs of preventing and caring for genetically defective individuals. Additional public policy questions will arise when genetic therapy that can alter gene structures is available. This is likely to be complex and thus expensive. Policy will be complicated by demographic factors. An increased percentage of older women are now giving birth to children, and because those older women belong to the large cohort known as the "baby boom," a 65 percent increase in the number of genetically defective births in the near future is predicted: older women are more likely to give birth to children with genetic abnormalities. Increased numbers and increased technology will unite to heighten the cost factor when future public policies about genetic defects are made.

At a time when worries about expanding health care costs are heard at dinner tables as well as government offices, financial constraints are likely to have a primary role in public policy decisions. The willingness of the government, either at the state or national level, to provide substantial sums either for additional research or for patient care is very limited. In 1976, the U.S. Congress authorized $90 million for research, testing, and counseling for genetic diseases, but the funds were not appropriated. Spokespersons for any number of health needs are clamoring for their share, and those who want money to finance research on cures for genetic diseases will be fortunate even to be invited to the table. At a time when cost-benefit analyses determine courses of action, the costs of caring for those with genetic diseases are far easier to calculate than are the benefits, which are uncertain, amorphous, and difficult to quantify. Prenatal screening and selective abortion constitute a fiscally sound method of dealing with genetic defects. To the extent that policy makers perceive genetic defects as an individual problem, they are unlikely to give it high priority for funding of any kind, whether screening, counseling, selective abortion, or research into treatment. On the other hand, to the extent that they perceive it as a public health problem, they are likely to fund prenatal screening and abortion but not long-term care, nor research into cures or treatments (like genetic surgery) that are complex and very expensive.

What's a Patient to Do?

In the case of Barbara Booth we saw her struggle alone, then seek help from physicians, therapists, and counselors, and finally confide in her husband. It is helpful to review certain features of her case before turning to more general considerations germane to patients in similar situations.

Barbara's family physician advised Barbara not to consider having children, guided by his personal knowledge of her father and her father's tragic death. Although he provided her with accurate information, he was concerned as a family friend and physician to shield her and her prospective children from the anguish that Jack Simmons and Barbara herself would go through. He was not motivated by concerns about the quality of human genes, about eugenics policies, or about the future prospects of research in this area. His aim was simple and true: to prevent suffering. Yet, Barbara herself had seen her father's condition (although not from the same perspective as Dr. Sloane). His protective feelings toward the young girl were both understandable and admirable, but his advice did not help her to come to her own answers; for many years, it actually kept her from thinking about the question.

The genetic counselor to whom Barbara is referred by her psychotherapist does provide her with accurate information, but he also urges her not to have children. His reasons, unlike those of Barbara's family doctor, are not based on the need to avoid personal unhappiness whenever possible. Instead, he is concerned about social responsibility. When he tells Barbara that by making this great personal sacrifice she can help to eliminate Huntington's chorea from the world, he is not concerned about her specifically, but about the fate of the world. He is appealing to her altruistic sense, not to her ordinary sense of self-interest. A counselor who is primarily concerned about the individual's own situation (rather than society's situation) might be more inclined to urge that the husband be informed about the genetic facts. An interest in maximizing individual choice would logically include the spouse, since any child that is or is not born will be the child of both.

Barbara has all the information she needs, but information does not provide her with a way to make decisions. Nor has advice from professionals about what she should do helped her. It is only when she is able to share the decision with her husband that she is able to come to a decision with which she can be comfortable. Many individuals at risk for Huntington's disease do have children, despite the risk and despite the strong opinions of many genetics specialists that they should not. For Barbara, as for many others who face the kind of risk she does, life must be lived one day at a time. Death and disease will come when they come, but until then, the ordinary pleasures of life are their lot.

Barbara withheld information from Mark because she was afraid of the effect that such knowledge would have on him. She might reasonably be concerned that if he knew she might have the disease, he would be less interested in her. Beyond that, she has left home and attempted to erase her past psychologically to help cope with the awesome uncertainty in her life. To maintain her fragile sense of herself, she needs to be treated as a normal person. If Mark were to know, he could not treat her that way, even if he accepted her without stigmatization.

Mark and Barbara's ultimate decision to have children represents their belief that when harm is not inevitable, it is morally permissible to give birth to a child. Should the child develop Huntington's disease, they have a significant moral responsibility to provide enormous psychological and other support. This will be impossible for Barbara, however. If the child is a victim of Huntington's, Barbara will also have the disorder and probably will not survive long enough to know about her child's fate. Mark's knowing involvement in their decision to have children becomes all the more important in this light, since the burden of support will fall on him.

Dealing effectively with genetic defect risks means acquiring information. Individuals must first know whether they are at special risk and, if they are, must know what they can do and are willing to do to control that risk. Currently, there is little legal regulation of individual choice because mandatory screening is unpopular and abortion laws are liberal. Individuals should decide how they think and feel about personal eugenic decisions and learn what they can do to realize their preferences.

Before patients can do anything, they must know whether they are at special risk for having children with genetic defects. Despite some efforts at public education, most people have little idea about whether they are in a high-risk category. Every pregnant woman is at some risk, of course, but few receive any information about additional risks that derive from the prospective parents' ethnic background, family history, or age. Since that appears to be a technical/

medical matter, most people assume that providing this information is the physician's responsibility. However, that has not proved to be a reliable assumption. Even though physicians know that there is an increased risk of Down's syndrome for pregnant women over the age of 35, only a small proportion of these women know about or use amniocentesis. This is so even though doctors have been held legally liable for failing to tell older women of their risk of a Down's birth and the availability of amniocentesis.

If physicians cannot always be expected to inquire about risk factors, patients can offer specific information about their own background and inquire as to whether it places them at special risk. In order to do so, patients must assess and present their own background honestly. Age and ethnic background can be important clues. Family incidence of genetically defective births provides very important information, but many couples fail to mention it to their physician either because they are embarrassed by the information, or because they psychologically deny its relevance to their own situation. This is illustrated by one highly educated patient who, upon being told that she was at additional risk because a cousin had given birth to a child with a genetic defect, unhesitatingly replied that she scarcely knew the cousin! Despite educational efforts to the contrary, many people regard genetic defects as shameful. If patients are to get the information they need from their physicians, they must provide the information the physician needs.

Ideally, if individuals espouse eugenics values, they should know in advance of marriage or pregnancy the nature of any particular risk they run. Individuals who have family histories of defective births or who are among those ethnic/geographical groups with particular risks should learn about whether there are carrier tests that can be performed to give them clear information about their status. Before they undergo carrier testing, they should be aware of the psychological burdens that a positive carrier test may give them. Knowing that one is a biological carrier of an undesirable genetic trait may be very harmful to self-esteem and may make serious male-female relationships more difficult. Mandatory carrier screening implies that everyone should know their carrier status, regardless of the personal costs to those who are screened. The current emphasis on voluntary screening implies public acceptance of the argument that the personal costs of knowing may be too burdensome for some individuals. Persons who choose carrier testing should first consider whether they want those burdens.

If prenatal testing is available and appropriate, then patients must decide whether they want that information. There are several benefits to having this information. First of all, if the test is negative, the parents' anxiety is relieved. If the test is positive, then abortion can be pursued if that is acceptable. If testing is conducted late in the pregnancy (as amniocentesis must be), then abortion is likely to be accompanied by greater levels of stress. Some have argued that prenatal tests, whether through amniocentesis, chorionic villi, ultrasound, or a combination of these, are inappropriate if the couple is not prepared to accept abortion. Others, however, have persuasively argued that even those who oppose abortion can benefit from information gained through prenatal tests. In some instances there is a medical benefit in that, for example, a cesarean birth may put the handicapped child at less risk than an ordinary vaginal birth. In others, the benefit is psychological. The prospective parents are able to use the prebirth time to learn more about the implications of the handicap and how they can best work with the child to improve its life, or to consider the possibility of adoption. Before undergoing prenatal testing, patients need to think about what they will do with the information when they receive it. It is advisable to make at least a tentative decision in advance, although the emotional reality of genuine information may lead them to other decisions.

Before deciding to abort a fetus with a genetic defect, the prospective parents need to find out what that particular genetic defect actually involves, what kind of treatment is available, and what kind of lives children with that defect actually live. There is enormous variation in genetic disorders. Many are not fatal; many do not involve immediate suffering; many do not involve acute suffering; some are not even illnesses. As the disorders themselves vary, so will patients' attitudes toward them. For some parents, the birth of a Down's syndrome child will not be thought an undue hardship, either for the child or themselves. For others, it will appear a monumental burden.

Decisions made by those at risk for Huntington's disease appear exceptional because they mean balancing many years of normal life against the tragic death that will follow. Other genetic disorders are similar, however, in that life, though impaired, may yet be rewarding both to the family and to the child. Decisions to have no children because of genetic risk or to abort a genetically defective fetus can seriously affect peoples' self-perceptions and lives. Before making such decisions, they should know what it is that they are rejecting and not reject it simply because it is not "normal."

Those who are at risk may want to consult genetic counselors. Many physicians are not well-trained in this area but good information is available. If a family physician cannot recommend either an M.D. or Ph.D. genetic counselor, then the county or state medical association can provide referrals to those who are adequately trained. Most genetic disorders have support groups (usually foundations) that can also provide information. When consulting a genetic counselor, clients should be clear about what they want. Some counselors have a very strong point of view about whether risking the birth of genetically defective offspring is acceptable. Others are more inclined to provide information and let the client make the decision. Still others may provide information selectively. If the individual or couple make clear the kind of information and assistance they want, then the counselor is more likely to provide that kind of help. If they feel they are being pressured or persuaded unduly by the counselor, they should realize that this is a risk of genetic counseling and that they need not accept the advice that is being given. Although genetic counselors have better information about treatment and transmission of genetic defects than do other individuals, they have no better idea than anyone else about what to do with this information because these decisions are ultimately based upon personal values. Individuals seeking screening must find the decision that fits their own values, not one that fits the values of the counselor.

Individuals who are at risk must also think about what information they owe others. Personal privacy is highly valued in this culture, but the success of intimate relationships depends upon each person relinquishing some degree of privacy. The language we use (e.g., *defect*) indicates social attitudes, and individuals may fear disclosing the information because it will stigmatize them. The fear is a realistic one, but individuals need to consider whether their familial commitment to others does not oblige them to disclose the information.

These conflicts between family members regarding the right to have knowledge shared can take many peculiar forms. Huntington's chorea now provides a particularly problematic variant of this kind of conflict. In 1983, an experimental test was developed that in a limited number of cases can establish whether a person has the gene that carries the disease. However, this test requires blood samples from several generations. A Huntington's family might reasonably have three generations living at one time with knowledge of the disease only in the first generation. If a third-generation member were to have the test to determine whether he or she carried the disease, this information would also (at least half the time) provide information to some members of the second generation, even if they didn't want it. If a granddaughter has the test, blood samples must also be drawn from her parents and grandparents (as well as others in the family if possible). If the test concludes that the granddaughter has the gene, then it is inevitably the case that she inherited it from a parent. The parent then will know his or her status, even if he or she wished not to know it. If the test is negative, of course, then the second generation's status is still unclear. Here, the granddaughter's desire to gain information may conflict with the parent's desire not to know.

Of course, the ultimate information (that is, whether they actually have the disorder) is not yet available for Huntington's patients. But even if it were (and it probably will be quite soon), some will not want information. They do not want to know because the knowledge that they will succumb to the disease will unduly burden their life long before the illness strikes.

Conclusion

Those at risk for genetic defects also need to understand the public policy issues. American attitudes toward eugenics shift frequently and public values can substantially shape personal views. Whether this society regards the birth of genetically impaired children as an act of social responsibility (providing compassionate respect for all human life) or of social irresponsibility (inflicting undue suffering upon a child and excessive costs upon society) is very much unresolved. Individual choices will very much be determined by the public mood. At present, it is going in two directions. On the one hand, the pro-life supporters are attempting to discourage all abortions, and second trimester abortions may be restricted as a result of their efforts. If so, that will make it more difficult to exercise choice through selective abortion. Pro-lifers as well as others have also worked very hard to establish federal and state legislation that will ensure the survival of genetically abnormal infants through the *Baby Doe* legislation. On the other hand, those who are pressing for cost containment suggest that prolonging life for infants who have marginal quality of life is an unwise use of limited health care resources. A philosopher writing about economics has emphasized the importance of preventing congenital defects as part of cost-containment philosophy and strategy. These trends go in two directions and neither is entirely consistent with the current emphasis on individual autonomy. Calls for attention to the "welfare of the whole community" are increasingly being heard and such claims might lead to mandatory eugenics policies.

Although genetic technology and research do not entirely depend upon the continued availability of abortion to be effective, the two issues are very closely related. It is a technology that can easily serve either individual preferences or social eugenics. Many argue that the threat of eugenics policies is unrealistic because the government would never be able to mandate abortion programs, for example, even if prenatal screening programs were required, because of public opposition. It is probably true that imposed eugenics policies are unlikely. However, because genetic counselors are in a position to influence the reproductive decisions made by couples at risk for genetic defect, *unofficial* eugenics trends could result. Since many Americans (including those likely to be found in counseling positions) currently display a deep commitment to a limited number of acceptable life-styles, it is very likely that any kind of defect that is inconsistent with the approved and desirable life-styles will be rejected. For some, this seems sensible, practical, and reasonable, not least because it represents human progress and another step toward the perfectability of mankind. For others, it appears to be a denial of toleration of human differences, compassion toward those who need our help, and recognition that perfection is realized only in dreams and in machines.

The implications of genetic screening as it is now practiced are that humans should have "better" children. The question may be only who is to decide what is better. If society thinks that children with genetic defects should not be born, then they will provide funds for screening programs, support for selective abortion, and minimal funding for family assistance programs. If society thinks that individuals should decide for themselves what children they want to bear, then they will provide more funding for special family assistance programs and increase medical research into cures. Encouraging individual choice also includes encouraging and respecting highly idiosyncratic choices and includes within it the legitimacy of using abortion for sex selection. Although the President's Commission for Ethics in Medicine and Biomedical and Behavioral Research believe that this practice is appalling, others argue that it is consistent with other genetic screening policies.

Society may be more likely, of course, to continue along its schizophrenic path, offering voluntary screening, discouraging defective conceptions, encouraging selective abortion before birth, and insisting upon maximum treatment after birth. Whether all this will lead to a better result is open to question. If we fail to change matters by screening, counseling, and providing medical therapy, doubtless we will move on to higher forms of technology. Unfortunately, the technological fix in genetic improvement is likely to be just as illusory as it has been in other areas of health care.

CHAPTER 5

The Kindness of Strangers
Embryo Transfer
and Surrogate Mothers

Americans have always had a great belief in personal freedom, a belief in the importance of having it their own way. We admire those who have it their own way because they have demonstrated their control over fate, their ability to master events, rather than to be mastered by them or to be forced to bend to necessity. Our myth is that cowards and failures adapt, while the valiant shape life to fit their desires. The development of in vitro fertilization and embryo transfer demonstrates that longing for control, and because the importance of control is so woven into our national values, we hear very few voices questioning the wisdom of technological baby making. Nonetheless, although science's newfound ability to create and to relocate human life may be among its most colorful masteries of nature, it is a mastery that is replete with ethical and societal problems. Before we plunge into full-scale baby manufacturing (delivery destination as per order), we would be advised to consider where our reverence for doing it our way—instead of nature's way—will take us.

This particular story began twenty-five years ago with a scientific advance: "the pill," the first really effective contraceptive method short of surgical sterilization. Up until that time, nature was, by and large, woman's destiny. Unless she was celibate, she had children not when she chose to have them but when she became pregnant. The pill changed all that. Later, questions about the safety of the contraceptive pill became widespread, but by that time, the essential message had already been spread: women could and should control their lives by deciding when they would become pregnant.

The introduction of the first oral contraceptive occurred at a time when several states still legally forbade the sale or use of any device or chemical substance intended to be used for contraception. In 1965, the U.S. Supreme Court ruled on a lawsuit challenging Connecticut's right to prohibit the use of contraceptives. In the landmark decision of *Griswold v. Connecticut*, Supreme Court Justice William O. Douglas announced for the Court that the Constitution prohibited the state from interfering in such intimate matters. The newly enunciated constitutional "right to privacy" covered every married couple's right to make decisions about their marital affairs. Seven years later, the court extended this protection from married couples to single persons, stating explicitly that every competent adult had the right to decide whether to bear or beget a child.

In 1973, eight years after the Connecticut case, the Supreme Court took up the problem of abortion. Again, they reiterated the right of privacy as a fundamental American value that provided a woman with the opportunity to decide whether or not she wished to bear a child, even if she was already pregnant.

The third important legal decision about the right to parenthood was made not by the Supreme Court but by a number of state courts over the question of involuntary sterilization. Prior to 1969, an ordinary woman who requested contraceptive sterilization was routinely turned away by obstetricians if the woman had not already had "enough" children. Physicians had a rough formula for deciding what was enough: the age of the woman times the number of children she had already borne had to equal at least 120. Otherwise, unless pregnancy placed her life at risk, sterilization was not available to her. On the other hand, physicians were performing sterilizations of certain women—the criminal, the mentally ill, the retarded, and (by some accounts) the poor and the foreign-born. These attitudes toward sterilization began to shift in the late 1960s and by the 1970s the situation was fully reversed. Sterilizations for *normal* women reached an all-time high, becoming the most common method of fertility control in the United States; and sterilization became almost totally unavailable for women who were mentally ill, mentally retarded, or institutionalized. The courts had concluded that because the right to bear or beget children was so fundamental, no one could interfere with a woman's decisions about her reproductive capacities. The normal woman who chose sterilization had to be given adequate information to ensure that she understood the implications of her decision. If she was competent and aged 21 or older, however, a physician could not deny her request simply because it appeared unwise. Nor could a husband interfere with her wishes. In the case of a woman who was incapable of giving informed consent, the courts judged that the capacity to bear children was so important that no one else could consent for her. According to the courts, neither parents, guardians, institutional custodians, nor judges themselves might consent to sterilization for the incompetent woman unless the state legislatures had passed laws specifically permitting guardians or courts to consent when they believed sterilization was in the woman's best interests.

As a result of these legal changes and scientific advances with respect to contraception, sterilization and abortion, America entered the 1980s with an extraordinarily heightened concern about women's reproductive rights. After women had been at the mercy of their reproductive natures for eons, the courts now expressly stated that they might neither be forbidden to bear children nor be obliged either to conceive or to bear children they did not want. Legal writers conducted lengthy studies of the newfound "right to reproductive freedom," a by-product of the "right to privacy" that Justice Douglas first articulated in the Connecticut contraceptive case. Women received officially approved access to control over their reproductive lives. With that control, they entered those realms in which people shaped their destiny, in which people had it their own way.

While lawyers, feminists, judges, and physicians worried about securing women's right to bear and beget children (a right that primarily focused on their right *not* to do so), another group of people lost their primary method of parenthood—adoption. Infertile couples—including about 15 percent of the population—did not have the luxury of worrying about a *right* to bear or beget children. Until 1973, when the Supreme Court legalized abortion, infertile couples had most frequently remedied their childless state by adopting infants or very young children whose natural mothers were unable or unwilling to care for them. After the legalization of abortion, however, adoptable infants practically disappeared. There continued to be children available for adoption, of course, but they tended to be minority children or handicapped children or both, not what the average adopting couple had in mind when they set out to satisfy *their* need for "reproduction."

In the ten years since abortion drastically reduced the supply of desirable, adoptable newborns, couples and even single individuals have been creative in finding alternatives. Legal protection for artificial insemination has helped those couples who suffered from male infertility. Those willing to accept an international flavor to their families have imported South Korean, Indian, and Colombian children. In addition, a well-organized black market in infants that violates all the laws against baby selling reportedly operates in the United States, for the benefit of the affluent, infertile couple.

Entrepreneurial lawyers, who claim to be interested only in helping childless couples achieve their dream, have offered their services to arrange surrogate mothering. In surrogate motherhood, a woman agrees to be impregnated by artificial insemination with the sperm of the husband of the childless couple. The pregnant woman then bears the child and, at birth, gives it up for adoption to the childless couple. The surrogate mother receives a fee for her expenses and the lawyer receives a fee for his or her services. The couple adopts a child who is the genetic child of the husband. The procedure is distinguished from baby selling because the biologic mother is supposed to be devoting her services primarily for charitable reasons and the fees involved are merely to cover expenses such as hospitalization, prenatal health care, and ordinary food, clothing, and shelter for the nine-month period. Some childless couples unable to adopt the kind of child they wanted have found this a reasonable way to achieve their reproductive rights. It is, however, very expensive and fraught with problems that defy legal regulation. The biologic mother who changes her mind and decides to keep the child is only one such problem. In such an instance, the ongoing relationship between the child and the biologic father and biologic mother as well as the financial responsibilities for the child are mind-boggling problems. The difficulties are even more intractable when the child is born with some kind of handicap and no one wants it, as recently happened in a surrogate case.

The problem of infertility has not, however, been left only to nonscientific solutions such as adoption or surrogate mothering. Medical science has also been hard at work on the question and in 1978, British doctors Steptoe and Edwards announced the first success with in vitro fertilization. Baby Louise Brown appeared on the front pages of newspapers all over the world: the first infant ever to be born as a result of a conception that took place outside the human body.

In vitro fertilization may be used when the childless couple's inability to conceive is due to problems with the fallopian tubes (usually obstruction from scarring) that keep the sperm from meeting the ovum. Steptoe and Edwards, in a method that had produced over three hundred infants by 1984, remove one or more ova from the prospective mother by a surgical procedure called a laparotomy and fertilize it (or them) in a petri dish with the husband's sperm. (The news media seem to like the idea that this fertilization takes place in a test tube, but, alas, it does not.) The fertilized egg is then placed in the woman's uterus for implantation. If the conceptus does not implant, then the process is repeated with additional ova (which may have been frozen) until implantation does occur. This technically sophisticated work results in the biological mother's giving birth to an infant whose chromosomal makeup is entirely hers and her husband's.

In vitro fertilization, then, considerably improved upon adoption, surrogate mothering, and artificial insemination. It provides full genetic identity with the parents, and also permits the woman to experience the pregnancy, to bear the child, and thus to regulate the prenatal environment of the developing fetus. Its advantages over surrogate mothering include its price. It is cheaper though less reliable than the surrogate route. Whereas surrogate fees were reported in 1984 to be around $25,000 (including attorney's fees), in vitro fertilization could be undergone for as little as $4000 or as much as $11,000. Ordinary medical insurance provides coverage for neither route to parenthood, but a $25,000 investment in a surrogate might provide more rapid results since there are few centers providing in vitro fertilization, many women who want the product, and the success rates are very low: in the vicinity of 25 percent. In fact, because of the low success rates, some physicians have begun to reintroduce four fertilized ova at a time, hoping that at least one would take. In some instances, the result has been quadruplets—rather more than the parents had in mind.

In vitro fertilization would not, however, provide everyone with access to reproductive rights even if the cost were lower and the services more available. The process requires that the woman have usable ova to be fertilized. For those couples whose infertility springs from the fact that the woman has no available ova, in vitro fertilization has nothing to offer. In 1984, these couples were given new

hope when a group of researchers at UCLA-Harbor Hospital announced their success with a procedure called embryo transfer
(sometimes called ovum transfer), a technique long used by animal
breeders. In embryo transfer, a "donor woman" is impregnated by
artificial insemination and the fertilized ovum is then transferred to
the infertile woman. When physicians successfully manipulated the
birth of the first human infant by this procedure, the door to reproductive rights opened for yet another group of women and men—at
least in theory.

Embryo Transfer

As it happened, researchers did not at first use embryo transfer for
those couples in which the women had no available ova. Instead,
they focused on the same population as in vitro fertilization had—
those women who had intact ova but who were unable to conceive
because of other defects, especially blocked fallopian tubes. This
population was easier for a first attempt because, since their ovaries
were functioning, embryo transfer could be achieved with natural
hormone production. Women without functioning ovaries do not
produce the natural hormones necessary for pregnancy, and physicians must introduce synthetic hormones in order to maintain the
state of pregnancy. This is a more difficult—though not impossible—problem, so it was natural to begin the experimentation on
embryo transfer with the easier group of infertile women.

Infertile couples and donor women were solicited through public
announcements, including newspaper ads, and were very carefully
screened with respect to physical history and emotional stability.
Screening techniques in all programs that involve allocation of very
scarce resources (as in the early kidney dialysis committees) are often very controversial because they tend to rely so heavily on traditional, conservative middle-class values. Thus, there is a tendency to
prefer subjects who are younger, Caucasian, middle-class, financially stable, educated, heterosexual, and married. In the initial
stages of a medical-experimental program like the embryo transfer
project, there is virtually no possibility that, for example, a lesbian
homosexual couple or a single woman or an unmarried or older
couple (40-year-olds, for example) would be chosen to participate.
The experimenters are usually extremely sensitive to the controversial nature of their work and are quick to avoid any application that

is even remotely unusual or questionable. Thus, both the recipients and the donors in embryo transfer were very likely to be, at least superficially, very socially acceptable people.

The embryo transfer procedure is not particularly complex in theory, although the actual logistics can be fairly frenetic. Simply put, the object is to impregnate the donor woman by artificial insemination and then to transfer the fertilized egg from the donor woman to the recipient wife. The semen used in the artificial insemination usually comes from the recipient husband, though it does not need to. The first requirement for making the transfer effective is that both donor and recipient women must be at the same point in their menstrual cycle. Thus, there must be enough donor women so that at least one of them will have a synchronous cycle. The second critical point is the removal of the fertilized egg. Five days after fertilization has taken place, the fertilized egg is "washed out" of the donor's uterus. At this point, it is inspected microscopically in order to make sure that it has been fertilized and to observe its development. Little can be observed at this point with respect to the fertilized egg's genetic normality, although "normal" development can be observed. If the lavage (the "washing out" process) is successful, the third critical stage is reached: reintroducing the fertilized ovum into the recipient's uterus and its becoming implanted there.

The process can go wrong at any of these points. If there are not enough donor women, the cycle of the proposed recipient woman may never be matched accurately. If the artificial insemination does not take—and frequently more than one attempt is required to be successful—then no fertilized ovum is available. If the ovum is fertilized, but cannot be rescued through the lavage process (which happens about 15–20 percent of the time), the donor woman's pregnancy must be dealt with in some way. If the fertilized ovum is successfully washed out, it must be developing appropriately or it will be unlikely to implant. Since a very large number of conceptions are abnormal (as many as 60 percent, according to some estimates), the procedure has a great probability of going on the rocks at this stage. In the UCLA project, the first report indicated that slightly over half of the "washings out" were unsuccessful and no ovum was found, fertilized or otherwise. Ten fertilized ova were recovered, but only two appeared to be developing normally. The eight slow or abnormal developers did not establish a pregnancy. Finally, the transfer process may go awry: the fertilized ovum may be damaged and may either fail to initiate a pregnancy or may initiate a faulty pregnancy that will either spontaneously abort or will give rise to a defective birth. This final concern that the artificial manipulation of the conceptus may in some way damage the rapidly dividing egg, resulting in a "successful" but abnormal birth, is a particularly troubling one. Researchers point out, however, that comparable worries about in vitro fertilization have so far proved unfounded.

The scientific aspect of this program is far better understood than are its social implications. Because the embryo transfer procedure has been used for many years by cattle breeders, scientists and technicians are not unfamiliar with both the practical problems and their potential solutions. Researchers have pointed out that human beings are now the fifteenth mammalian species in which embryo transfer has been successfully achieved, but this attempt to play down the problematic quality of the procedure, suggesting that it is merely a standard technique, is deceptive.

Homo sapiens may be the fifteenth species, but none of the others worry about legal rights or moral rights. None of the participants from the fourteen other species are able to choose to enter such a program nor must they make any decisions about what to do when, for example, a fertilized ovum is retained by the donor, or when the infant is born with severe deformities or handicaps. Humans have created a market for animals in which animals are objects to be bought, sold, and bred in whatever efficient and economically productive way is possible. Those who argue that procedures developed for animals can be transferred to the human world without problems misread the relationship between science, society, and morality. The social problems of embryo transfer are substantial, but as with many new medical technologies, we are quick to leap, but reluctant to look.

Embryo transfer in humans is so new that we do not have many cases to look at, but we do know something about the potential for problems. The following case study is fictional but the problems it presents are all familiar. American experience with surrogate mothers in the past few years has demonstrated that problems appear quickly, and the problems are often bizarre. Embryo transfer procedures are likely to provide comparable dilemmas, especially if the technique becomes commercialized.

Case Study

Bert and Betty Jones married immediately after college, established an accounting business together and did not even begin to think about having children for ten years. When Betty was 32, they realized that time was running out on them and they decided to have a child immediately, or at least as soon as the recently expanded business took better shape. Two more years passed and the demands of work only increased. Betty realized that the business would never leave room for a baby. They would have to begin their family even if they didn't have enough time. She convinced Bert that the actual *presence* of a child would alter their business life in a way that the *idea* of a child never could.

A year later, Betty was not yet pregnant. She consulted her physician and she and Bert were referred to an infertility specialist. Another year passed, the pregnancy still unattained. Worse yet, their experiences with the infertility specialists left them depressed and harrassed. Each new specialist they saw treated them sympathetically; each had some new suggestion about what might be tried. The couple underwent numerous tests. They made temperature charts. They changed their style of clothing so that nothing fit too tightly. They undertook intercourse on a demanding schedule that was carefully supervised by a host of specialists. Betty took complicated regimens of expensive medications that required regular blood level checks. They began to feel that they saw more of each other in doctors' offices than they did at home. Their attempts to have a child seemed to have become a public performance. Each time some new procedure was suggested, their hopes would rise since the physicians were so confident that this would be the answer. Each time that it didn't work, the doctors seemed to feel that Bert and Betty had failed them. The experience frustrated them, saddened them, and finally alienated them.

Bert especially began to feel that no matter how much pleasure a child might bring to their lives, it could hardly outweigh the misery that trying to have a child was bringing them. He felt like a fool caught in a bear market, endlessly throwing good money after bad. In his and Betty's case, though, it was not only good money that was going down the drain, but good time and good feelings. Bert suggested they abandon the effort. Betty resisted his entreaties briefly, but then she too acquiesced. Life returned to normal. The business grew. They were active, involved in day-to-day events, took a long-overdue vacation, and rearranged their expectations.

Two years later, at her dentist's office, Betty read an article about new methods of treating infertility, including in vitro fertilization and embryo transfer. She was surprised to find that she continued to think about the article for several days, for she thought she had put all that behind her. She decided not to discuss the possibility of new treatments with Bert, but did write to the hospital mentioned in the article, asking whether such treatment was available in their area. A month later, she received a xeroxed list of medical centers that included the Fertility Research Center, a half-hour's drive from their home.

Bert was reluctant, but agreed to go to the center, drawn by his love for his wife. Despite his agreement, however, he feared the prospect of placing himself in the hands of physicians, of giving them power over his happiness and sense of well-being. Betty made an appointment for them both to see a Center counselor.

Karen Jensen, a 28-year-old widow with a 5-year-old daughter, first heard of the Fertility Research Center when she noticed an uncharacteristically large classified advertisement in the Personals section of the local newspaper. The Center was advertising for women, aged 25 to 35, to help infertile couples bear children. The advertisement stipulated that there was no risk, that compensation for time was available, and that the procedure was comparable to sperm donation for men. She read the ad with interest, for she understood the great desire to have children and knew the enormous pleasure that her own child brought to her. She still deeply regretted the loss of her first child. At age 19, Karen had become pregnant while in college. After several weeks of agonizing indecision, she had gone to an abortion clinic. She had never forgotten her sorrow as she lay there, looking at the cold green ceiling, hearing the rush of the suction machine as it drowned out most of the diffident physician's words, and feeling the nurse's hands compassionately pressing on her own cold hand, while tears of loss ran down her cheeks. Thinking back on that loss, she found herself tearing out the ad. She would call and ask for more information.

A month later, Bert and Betty Jones and Karen Jensen were all participants in the Fertility Research Center program. They had successfully completed personal interviews, psychological screenings, medical histories, and informed consent procedures. Karen was pleased to be able to contribute to another couple's happiness. She had been uncomfortable when the psychiatrist pressed her about her reasons for the earlier abortion. As the session with him progressed, however, she felt less defensive, more accepted simply as a woman who wanted to help two other human beings in a simple way. Toward the end of the interview, when he pointed out the statistical possibility of a retained pregnancy, he once again seemed to be testing her acceptance of abortion, since that would be the appropriate way to conclude the failed embryo transfer. By then, however, she had acquired the rhythm of the interview, and felt practically a part of the team. Abortion as a medically recommended way of resolving the transfer failure made sense to her. The compensation was minimal, but she had no great need of money and there was relatively little demand for her time. Physicians had explained the procedures; counselors had explained the negligible risks. She signed on happily.

Betty, too, looked forward to acceptance. Intuitively, she felt that this was the procedure that would work for them. She wished the child would be genetically both hers and Bert's, but she felt that genes were not really as important as carrying the baby within her own body during its nine-month gestation. Bert continued to be hesitant, but was pleased by the fact that any baby would have his full genetic heritage, would really be his own child. He had never cottoned to adoption since it seemed to him that the child would always be at some level a stranger. This would be better . . . if it worked. He was prepared to give it a six-month try. After that, he wanted out. He would be happy to have a baby; but he would be happy if they didn't have one, too.

Once they were formally accepted, the tedious part began. Regular blood tests to check hormone levels were necessary in order to track ovulatory cycles. When donor and recipient cycles coincided, artificial insemination was attempted on more than one donor. The doctors insisted on this procedure in order to increase the chance of getting at least one fertilized ovum in the washing-out process and also to make it impossible for the donor women to know whether they or their colleagues had actually donated an ovum. As with sperm donors, it was a method of insuring anonymity.

When Karen was called for the insemination, she went immediately to the center. The transfer of semen was made rapidly, in a businesslike manner. Lying on the table, she thought about the bland impersonality of the procedure. How different from the heated union of nature's design. Perhaps this rational, thoughtful, reflective process was better; so carefully considered, so well-planned. Yet, the blood seemed to long for something more. It was lonely and cold as she lay alone on the hard table in the clinic office, while the foreign, anxious sperm began their search.

Afterwards, the unexpected sense of sadness disappeared quickly and the five days until she returned for the lavage process passed quickly. She had previously been shown the instruments used to retrieve the egg as well as those used to reimplant it in the recipient mother and fully understood what was to happen. The procedure was over quickly. Everyone thanked her when she left. She felt moderately puzzled by their thanks, since she had no sense of having done anything that merited thanks. Perhaps it was the ultimate gift: a joy to the recipient and no loss to the giver.

Two days later, Karen received another call from the Center, asking her to return for one more blood test and a subsequent appointment. She gave the blood, made an appointment, cancelled it, then made another one. By the time she saw the physician, her ordinary menstrual period was several days late, but she attributed it only to the disruption caused by the artificial insemination. Dr. Steiner, however, thought otherwise. The lavage procedure had failed to retrieve an egg, fertilized or otherwise. Her blood tests indicated a retained conceptus. The Center recommended that she come immediately for menstrual extraction, and for that purpose had arranged an immediate appointment with a Center counselor.

Karen was moved from one office to the next, almost struck dumb by the news. Janet Dailey, the counselor who had originally interviewed her, wanted to know how she felt. Karen hardly knew, she was so confused. She had known about the possibility, but had not really given it much thought, for it had seemed so unlikely. Now, she was angry, feeling that the doctors or science in general had betrayed her. The anticipated pleasure in helping others had boomeranged, and now Karen was the one who needed help, who was dependent upon the kindness of strangers. Janet detailed the advantages of abortion, but Karen was unable to be sure where her preferences lay.

She returned for a second appointment, four days later, still uncertain, but inclined to want to go through with the pregnancy. Janet was concerned about the effect of an undesired abortion on Karen. She was emotionally strong, but Janet thought it would be a substantial burden on her for a very long time. Karen pointed out that the obvious solution would be for her to continue with the pregnancy. Then, when the baby was born, it could be adopted by the couple who had fathered it and who had intended to mother it as well. Janet reminded Karen of the confidentiality protection afforded all the Center patients. Because of this, it would be totally unethical for Karen to know who the father was or for the father to know Karen's identity, and certainly unethical to inform him and his wife of the current problem.

Janet realized that, as Karen herself said, surrogate mothering would provide an ideal solution to this problem. No fertilized ovum had been harvested for Bert and Betty, and Karen was the only donor who appeared to be pregnant. Janet knew both the Joneses and Karen from the many counseling sessions they had undergone. She thought they could all handle the situation. She was deeply touched by Karen's unwillingness to undergo another abortion. During the screening process, they had gone over this aspect of embryo transfer thoroughly, but Janet knew that what looks reasonable in theory may be unbearable in reality, that people cannot always predict their reactions. Karen had made an inaccurate prediction; the Center counselors had believed her, perhaps because they wanted to. Karen had been wrong, but so had the counselors. Now, the question was how to get past that error with the least harm.

Janet knew that it was against all official policy to let Karen know the names she wanted. Yet, it seemed to her that that was the humanly proper thing to do. Uncertain and ambivalent to the last moment, Janet left Karen alone in the office for about five minutes, after letting Karen know, at least indirectly, that the names she wanted were in the file folder on Janet's desk. She left it to fate to decide what should happen: if Karen understood the opportunity she was being given, then she could take it. If she did not understand, then it was better that she not have it.

Karen understood, immediately copied down the names, and left soon afterwards, thanking Janet for her help and assuring her that she would decide shortly. Karen thought for two days more, then wrote to Bert and Betty, offering them the baby, no strings attached. She apologized for not being able to tell them how she had obtained the information that Bert was the child's natural father. If they did not believe her, however, or did not want the child, then they need not contact her. She would schedule an abortion for ten days later, but hoped that she would hear from them before that time.

Writing the letter made her even more miserable. Mailing it, she felt like a blackmailer, risking immediate arrest and imprisonment. Waiting for a reply, she could no longer tell whether the drama she seemed to have the leading role in was her own or someone else's. It felt alien to be so concerned about a decision that, morally, belonged to someone else.

Bert and Betty received the letter, Betty was unsure of what it might mean; Bert was convinced that someone was trying to make a fast buck at their expense. He again regretted their involvement in the Center and urged Betty to pay no attention to the letter. It was just one more pothole in the road to parenthood, a road so bad it deserved to be closed down. Betty thought the letter writer sounded sincere though rather emotional. Her intuition was sufficiently positive that she wanted to give the person an opportunity to explain herself further. With or without Bert, she decided to see Karen. They arranged to meet for dinner.

The meeting was awkward; all three were uncomfortable. Karen tried to explain herself as directly as she could. She told them of her own daughter; of her sorrow about the abortion years earlier and how that had inspired her to enter the program. She still refused to tell them how she had discovered that Bert was the natural father of the child. They would simply have to believe that she had seen the records. If they wanted the baby, they could always have blood tests or gene tests done after the birth that would prove she was telling the truth.

When she was through, all three sat in silence, held back by the magnitude of the problem, but also held together by their common bond. Karen longed to reach out to them, to take their hands in hers, to answer the troubling question literally by touch.

"The baby is yours," she finally offered. "In every way. I don't want money. I don't want visitation rights. I don't even want to become your best friend. I just want to know that someone wants this baby and can offer the right kind of life: a full set of parents who really care. You are this baby's father, Bert; do you want to be its mother, Betty? That's the only question."

Betty looked at Bert. He nodded slightly and then, with tear-filled eyes, she nodded to Karen.

"Yes, " she finally managed to say. "We do."

The Decision Makers: Their Perspectives and Interests

Medical Perspectives

Infertility treatment, like much plastic surgery, is *elective* treatment, undergone at the patients' request to alter their lives but not, in any ordinary sense, to improve their health. As a result, despite the fact that most physicians who specialize in infertility treatment sincerely desire to help the couples who come to them, the field is ripe for commercialization. Economic interests may cross over and affect medical perspectives. Infertility physicians frequently use the word "desperate" to refer to their patients. An economically motivated physician faced with a desperate patient may go to extraordinary lengths to provide assistance.

Until relatively recently, infertility was a personal blight with which one came to terms. Now, infertility has increased dramatically, and those who are deprived of their reproductive rights are seen as a population in desperate need of medical help.

The demand for infertility treatment is very high, frequently estimated at as many as two million couples. The demand is likely to increase since infertility is rising among younger women as a result of an epidemic of pelvic infections. As well, infertility is more frequent in older women, and the age of childbearing is moving upward. Women who might have conceived easily when younger may find that, by waiting, they have acquired infertility problems that require complex medical treatment. Infertility rates also increase as a result of voluntary sterilization. A significant part of the population that desperately wishes to conceive are infertile because they chose sterilization as a method of birth control and then, for a variety of reasons, changed their minds about wanting additional children.

Because of this demand, the medical practice of infertility treatment has become a new frontier, although the standard treatments are not very effective. A recent study compared the results of treating infertile couples and not treating another group of infertile couples, when both groups of couples desired pregnancy. In the treated group, 41 percent of the couples became pregnant; in the untreated group, 35 percent became pregnant. One reason standard methods of treatment are not very successful is that they are indirect: they simply try to improve the conditions for fertilization. Treatments that guarantee fertilization are much more effective.

In vitro fertilization and embryo transfer enable doctors to respond more directly to their patients' desires for children by permitting them to control fertilization more closely. In addition, these techniques are on the cutting edge of scientific knowledge. They are somewhat experimental and risky, but physicians have an interest in continuing to find ways to ensure pregnancies because the work holds the promise of scientific and intellectual achievement. Embryo transfer, of course, only repeats the achievements of cattle breeders, but within *human* medicine, it is new and provocative.

The high demand for this service also means that physicians have a substantial economic interest in these procedures being continued. Infertility treatment is time-consuming and expensive. Each *successful* pregnancy through in vitro fertilization is estimated to cost $50,000. We lack good cost figures for embryo transfers because this procedure's use is so new, but it, too, is likely to prove very costly. The lowered birth rate in the United States also affects physicians' economic interests. Fewer babies leads to smaller work loads for obstetricians, from whose ranks the infertility specialists are drawn. When an abundant supply of physicians meets a low birth rate and a high infertility rate, the pressure to provide more infertility services cannot help but be expressed. There has been a noticeable increase in the number of physicians specializing in infertility.

As long as demand for the advanced forms of infertility treatment exceeds treatment availability, elaborate screening procedures will be necessary. Physicians will necessarily provide the medical criteria for screening, which will include causes of infertility and information gained from medical and genetic histories. Psychosocial screening criteria, on the other hand, are much more likely to be developed and judged by psychologists and perhaps by specially trained nurses and social workers. Psychosocial screening focuses on far more amorphous matters, such as psychological stability and emotional makeup. In order to be effective, this kind of screening requires substantial disclosure of private matters. As a result, the professional-client relationships that develop around these disclosures will inevitably be filled with ethical conflicts. When professionals encourage or require patients/clients to reveal personal, intimate details of their lives in order to receive medical services, the revelation creates a special kind of relationship, one in which the professional may feel particularly protective toward the client or particularly obligated to help the client in times of distress, and in which the patient/client may expect that kind of assistance.

As the physicians withdraw to more remote technical or scientific roles, support staff will take on these personal relationships with the patients and the support staff may identify with patients, not research goals. Confidentiality demands, for example, may appear reasonable and compelling when medical treatment involves only one person. When two or more people are involved, however, and when complex relationships exist between them or are created by the treatment itself, claims of confidentiality may not be easy to weigh among participants, especially when all parties have a very strong emotional investment in the information and the outcome.

Legal Perspectives

In vitro fertilization presents relatively few legal problems because the offspring, when conceived, is the genetic product of the couple who expect to become the parents. Potential legal problems exist should the child (or children) be born with defects that at least arguably result from the external manipulation of the embryo. Thus far, there has been no indication that external fertilization and subsequent implantation lead to increased risk of abnormal births. Furthermore, the pregnancies are customarily followed very closely for any sign of abnormality and, in many instances, amniocentesis* and ultrasound† diagnostic tests can detect abnormalities before birth. If an abnormal fetus is diagnosed, then an abortion can be performed if the parents choose. There is always the chance, however, that an abnormal fetus might not be discovered before birth, and this could lead to a malpractice suit.

On the other hand, the legal status of ovum donation and embryo transfer is far murkier. In some respects, it parallels sperm donation. Most states have passed statutes that legitimize the practice of artificial insemination, declaring that the donor has no legal relation nor obligation to the resultant offspring. If egg donation were to be seen as the same procedure as sperm donation, then presumably the woman who donated the egg would also have neither claim nor obligation to the child born of the recipient mother. No states have yet passed laws protecting egg donors in this way, primarily because the procedure is so recent. In the absence of such statutes, the parallel with sperm donation could be argued but would not necessarily be conclusive.

Legal problems involving embryo transfer are likely to arise in those instances where an abnormal child is born or where the artificially fertilized ovum is retained, resulting in an ongoing pregnancy for the donor mother. Although researchers reportedly require do-

*Amniocentesis is a procedure that involves taking a sample of uterine fluid and testing it for known chromosomal abnormalities or for other unusual properties that would indicate that the fetus was not normal.

†A widely available imaging process using sound waves.

nor women to sign agreements that they will undergo abortion in the case of retained fertilized ova, that is not a legally enforceable agreement. Constitutional protections around reproduction make it impossible for anyone to be *required* to submit to abortion, regardless of what they have signed or why someone has asked them to sign it. The legal problems of an ongoing pregnancy for a donor woman are significant since, at least conceptually, both the ovum and the sperm are donated: the ovum donated to the couple by the woman; the sperm donated by the couple to the woman. If the donor woman has the same status as the male sperm donor, then she has no rights or obligations to the child. Because the donor woman has been impregnated by artificial insemination, the male has neither rights nor obligations to the child-to-be. The failed transfer presumably alters the woman's status as a donor, leaving her with full parental control of and responsibility for the offspring. If the donor woman is herself married, her husband is presumed to be the legal father of the child unless there is conclusive evidence proving that he is not the father. At least in theory, the donor woman with a retained pregnancy has complete control over the fate of the offspring. There are, however, enough conflicts and legal ambiguities to keep a division of lawyers busily at work for years.

The law may also need to be concerned about the interests of the child born of the embryo transfer arrangement. Children may have both an interest and a need to know about their genetic parents. Although this situation differs from ordinary adoption, it has significant similarities. Recent years have seen considerable agitation from adopted children—as well as mothers who have relinquished children for adoption—seeking access to information about their biological parents. Although the recipient mother in embryo transfer may more closely approximate the role of the biological parent since she actually gives birth to the child, she is not the genetic parent. Scientists have continually struggled with the question of whether nature or nurture, genes or environment, is more important in a child's development. Without a conclusion in favor of nurture—and they have not reached any such conclusion—we can reasonably expect that people will have a continuing desire and even, perhaps, a deep-seated psychological need to know about their genetic parents. It is also conceivable that with increased understanding about how genes function, much more detailed information about genetic history will be routinely necessary for each individual's personal health care.

Ethical Perspectives

Philosophers have three primary concerns about these extraordinary reproductive processes. The first is that both the research and the procedures themselves use and, in some cases, intentionally destroy embryos. Since embryos are forms of human life, this kind of research and technology may fail to show adequate respect for human life and may constitute wanton destruction of human life. The second concern is that the technology responds to individual parental desires and hopes without sufficient concern for the social matrix in which parents and children exist. This argument is primarily concerned with attitudes toward reproduction and child rearing, and suggests that extraordinary forms of procreation are likely to lead to a society in which children are seen merely as objects to be possessed, rather than as humans worthy of respect in their own right. Because these reproductive procedures are so sensitive to producing "normal" children, they are likely to lead to increased knowledge of and interest in producing "perfect" children. Furthermore, the donor procedures lead to considerable confusion about what it means to be a parent, further separating biological norms from arbitrarily (or socially) defined ones.

Philosophers' third concern, which is distinctly related to the second one, is that children born of these procedures will be physically or psychologically harmed by the abnormal means of conception. Although evidence from in vitro fertilization suggests that there may be no added risk for physical harm from external fertilization, research on freezing embryos for later transfer presents new possibilities for harm. It is clear that research in this field will extend in many new directions: the present questions are only the beginning. The fear of psychological harm to the child stems from the unusual birth circumstances and, in the case of embryo transfer with a donor egg, the potential competition between parents because the father is more closely related (at least genetically) to the child than is the mother. In a culture typified by unstable marriages, the latter concern is surely a reasonable one.

Policy Perspectives

Currently, the United States has no public policy on in vitro fertilization or ovum transfer, and the issue of surrogate mothers has proved so complex that little progress has been made in that area, although there is legislative discussion. In 1975, the Department of Health, Education and Welfare issued a policy that no in vitro fertilization research could be funded unless HEW's Ethics Advisory Board approved the project. In 1979, the Ethics Advisory Board did make a series of recommendations serving to protect subjects of in vitro fertilization research (both the parents and the prospective infants). The department took no actions on those recommendations at that time or subsequently, nor has its successor, the Department of Health and Human Services. As a result, no federally funded research has been done and no federal policy discussions have been held.

Because in vitro fertilization, both in practice and research, creates and sometimes destroys human embryos, the American right-to-life movement has strongly opposed it. As long as the abortion controversy is so intense, it is unlikely that the federal government will be willing to take on policy questions relating to these extraordinary forms of reproduction. The government's failure to provide funds or policy discussions, however, has not interfered with research or with clinical applications, other than to slow them down. In vitro fertilization is now considered to be an acceptable form of treatment for infertility, although the demand for services vastly exceeds their availability.

A continuing policy concern about both in vitro fertilization and embryo transfer will be the risk of harm to the children who are produced by these methods. In the late 1970s, many critics of in vitro fertilization research argued that the risk of damaging embryos by external fertilization and subsequent artificial implantation was, at least theoretically, sufficiently high that the practice should not be permitted. In essence, they were asserting that these children-to-be were themselves subjects of medical experimentation in which they were placed at unknown and potentially serious risk of injury. Although parents may, in many instances, consent to children's involvement in research, in this case the parents were not yet parents and their desire to become parents might all too easily blind them to the risks involved. After five years of limited experience with children born from in vitro fertilization, there do not appear to be significant additional risks of producing seriously damaged infants. The first of these children, however, was born late in 1978, and the great majority of them are much younger. Thus, there is still the possibility that this form of procreation may hold within it less immediately obvious damage (e.g., subtle neurological injury) that may take many years to detect. Unfortunately, because the practice has increased so rapidly and without government oversight, we have no guarantee that good follow-up will be provided on these children, ensuring data collection that will enable us to know whether in vitro fertilization does involve harm.

In the case of infants born by embryo transfer, the probability of long-term follow-up is even less likely. Because embryo transfer involves donation from a third party, the fact that the child was conceived by this method is likely to be kept secret, just as is pregnancy resulting from artificial insemination. Parents are, therefore, unlikely to be willing to have their child identified as an embryo transfer child for purposes of long-term study. These children will be closely followed through the birth process to ensure the child's normality at birth and will then be quietly absorbed into the general public, another happy family by virtue of modern medical technology.

Policy makers will also need to address the twin issues of costs and allocation of resources. Currently, the cost of each successful pregnancy through in vitro fertilization is estimated to be $50,000. An initial fertilization attempt may cost around $10,000, and additional attempts—the first one is rarely successful—cost $4000 to $5000. The developers of embryo transfer have stated that one reason for their research was that they believed it would be a more reliable method of providing pregnancy than in vitro fertilization had proved. The in vitro fertilization success rate is between 15 and 20 percent. The first embryo transfer results were significantly less successful than those of in vitro fertilization, but in theory the procedure could become much more efficient. By 1984, the world had only two reported human embryo transfer births and thus we have no reasonable figures for what costs might be when it becomes available for wider use. In vitro fertilization requires hospitalization in order to surgically remove ova by laparoscopy and this contributes to its higher cost. Embryo transfer, on the other hand, is an outpatient procedure and thus looks to be less expensive, even were it to have only the same success rate as in vitro fertilization. The donor woman must be reimbursed for her services, however, and public policy may very well be needed to determine how to assess the value of her contribution.

A final factor in cost assessment will be the legal resolution of attempts to patent both procedures and equipment devised for embryo transfer. Because the project was funded by private business rather than by government or nonprofit groups, the company that paid for the research is seeking to recoup its investment by patenting and licensing the work. Most scientific research in the United States is federally funded and the products thus lie in the public domain. Patenting medical equipment is common, however, and patenting medical procedures is not unknown, so the courts may recognize entrepreneurial enthusiasm in this area. If so, that will affect both the price and the availability of the services.

Since there are approximately two million infertile couples in the United States who might seek treatment, the potential demand for both these services is very high. The current demand cannot be met by the available supply, although an unregulated market may quickly increase the number of physicians interested and able to perform these procedures. As long as demand outstrips available services, however, there will have to be some method of choosing who will benefit. For example, does an infertile couple "deserve" more than one child by extraordinary means? Does a woman who has been voluntarily sterilized "deserve" assistance when her circumstances or attitudes change? Do older infertile couples "deserve" a higher place in the queue than younger infertile couples?

Some have argued that the infertility problem is yet another indication of how confused American priorities have become. At a time when perhaps as many as a million couples want to have children and are unable to do so, over a million pregnant women are undergoing abortions because they do not want to have children. Yet, as one reproductive specialist has commented, people are no longer willing to accept adoption as an answer to infertility when medical science can provide them with a child who shares at least some of their genetic identity.

What's a Patient to Do?

The case study involving Betty, Bert, and Karen brings out not only the psychological complexities but also the uncertain outcomes of experimental infertility services. Participants as well as professionals must enter this area with an ability to adapt to uncertainty and to cope with complexity, risk, and an ambiguous future.

The uncertainty begins with the difficulties Bert and Betty have in their efforts to effect a pregnancy; but it is compounded by their experiences with the infertility specialists. Paralleling the uncertain outcome concerning pregnancy are Bert's reservations about trying yet another procedure after so much disappointment. Betty is more willing than Bert to keep trying. This difference of attitude may well create tensions in their relationship—just as not having or trying to have children might.

Karen Jensen acts from complex motives. In part she is willing to benefit others for minimal economic compensation, but she primarily seeks psychological compensation to lessen the sense of loss from her previous abortion. She is aware of the potential benefits and has been informed of the statistical risks of, for example, a retained conception. She knew beforehand of the possible costs, but did not fully appreciate them. Or perhaps she unconsciously hoped for the pregnancy to replace the aborted child.

Karen, Bert, and Betty have all given informed consent before entering the infertility program, but none of them has given any serious consideration to the complexities of the possible results. Because the program is run by professionals, they assume that the professionals will take care of things. When they find themselves in an unexpected situation, they are no longer willing or able to depend upon professional guidance, since the question, for example, of whether Karen should act as surrogate mother for them is not a question with any particular medical content. Furthermore, they show every indication of proceeding without any further degree of understanding. Although the state may not recognize surrogate parenting, the three have entered into a private agreement with little thought of the possible complications. The situation may appear resolved to them, once the surrogate agreement is made. However, experience with surrogate parenting in the United States so far has demonstrated substantial complications, especially with surrogates who decide to keep the children and defective babies who are wanted by no one.

The physicians play a scientific and technical role. The traditional doctor-patient relationship is, by and large, turned over to allied health workers, to nurses, social workers, and psychologists, who "handle" the patient while the physician deals with the problem technically. This structuring explains the physician's role as the process manager and the conductor, as it were, of the event, creating offspring by means of the reproductive equipment of his or her patients. Although many doctors are much more personally involved with their patients, these technologies do not require such involvement and permit the physicians to occupy themselves fully with the role of applied scientist. In fairness to physicians and other professionals, it should be pointed out that when they obtain informed consent, possible complications are explained. But people change their minds. And the donor of the egg owes nothing to the professionals or the possible recipients, so she is relatively free to reject the original plan to abort a retained conceptus and to opt for keeping the child or serving as a surrogate.

The physicians have a substantial interest in confidentiality being maintained, both because confidentiality is a cherished medical value and because surrogate mothering is neither legally nor culturally acceptable at this time in most communities. Thus, they need to protect confidentiality in order to prevent surrogate arrangements from being made in the event that the embryo transfer procedure does not work as planned. The patients' interests in having their confidentiality protected is also very significant. In part, this stems from an unwillingness to be publicly identified as infertile, in part from unwillingness to be identified with unusual reproductive treatment methods, in part from an unwillingness to have the child-to-be ever know about the unusual circumstances of its conception, as well as from a general interest in preserving confidentiality about intimate medical matters. The patients' interests in keeping their identities secret from one another may not, however, be absolute. Medical policies frequently not only seek to assure confidentiality; they insist upon it, even if the patients do not wish it. (For example, for years, physicians have insisted that medical records were confidential and thus patients themselves might not see them.) Here, Karen Jensen and Bert and Betty Jones had the potential to benefit from disclosures about their identity and the progress (or the misprogress) of the treatment. If the goal of the procedures is to provide a child for the infertile couple, then, if all agree, it can be argued that it would be reasonable to violate the confidentiality in the event of a retained pregnancy. A surrogate pregnancy is different from an embryo transfer pregnancy, but not so different that the one is clearly unacceptable while the other is clearly acceptable with respect to cultural values. Physicians are unlikely to provide this option because it may provoke public disapproval and thus interfere with their own interests of continuing research. Support staff, however, may be tempted to make different judgments about the importance of confidentiality simply because they are more closely identified with the patients, more sensitive to the patients' psychological and emotional status, and more oriented toward the final goal of providing the infertile couple with a child. Even if such a variation violates professional codes or staff agreements, we know that other forces do influence human behavior.

Karen, although ambivalent, ultimately treats the developing embryo/fetus as if it were an object, and one that belongs to them rather than to her. Her final statement (if they don't want it, she will abort it) embodies that sense of the fetus as object. Her previous abortion experience, however, indicates the kind of struggle she feels about the ambiguous status of the unborn child. She denies having any natural or emotional involvement with motherhood when she assures them that she wants no relationship or involvement with them or the child in the future. Before she actually became pregnant, she was equally certain that she would have no qualms about aborting the embryo. The statement may or may not be accurate, but we might culturally be concerned about women's (or men's) ability to sever themselves easily and cleanly from their biological offspring. We might prefer a society in which attachments to natural offspring, even if not always able to be maintained, are valued, rather than held to be of indifferent meaning.

The desire to have children is not only normal but of extreme evolutionary importance and is doubtless deeply planted within the human biology and consciousness. When thwarted in their desires by genetic causes or environmental events, couples may feel desperate and may experience significant personal and marital stresses. Where infertility exists, it frequently plays a large role in divorce and marital disharmony. The desperation these couples feel makes them willing, as they often say, "to do anything, to try anything." They are, as a result, very vulnerable to professional manipulation, which may stem from the professionals' scientific curiosity, financial ambitions or misguided attempts to be of help to needy patients. Professionals who may take witting or unwitting advantage of these couples include physicians and lawyers.

These couples are likely to accept not only excessive rates for themselves but also excessive risks for their prospective offspring. The couple who "goes through hell" to have a child and then gives birth (however birth is achieved) to a defective child as a result of inadequate genetic screening of the donor or of potential damage from the procedure itself is likely to be bitterly disappointed. Even though medicine has made brilliant progress in its ability to detect abnormalities, its methods are not error-free and physicians are not able to detect all problems. Inevitably, some children will be born less than perfect and even less than adequate by almost any standards. Because these procedures are so controlled, so removed from natural processes, couples tend to believe that the degree of control is higher than it actually is. One of the significant broad-scale social risks of these procedures is that they imply a degree of quality control that may make humans very discontented with standard products of natural procreation methods. On a smaller scale, the scientific trappings may make patients think that the results are more predictable than they in fact are.

Patients may not be willing to think of themselves as participants in a large social experiment, but that is their role. The society has no idea of the long-term results of "child-production" (rather than reproduction), and researchers may require infertile couples and their unconsenting children to become public property in order to understand the effects of artificial procreation. Studying it will itself alter the effects, and it is the child that will bear the greatest burden of the study.

Couples who choose to participate in abnormal forms of reproduction should carefully assess their ability to handle the possible unexpected complications. They should be sensitive to the fact that their enormous desire to have children will tend to blind them to the risks of negative consequences or questionable procedures. They may find that professionals are less interested in helping infertile couples to understand and cope with the vagaries of fertility treatment than they are in accruing further scientific understanding about reproductive processes at the infertile couple's expense (in time and emotions as well as money). They may find that the fertility treatment places greater stress on their marriage than infertility does.

When dealing with the health care system, embryo transfer patients need to realize that they are not patients in the usual sense of having an illness. Instead, they are trying to acquire something. In many respects, they are more like consumers than like patients. Like patients, however, they are dependent, vulnerable, and often desperate. Before investigating infertility services, people need to be very clear about what they want and why they want it. Prior to seeking the more experimental forms of reproduction, they may want to obtain counseling in order to consider the genuine sources of their desire for children. Because extraordinary forms of reproduction have such potential for stress, couples need to be very sure that they want a child. No child should be expected or asked to justify the difficulties that unusual reproduction entails.

In addition, couples who contemplate these forms of infertility treatment need to have a very clear sense about the options and the possible complications of each. Because they are very desirous of the results, people tend to underestimate the seriousness and the degree of difficulties that can arise. This is true of both the infertile couple and those who donate their bodies and time. Although surrogate mothering and embryo transfer can be understood intellectually as a generous gift or as a responsible piece of work, pregnancy triggers many deeper feelings that transcend intellectual analyses. A couple that contemplates surrogate motherhood as a means of having a child should consider ahead of time what they would do if the mother chose to keep the child. Some attorneys who specialize in this area argue that the couple and the surrogate mother should have very close contact during the pregnancy so that the surrogate feels a personal rather than a contractual obligation to transfer the child to them after birth. Others have suggested that this personal relationship might also foster a reverse obligation. That is, the couple might feel an obligation to permit a later relationship between the surrogate mother and the child should she want one as the child grows up.

When couples have suffered through ineffective fertility treatment, they are likely to chase after every new development, believing that this is what they have been waiting for. As a result, they may be willing to make decisions more quickly than is advisable. When traveling unknown territory, it is wise to move slowly. Couples should really understand the roles and interests of the professionals and not assume that everyone's primary interest is in producing a baby. If researchers, lawyers, surrogates, counselors, or other parties have primary interests that differ from the infertile couple's, that does not mean that the procedure is wrong or ill-advised. Nevertheless, the couple, as consumers, should be very clear *where* interests differ. If, as in our case, a retained pregnancy occurs in an embryo transfer procedure, should the pregnant donor be able to transfer her role to that of a surrogate if she wants to and the infertile couple agree? If not, whose interests are being served by the service? If the surrogate transfer is made to the adopting parents and the surrogate reappears in their life, does the attorney have any obligation to the couple to help resolve this problem?

Extraordinary reproduction (other than surrogate mothering) now occurs most often in a research or semiresearch setting. Couples who are participating in research need to know about what will be expected of them in relation to the research goals. Will there be long-term follow-up? How is that follow-up to be explained to the children as they grow older? Are they obliged to participate in follow-up studies? Will their own and their children's identities be kept secret? Will they be protected from the news media? If it turns out that the children are harmed by the method of reproduction, what help will the research institution provide? Couples need to think about the risks to themselves and to their children before assuming that the benefits of parenthood alone justify whatever reproductive assistance they are contemplating. In this area, more than most, health care consumers need to know the current background, the controversies, and the legal realities. To accept a surrogate contract in the absence of legal clarity about the various parties' rights may be a legitimate choice. Nevertheless, couples should not depend for information solely upon the attorney who is in the business of arranging surrogate contracts, since he or she has a vested interest in the project's going through. Entering a newly operating commercial embryo transfer program may be an appropriate choice. Yet, couples should make the effort to ascertain the probability of positive results and to verify the credentials and experience of those who are providing the service. To have a child by in vitro fertilization may be the high point of a couple's life. Nevertheless, to enter such a program without understanding its long-term uncertainties is to court disappointment.

Entering into these extraordinary forms of reproduction means accepting the risks of experimentation. Because the mechanisms and procedures are easy to understand, people may tend to think that the process itself is of little concern. It is experimental in a medical sense, but more importantly, it is a psychological experiment on parents, on donors, and on potential offspring. We have little information about how people respond to these reproductive variations. Those who want to be parents have a duty to contemplate the impact of the phenomenon itself on their offspring. Wanting children may not in itself be sufficient justification for having them.

Emotional attitudes toward reproduction lie at the heart of human life. When reproductive methods are consciously manipulated, reactions both of the donors and the parents-to-be, of the future child, and of the society at large are likely to be strong and longlasting. Those who choose to participate in that manipulation should be fully aware of the primal forces that they may be unleashing.

Conclusion

Embryo transfer represents the latest advance in what some critics have referred to as the manufacture of humans. Like in vitro fertilization, surrogate parenting, and artificial insemination, it enables couples who cannot reproduce naturally to do so with technological aid. It has been argued that helping infertile couples who desperately want to become parents exemplifies medical high-tech treatment at its finest. In judging this new development, however, it is not sufficient simply to prove that those who developed the technology had good motives or that those for whom they intended it have good desires. The technology will not cease to develop nor will it always be used in the same way. Already, a case has arisen about the legal (and moral) status of frozen embryos whose biological parents were killed in a plane crash. If embryos can be successfully frozen for ten or twenty or two hundred years (which is theoretically possible), science and politics may once again draw us into a variation on the theme of eugenics. We already have special sperm banks to promulgate the heritage of Nobel prize winners and other high achievers in the society. Perhaps others—the rich or powerful—will attempt to use frozen embryos to assure their genetic continuity with future generations. At the beginning of this chapter we mentioned the urge of Americans to have it their way; perhaps there is also an urge to have their own forever. The yearning for genetic immortality seems to be deeply rooted and widely shared.

CHAPTER 6

Treating
Handicapped Newborns
The Fate of Damaged Goods

Some infants are discernibly different at birth or soon after, and cultures have tried to understand what that difference *means*. These different infants have sometimes been considered to be the chosen of God, marked by him for specialness. They have, less favorably, been considered to be children of the devil or a tangible form of God's punishment of the parents, especially of the mother—sometimes a public mark of sin. They have been thought to be a special gift to the family, to be specially fortunate, to bode good fortune, or, more recently, to be a serious burden. There have been equally varying ideas about how to treat physically deformed or mentally deficient children. When they have been thought to be special, to have a special kind of knowledge—the wisdom of the innocent child, for example—they have been cared for and cherished, sometimes even occupying special cultural roles. At other times, when the culture defined their difference as a matter of inadequacy or wrongfulness, they have often been victims of either explicit or covert infanticide. As Spartan culture approved abandoning such children on barren Greek hillsides because they were unable to endure the rigors of militaristic life, so in other times and other places, societies have condoned the actions of mothers, fathers, and midwives who have "covered" or smothered deformed infants at birth in order to prevent the public shaming of the parents and family or to spare the infant from probable suffering.

143

Living in the age of science, we believe that we have found the correct way to determine the "meaning" of events. We look for causal factors in the structure of the physical world and believe that such explanations determine and limit the meanings and values of events. We do not consider the birth of a deformed child to be either good or bad news from God or any other external agent. It is merely a fact, an event, caused by certain physical, perhaps random, statistical phenomena that we may or may not understand at the moment but that are ultimately understandable. There is no further meaning in the birth of such a child. The parents' emotional concerns are understandable, but they are not, in the strict sense, important to meaning or understanding. Despite the surprise and inevitable disappointment, a handicapped newborn is merely a child that varies from physical and mental norms in specific, definable ways. But it is nonetheless a child in every significant way and is presumably to be cared for as any child would be. We recognize that it is different, but its differences does not make it any less one of us, any less a person, any less an infant deserving of the loving attention of its parents and its community. That is our scientific, intellectual assessment of the child born with handicaps. Yet, its difference is such that no one congratulates the parents upon the birth of such a child. Instead, we feel pity and sorrow for them and extend our sympathies for their tragic situation, very much as if the child had been born dead. Our ambivalence is reflected in these contrasting attitudes.

Science may have enabled us to see how the deformed child is truly one of us, but our interpretation of that commonality continues to stress defectiveness, inadequacy, and imperfection. As a result, we are very ambivalent about these children. In our language as well as in our lives, we struggle with the problem. We hardly know even how to refer to them. What word or words will give them membership in our group yet acknowledge their difference? They have been referred to as like us but *deformed*, as like us but *handicapped*, as like us but *special*, as *exceptional*, as *disabled*, as *defective*, and most recently as *differently* or *differentially abled*. Every word we use captures the less than perfect quality of these children, these people. And because we are so ambivalent, whatever phrase we use begins to be colored by our deeply felt disapproval and dismay about imperfection. The word or phrase then develops connotations of disapproval, and the search for another neutral word or phrase must begin again.

Science has provided us with new information, and technology has given us new machines and new techniques to diagnose and treat the handicapped newborn. It seems quite straightforward: the physicians are trained to provide lifesaving care; the support staff is ready to assist; the equipment fills the neonatal intensive care unit. And yet, some physicians hesitate to act and some parents are reluctant to consent to treatment. Those who believe that all human life must be respected and that all life-prolonging treatment must be used argue that those who shy away from treatment are morally insensitive and self-centered. The implication is that these parents who want to refuse treatment for their infants are concerned only — about their own well-being. Refusals, it is charged, are based upon their inability to accept the child's lack of "perfection" or the additional burdens that having a handicapped child will bring to their life. The parents and physicians who believe that treatment should not always be provided to handicapped newborns claim that their refusal is based only upon concern for the infant's best interests. To be condemned to a life that consists of little but medical interventions cannot benefit any infant, they say. Some lives, they claim, are truly not worth living and moral insensitivity characterizes anyone who knowingly inflicts a burdensome life upon a baby.

Until relatively recently, both the public and most physicians assumed that newborns whose lives could be saved by modern medical techniques were being treated whenever possible. In 1971, there was extensive discussion about a Down's syndrome infant with an intestinal malformation who was allowed to starve to death at Johns Hopkins Hospital, although surgery was available and uncomplicated. Then, in 1973, two widely respected pediatric physicians, Raymond Duff and A.G.M. Campbell, announced in the *New England Journal of Medicine* that infants with birth defects were left to die at Yale–New Haven Hospital when physicians and parents agreed that nontreatment was the appropriate course. The physicians were primarily concerned with defects like Down's syndrome and with spina bifida (the two conditions that figured in the Baby Doe and Baby Jane Doe cases). The publication of this article marked the beginning of openly divided medical opinion on whether the lives of seriously ill newborns should always be saved.

Many physicians and members of the public were appalled by this conduct, declaring it a basic denial of the physician's calling; others called up memories of Nazi doctors who killed handicapped children and equated the Yale activities with these atrocities. Still others, however, agreed with Duff and Campbell's reasoning, which appeared to be based on a sincere concern for the quality of life that the infant and its family could expect to live. There the conflict stood until a few years ago, when two cases—one involving a Down's infant and the other a baby with spina bifida—led to a dramatic shift in parents' rights to consent to treatment for their seriously ill newborns and seriously curtailed the ethical debate about when treatment was appropriate.

The Cases of Baby Doe and Baby Jane Doe

In 1982, a baby with Down's syndrome was born to an Indiana couple. Soon after, the physicians realized that the infant had additional problems: an esophageal malformation (making it impossible for the infant to eat) would lead to the baby's death if surgery were not provided promptly. The family obstetrician recommended that no surgery be provided. The pediatrician disagreed. The family did not want treatment because, as the judge recounted the father's testimony, "he and his wife felt that a minimally acceptable quality of life was never present for a child suffering from such a condition." The presiding judge of the Monroe, Indiana, Unified Court System agreed that surgery need not be provided because "the possibility of a minimally adequate quality of life was nonexistent." The case was quickly appealed, but even the Indiana state supreme court refused to interfere with the judge's decision. As lawyers flew to Washington, D.C., to request the U.S. Supreme Court's intervention, the infant died.

The case received widespread publicity, not least because interest in the question of when lifesaving treatment should be provided to handicapped infants had been growing as more and more treatment became available and more parents learned about the extent of aggressive medical care and, along with their newborn infants, endured its rigors. Editorial writers contemplated the pros and cons of the situation, readers wrote in to attack the judge's intelligence and humanity, and parents involved in similar situations detailed their own agonizing experiences with infants whose lives had been saved but only at the price of great suffering and increased handicaps. Many believed that parents should decide when treatment was desirable since they would have to bear the burden of caring for a seriously handicapped child. Others claimed that the child had a moral and legal right to receive all lifesaving treatment possible, even if the family would be obliged to shoulder additional burdens. After all, they argued, we do not ordinarily countenance parents allowing their children to die simply because they are burdensome.

For the most part, however, there was consensus that a normal infant with an esophageal atresia would be treated. Therefore, if a Down's infant had a similar condition, treatment was also appropriate. Otherwise, treatment was being denied only because the infant had Down's and would suffer some degree of mental retardation. However, since the degree of retardation could not be predicted at birth and might be close to the normal range, it could not be argued that the infant's life would be worse than death. Its quality of life might be less than average (or possibly better than the average, even if its intelligence was lower), but there was no evidence that the infant's life would not be worth living. The courts, it was thought by many, were wrong. Baby Doe should have been treated.

Then in the fall of 1983, a second and more complex case arose: that of Baby Jane Doe. Baby Jane Doe was born in New York and was found at birth to have spina bifida, a congenital condition in which the spinal cord fails to close. It is associated with mental retardation and physical paralysis. The degree of retardation and paralysis varies from case to case, but is roughly correlated with the spinal area that is open. The higher the lesion, the more severe the retardation and the paralysis. In Baby Jane Doe's case, the opening was low, but the situation was complicated by the fact that she also had hydrocephaly (fluid buildup in the brain, which leads to an increased level of retardation and to death if not treated). Hydrocephaly frequently accompanies spina bifida and is normally treated by placing a shunt in the brain to drain the fluid. It was widely reported that Baby Jane also had microcephaly (an abnormally small head that is predictive of severe mental retardation). Microcephaly accompanies spina bifida less frequently and is untreatable. However, in Baby Jane's case, this diagnosis of microcephaly appears to have been incorrect, as her head size was in the normal range for babies with spina bifida.

Baby Jane Doe's parents were informed by their physicians that treatment was not available at the hospital, and the baby was transferred to another hospital. There, physicians suggested to the parents that conservative rather than aggressive treatment was appropriate. Instead of operating to close the spinal cord opening, they recommended that the opening be allowed to heal naturally and

that antibiotics be used to prevent the infections that would otherwise cause the baby's death. They did not recommend placing a
shunt to drain the fluid from the baby's brain. It was generally asserted that they based their decision on the likelihood that the infant
had little brain tissue, as a result of the microcephaly. Failing to provide a shunt could further damage whatever brain tissue did exist,
but the physicians did not believe that the infant would live long.

The parents accepted the physicians' recommendations and a series of court battles then ensued that once more thrust the issue of
when to treat handicapped newborns onto the front pages of newspapers all over the country. The court cases, which involved a right-
to-life advocate/attorney and the United States government, tried to
force the parents and physicians to provide treatment. They were
unsuccessful. The physicians' expectations that the infant would not
survive long proved to be wrong. The spinal lesion closed and the
baby appeared to be doing well. When it became apparent that the
infant was not destined for a quick death, the physicians recommended that the shunt be placed in the baby's skull to drain the fluids. Were a shunt not placed, her head would have continued to increase in size and become too large and heavy for the baby to move
and very difficult even for caretakers to move. The shunt was
placed; Baby Jane Doe went home with her parents. They were unsure how long they would be able keep her at home. If her care became too difficult, they might need to place her in an institution.
They had, as well, thousands of dollars in lawyers' bills as a result of
the ongoing lawsuits. After many months, the lawsuits came to a
close and newspapers and television lost their interest in the fate of
Baby Jane Doe.

The overall question did not go away, however. Members of the
right-to-life lobby went to the President and to the Congress with
their concerns. National organizations supporting the rights of
handicapped citizens felt, reasonably, that these two cases implied a
devaluing of those with Down's and spina bifida, and they, too,
went to the government seeking greater protection for handicapped
— newborns. As a result, federal legislation was passed in the fall of
1984, defining the withholding of medically indicated treatment
from a newborn as a form of child abuse. Any person who attempts
to withhold medically indicated treatment (parents, doctors, who-
ever) is to be reported to the appropriate state child abuse agency.
The legislation defines "medically indicated treatment" by specifi-

cally listing the only cases in which treatment can legally be withheld. Treatment may be withheld only when it is futile and will only prolong dying, when it is virtually futile *and* inhumane, or when the infant is irreversibly comatose. In all other cases, full medical care is to be provided regardless of the physician's or parents' assessment of what that treatment means with respect to the quality of the child's life or to the pain and suffering that the child must endure in order to survive.

This legislation became fully effective in October 1985. Those who helped to pass the legislation believe that they have righted a wrong and that the matter is finished. Others, however, are just beginning to understand the implications of this restrictive legislation and are being faced with the extraordinarily difficult moral choices that it has created. Although one might agree, even if reluctantly, that Baby Doe and Baby Jane Doe both should have received treatment, are we then to conclude that all seriously ill newborns should similarly be kept alive simply because it is within our power to do so? The U.S. Congress has concluded that this is required of us. Because of medicine's increasingly powerful technology, however, it is possible to preserve and prolong life for infants who predictably will never sit up or walk, speak, or engage in any meaningful relationship with another person, and may never leave the hospital, even though they may live for many months. Similarly, we can prolong the lives of infants with, for example, Lesch-Nyhan syndrome, Tay-Sachs, or Trisomy 18. These babies can live six to eight months or perhaps even a few years, but they are doomed and their deaths may be debilitating, drawn out, and painful as well as emotionally draining for those who care for them. It is possible to keep tiny infants alive when the highly aggressive treatment that they are receiving is in fact creating further damage to their bodies and minds. Very premature infants can be kept alive for remarkably long periods of time before they die from the treatment and as a result of their undeveloped organ systems. Must they, too, be treated with every new procedure just because it statistically might keep them alive, and even when previous procedures have left them blind and brain-damaged? Is there a time when parents can and perhaps should say, "No treatment!" or "No more treatment!"? The new law says that if a baby's death is not inevitable despite available treatment, then treatment must be provided, regardless of the infant's expected quality of life. Parents, physicians, and members of hospital ethics committees are not convinced of the wisdom of that standard, given high-tech medicine's capacity to treat and to harm those whose lives it prolongs.

Case Study

Sara and Jerry Merrill's first child had died shortly after birth, a birth that had been several months premature. The tiny girl's lungs had been insufficiently mature to breathe and, though the physicians did everything they could for her, it had not been enough. It was several years before Sara became pregnant again. Although she feared another premature birth, David was born at full term, a big, strong baby. Her third pregnancy was also perfectly normal. David and Stanley were 8 and 6 respectively when Sara and Jerry began to talk about the possibility of having yet one more child.

The decision to have a third child was a difficult one for them. Jerry was enthusiastic about it but Sara, at least initially, was unwilling to give up the freedom she had so recently gained, with both boys attending school. Before the children were born, Sara had worked as a book illustrator, and she had been contemplating the possibility of returning to work. Another child would make that impossible for many years. For several months, Sara appraised the difference between the often lonely but ultimately rewarding life at home with the children and the always frustrating though economically rewarding life at work. Life would be easier for all of them if she were to return to work, certainly, because of the additional income. In addition, she would again have the opportunity to use her skills and talents and to have them admired and approved by others. On the other hand, she had genuinely enjoyed being at home with the boys and, like Jerry, wanted a daughter. She balanced the difficulties and pleasures of the past six years with the memory of the very different difficulties and pleasures of the six years before the children were born as best she could, aware that such comparisons were impossibly faulty. Finally, she agreed with Jerry that they should have a third child.

The pregnancy moved along pleasurably but uneventfully. Sara, at 34, was in excellent health and she, Jerry, and both boys eagerly looked forward to the birth of this new child. As a family project, all four of them had redecorated the small room that would be the nursery, designing and painting wall murals, refurbishing furniture, and making new curtains. As they worked, Sara imagined the baby girl who would live amid all this newness.

The baby was due in early September and the family planned their vacation for late June, as soon as the boys were out of school. They would drive slowly to northern California, spend a week on the coast, then drive slowly back and wait for the baby. As spring ended, Sara felt so good that the prospect of the long drive did not seem at all burdensome. She rejoiced in their decision to have this baby and felt a full pleasure in her life, despite the growing cumbersomeness of her body.

They planned the trip for three days of driving, each fairly short. By the end of the first day, Sara was surprised to find how tired she was. The drive seemed to be harder than she had expected. By the next morning, she felt a little better, but after an hour in the car, she was again feeling acutely uncomfortable. Her back was beginning to hurt. The thought that what she was feeling was the beginning of labor suddenly leapt into her mind. At first, she tried to force the thought away, but as the minutes passed and the vague pain continued, she was flooded with memories of that first birth. "Jerry," she said, holding his arm tightly. "I think we're in trouble. We'd better find a hospital."

The vacation was over. Within a very short time, Sara was tucked into a hospital bed, Jerry's parents had driven up, picked up the boys and taken them home to San Diego, and Jerry was going back and forth between doctors and Sarah while everyone decided what to do next. They had been unable to stop the labor, although it was progressing very slowly. It might stop. It might not. If it didn't, the baby might not make it. A long labor and a tiny baby produced bad odds for the baby. Ultrasound showed them the baby was okay so far. The baby had the best chance if it stayed put for as long as possible . . . but if it wanted out, then a cesarean was preferable to a normal birth. Jerry explained the doctors' views to Sara and she unhesitatingly urged that they do whatever was best for the baby.

They waited and the doctors watched and within a few hours the doctors decided they had better move. They assured Sara that the baby was looking good and as she went under the anesthesia, the last words she heard were that the baby was going to be fine.

When Sara first saw the baby, she already knew that things were not going to be fine. It was three days before she could go to the neonatal intensive care nursery where the baby was attached to every machine that medicine had any use for. The tiny girl, weighing barely a pound and three-quarters, had just returned from surgery where they had repaired an open duct in her heart. The doctors and nurses had all assured Sara that the baby was doing fine, as if they had just attended to a minor cut. Sara imagined the tiny chest opened up and the doctor's ungainly adult hands taking stitches in this fragile creature's miniature heart. As she watched helplessly, her daughter's limp body began to stiffen, then to become rigid. She called to the nurse who immediately took charge, blocking Sara's view of the plastic isolette. When Sara again saw the baby, her body had returned to the previous limp stage. The chest was rising and falling imperceptibly as the oxygen was pumped into her lungs. There were tubes entering both arm and leg. Her inability to hold her child was painful, but no more painful than the sight of the helpless infant, kept on the edge of life by the machines.

When Jerry and Sara next met with the doctor, she was encouraging. "She's doing extremely well, you know. A baby that small usually has a very poor chance, but she's doing very well." Sara asked about the stiffening that she had observed. That, surely, was not normal. The young physician nodded, "Yes, that's not normal for a normal birth, but this isn't a normal baby. It's not unusual for a premature birth. They are a kind of seizure; they'll stop after awhile." Sara was uncomfortable with this answer and asked her whether the seizures would cause any harm, any brain damage. She patted her on the arm as she left the room, "I wouldn't worry about it," she cautioned. "We're doing everything we can."

As the days passed, the infant went through one crisis after another. The seizures increased in frequency and then, as the doctor had said, they stopped. Attempts to feed the baby by mouth were unsuccessful and the intravenous lines had to be replaced several times. When she began to run a fever, antibiotics were added to the IV lines. As the doctors pulled her through each new crisis, Sara became accustomed to their reassuring comment that the baby was doing fine. She wondered if they ever looked at the child and compared her color, her skin, the look in her eyes to those of a normal baby. She wondered if they ever thought about how it affected a baby's mind if its first introduction to the world was being cut open and sewed up. If this baby survives, Sara thought, she will never trust anyone.

Sara watched by the baby for hours, unable to do more than touch her, stroke her cheek or arms lightly, look at the dimness of her eyes when they were open. She did not try to move or to struggle against all the tubes that kept her going. She just lay there, limp and helpless.

Two weeks passed; further crises, further treatment, further reassurances from the doctors that they were still on top of the situation, that baby Ellen was doing fine. Sara knew that she was not doing fine. She was awake less frequently now. There had been an "incident," as the doctor called it, in which blood had flowed into her brain. The nurses were trying to reduce the level of oxygen, concerned that the baby would be blinded if she continued to receive so much oxygen. Yet she showed no signs of being able to breathe on her own, and when they reduced the oxygen levels, even the nurses were alarmed at the speed with which her skin took on a further bluish tinge.

At three weeks, Sara and Jerry were convinced that doing everything was doing too much. The baby's temperature was rising again as she tried to fight off yet another infection. The doctor had ordered further antibiotics. The couple met with her and asked that she withdraw the order. They had tried long enough to save this child. The treatment was doing no good. It was only keeping her alive, not giving her life. They were not willing to consent to further surgery, further treatment of any kind. They wanted their daughter kept free of pain, but otherwise, they wanted no more treatment.

Doctor Beal assured them that she understood how frustrating this was for them. It was hard for parents to stand helplessly by while their own child was going through such a crisis. But they should not confuse their own helplessness with the ineffectiveness of treatment. She went over the baby's chart with them, showing them how at each point of crisis, they had been able to intervene immediately, change the situation and keep the child stabilized. This was a hard battle for all of them: for baby Ellen, for her parents, and for the doctors and nurses. But they couldn't give up now, when they were making real headway.

They went over the same ground several times, but neither was able to convince the other of the rightness of their views. Jerry and Sara had already talked to several consultants, to a social worker, and to the nurses. No one could offer assurance that the baby would every be mentally or physically normal. They could see no real hope for the child except to keep her "going," but going where? "I really think we have to keep treating your daughter. Not just because I think so, but because the law says we have to. Perhaps," suggested Beal, "it might help if you talked this matter over with the hospital ethics committee."

Sara and Jerry had not known there was a hospital ethics committee and asked immediately for an opportunity to talk with them. A meeting was arranged for the next day, by which time the committee members would have had a chance to review the baby's chart.

The ethics committee had been meeting regularly for just over two years, recommending policies to the hospital administration on problematic issues like when to treat seriously ill newborns, when to withdraw respirators, when to accept patient refusal of treatment like dialysis. In addition, they were available to talk about specific cases with physicians, nurses, and even patients and their families if necessary. Many physicians in the hospital distrusted the committee because they feared that such committees would try to make decisions and force patients to abide by them. Of course, the committee could not, of itself, force anything, but the doctors knew that if the committee made a recommendation and the doctor did not abide by it, it would be very hard for the doctor to defend that decision if anyone decided to sue. If the ethics committee never heard about the case, then there was no way their opinion could be held against the physician.

Because so many of the doctors feared the potential power of the ethics committee, an implicit political deal had been struck: the committee could exist and do whatever it was going to do but patients were not to be informed routinely that such a committee existed. Nor were nurses or social workers expected to make the committee's presence known to unhappy patients. If physicians thought that the ethics committee would be helpful in any problem with patients, then they and they alone could inform the patient of the committee's existence. Of course, none of this was in writing, but everyone understood that the system worked this way.

Similarly, the doctor could bring the case to the committee without ever mentioning to the patient that she or he was doing so. Other hospital employees could also bring cases to the committee's attention if they thought something questionable was happening. Good doctors could prevent that from happening by making sure that everyone involved in the patient's care understood (even if they didn't agree with) the choices that the physician was making. Good doctors could manage the treatment team well. Poor ones were likely to run into trouble and find their cases the subject of ethics committee deliberations instigated by unhappy nurses or social workers.

Dr. Beal was not one of the staff physicians who opposed the ethics committee's work and as soon as she left Sara and Jerry Merrill, she contacted Bill Amis, the chairman of the ethics committee and a colleague in pediatrics, and asked for a fast ethics conference. She explained the situation briefly to Amis, concentrating on the Merrills' inability or unwillingness to understand how well the baby really was doing. "They're really upset about all this; you know how some parents get when they feel that they aren't in control. I told them that the law required us to keep treating, but they aren't convinced. I think they just need to hear somebody else tell them that it's best to keep going. This baby is doing great."

Nine of the fourteen members of the ethics committee met the next day to discuss the Merrill case with Dr. Beal. It was always hard for everyone to get to a meeting called on short notice, but they were used to functioning with less than a majority of the members present. In a real emergency, one or two of them could constitute a self-appointed subcommittee and act in the committee's name. Dr. Beal first went over the baby's chart, pointing out the numerous crises that Ellen Merrill had gone through and how, each time, they had been able to bring her back. From time to time, the committee members raised brief questions, asking for clarifications of technical points: How extensive had the intercranial bleed been? *An intermediate level.* Had the seizures stopped completely? *Yes.* How good was kidney function at this point? *Improving.* Was there any evidence of brain damage? *Not clear at this time.* Test results were enumerated, uncertainties discussed.

Most of the questions came from the three doctors on the committee, only one of whom was a pediatrician. The two nonhospital people on the committee, a minister and a philosopher from a nearby university, frequently asked to have the medical language translated into lay language. The nurses spoke infrequently, although all three of them seemed to be familiar with the case. The hospital lawyer made rapid notes while Dr. Beal was speaking, though he too had little to say during the case presentation. The ninth member present, a social worker, asked cautiously, "Why don't the parents want to continue to treat?"

Dr. Beal shrugged her shoulders. "I don't know, really. They're tired and frustrated, I suppose, and are afraid of getting their hopes up. You know how it is, parents see their own baby, so little and helpless. They feel awful about the respirator and the lines and all. They don't always connect the fact that what they see is what's keeping the baby alive. We've pulled this kid back three or four times already and I think she's getting stronger each time. We could lose her, of course. The odds are better than fifty percent and getting better every day."

Amis nodded reassuringly to Dr. Beal. "It sounds like you've done a terrific job with this baby, Paula. I don't think anybody can question what's been done so far. I mean, given the situation, we have to do everything we can and the kind of care this baby has received here has been great. You and I both know that ten years ago—even five years ago—this baby would have been gone in a few days."

Professor Wilkins raised her hand tentatively. "Dr. Beal, can you give us some idea about what this baby's quality of life will be like if nothing else goes wrong? I don't think I have a good idea of that."

Dr. Beal smiled at the philosopher, simultaneously shaking her head slightly, as if despairing at such questions. "Well, you probably don't realize that we can't really say much about that at this point. It will take some time. There probably has been some brain damage, of course, but it might be minimal. The oxygen levels have been pretty high and we haven't had much luck in getting them down. My best guess is that there will be some problems with her vision, but I could be wrong about that. We are noticing some inadequacies in her reflex actions right now, but I'm not sure. . . ."

Joe Simms, the hospital attorney, cut Beal off as she continued to recite the possible woes to which the infant might be heir. "Although I think Professor Wilkins's question is interesting, I'm not sure that it has any relevance for us here. As I understand the new child abuse law, the infant's quality of life is not supposed to be an issue when deciding about treatment. I'm not really clear about what there is for us to consider here. Dr. Beal assures us that treatment is available and that there's a reasonable chance of saving the baby's life. I think that if that is the case, then treatment must be provided. I don't really see any other course. It really doesn't matter what the parents think. If they are unwilling to give further consent, then we should get a court order for treatment."

A general nodding followed this observation and Amis asked whether anyone else had anything to say about the matter before they met with the parents to explain the committee's view of the case. The nurses on the committee had been exchanging knowing glances during Simms's comments. They were stirring restlessly and as Amis looked around the table, he caught the eye of Carol Thompson, one of the hospital's head nurses.

"Carol, did you want to say something?"

She nodded her head slowly, choosing her words carefully. "Well, I think there is a kind of problem with this case. I mean, a lot of the nurses are talking about it and they're not very happy about what's happening. They've resuscitated this baby seven or eight times already and they feel she's getting weaker all the time. You know, they'll do whatever they're supposed to, but I think we ought to realize that they're pretty uneasy about the baby's condition. A lot of the unit nurses think she's not going to make it and that if she does, she'll be in such bad shape, her family will wish she hadn't."

Dr. Amis tapped his fingers slowly on the table while Carol hesitatingly explained the nurses' position. He understood the nurses' feelings and indeed shared them. His own sense of the baby's prognosis was that it was a downward course that could easily be extended for six or even eight months if they worked hard at it. Maybe even longer if they got lucky. But their luck certainly wouldn't be the baby's luck unless you think that any life is better than none. They still had no sense of how much damage was done to a baby's spirit just by keeping it in a hospital for the long first months of its life. The nurses were great and loved these pathetic creatures as if they were their own . . . and in some ways, they were. The minute-by-minute treatment that the nurses were providing was what kept baby Ellen alive, but it was also placing enormous stress on her very being.

He also understood Paula Beal's enthusiasm at continuing treatment. He too had once been a young pediatrician, dazzled with his ability to make things happen, filled with the spirit of the medical mission, and intoxicated with the belief that his skill alone meant the difference between life and death. Like Paula, he would have kept right on treating any baby as long as there was anything left in his bag of tricks that might keep the infant going. And before that he had been a resident who had offered silent prayers, "Oh, God, if they are going to die, don't let them die on my service. Let them wait until they are transferred somewhere else." He had gone past that now, or at least he hoped he had. He had seen the survivors of his skill, the babies whom he had neatly cut open and stitched up again, their momentary injuries repaired. They had, some of them, come back to his office again and again, with their parents looking more and more harrassed each time, coping inadequately for the most part with the constant need for special care, special knowledge, and special strength. He saw their hopes dim, as well, as the baby's development dropped further and further behind schedule. Slowly, they came to grips with the reality that their son or daughter would never walk, would never go to a regular school, or would never fully participate in the most mundane aspects of life. For the most part, they were not parents who had high hopes for their baby's growing up to go to Harvard or to become the president of the New York Stock Exchange. They were young men and women who knew little of the world and even less of themselves. He remembered a teenage couple who were both working at a McDonald's and whose first child had spina bifida. The boy's mother had urged them not to treat the baby but the nurses and the social worker had persuaded the couple that treatment would save the baby's life. And so it had, but the baby was paralyzed and severely retarded and the husband got tired of McDonald's or being married or whatever. Then it was a thin unemployed little girl with a thin sick baby, and long years ahead.

Decisions had to be made in those days, of course, even if some of them—maybe a lot of them—proved wrong. Now Simms was right: it seemed there was little to decide. The Congress and the right-to-lifers had decided for every parent and doctor in America. Treat them until they die in spite of your treatment or because of your treatment. Only then can those babies get a rest from this world. Those little souls will be a long time coming back to this world after that kind of welcome, he thought ruefully. Well, maybe this family will do better. At least they aren't kids themselves. Even if the baby is pretty messed up, they can learn to love her . . . although it will be harder for them, knowing that she's alive only because we insisted upon it.

"Carol," he replied to the nurse who had been speaking. "I think what you are saying is very important. Joe is right, of course, about the law. It seems to me that we all have some hesitations, but continuing to treat this baby is not futile, and it's not experimental or virtually futile and inhumane. Those are the categories, and I think the committee is bound by the law. We have to recommend that treatment continue, but the nurses need to know why these decisions are being made. Do you think you can talk to them, or would it be better if the committee scheduled some kind of special in-service education program on this topic?"

"Now, if there is no other comment? Okay, do we have consensus then that treatment should be continued for this baby so long as there is reasonable expectation that she can survive?"

Around the table heads nodded, although no one spoke. Most of the members were not entirely happy about the recommendation but, on the other hand, they were not sure that they had any alternative.

"Well, then, before we close the meeting, are two or three of you available to talk to the parents with me this afternoon? And, thanks, Paula, for asking us to look at this case. Remember, though, that if things change, we'd be happy to talk with you about it again."

The Decision Makers: Their Perspectives and Interests

Medical Perspectives

In the case of handicapped newborns, physicians have a difficult role. Because physicians have been educated and professionally socialized to save life whenever possible, they are usually inclined to urge treatment whenever life can be prolonged. They are often criticized for this predilection (for example, when comatose patients are kept alive on ventilators even though they will never recover consciousness) on the grounds of insensitivity to the quality of life that the surviving patient endures. Similarly, they are sometimes criticized when patients who do not wish to be treated (e.g., quadriplegics who require ventilator support to live but who wish the ventilators disconnected are kept alive because the physician does not allow the patient to refuse treatment). In the case of newborns with birth defects and congenital anomalies, however, physicians have been criticized for *failing* to provide treatment. This deviation from their normal behavior may be caused by two things: (1) the patient's inability to express any wishes, and the parents' unwillingness to consent to treatment, and (2) the infant's mental retardation or physical deformities.

Because parents are permitted and required to consent to treatment for their children, physicians frequently treat the parents as if they were the patient. This leads to difficulties when there are potential conflicts between what may benefit the parent and what may benefit the child. The parents' wishes may prevail if the primary physician alone is left to judge. He or she may empathize strongly with the parents and with their unwillingness or inability to shoulder the burden that a mentally handicapped child may bring to them. Doctors are themselves members of a social class that strongly values intellectual achievement and thus they may well be inclined to devalue handicapped newborns—especially mentally retarded ones—even to the point of feeling quite sincerely that the child's life is not worth living simply because he or she is retarded. In addition, the primary physician in these cases—usually an obstetrician or a family or general practitioner—may have relatively little exposure to handicapped children and the many advances that have been made with respect to their care, development, and education. Thus, some physicians may not have very realistic ideas about the kinds of lives that are possible for these children or for their families. Inexperience or knowledge drawn from twenty years ago may lead them to believe that, for example, the mentally retarded can't live in society, or will inevitably cause turmoil in families, or are likely to impose a ruinous financial burden on the family, none of which are always or even usually true.

On the other hand, pediatricians in these cases frequently report that they see themselves as advocates for the children. In part, that is because the child is quite specifically their patient. In a hospital setting, the pediatrician who initially examines the suspected handicapped child may not even know the parents, which further focuses the pediatrician's concerns on the infant. Pediatricians, especially specialists who are drawn into cases of handicapped newborns, may have a wider range of experience and a deeper well of knowledge about handicapped children, including an awareness of both the difficulties and the rewards of their lives for themselves and their families. They may also be able to suggest alternative living arrangements, including the very real possibility of adoption. They may, on the other hand, be very anxious to improve their own treatment skills using their tiny patients as material for learning.

The experienced pediatric specialist who also knows the handicapped newborn's family may be in a unique position to decide what is best for all concerned. In some cases, such a physician may honor the parents' wishes to withhold treatment because he or she believes that the child's life in that family would be too harsh or unrewarding for the child or that, because of the family's inability to accept the child into their home and their limited financial resources, the child's prospective life in a low-quality institution would be crueler than a peaceful death at birth. A physician may decide this even in the face of law requiring treatment if he or she judges that everyone, including the parents and hospital staff involved in the infant's care, will agree. On the other hand, the pediatrician may be sufficiently committed to the infant's chances for a reasonable (if not ideal) life that he or she is prepared either to treat the child against the parents' wishes or to take the matter to court in order to request judicial approval for treatment. Finally, the physician may believe that treatment is not indicated but will provide it because the law requires it or because he or she cannot get agreement from family and co-workers.

Despite the suggestions that pediatricians are strongly oriented toward the infant's well-being and toward providing treatment, a 1977 survey of a large group of pediatricians and pediatric surgeons indicated that three-quarters of them would withhold lifesaving treatment at the parents' request in cases involving Down's syndrome with easily correctable life-threatening complications. This kind of statistic was used to justify the new congressional laws mandating treatment. It suggested that doctors were too sympathetic to parents' interests and insufficiently concerned with the babies' interests. Physicians now appear to have less discretion in making treatment decisions. They may, however, continue to see decision making as their professional responsibility despite the law's contrary view.

Nursing Perspectives

Nurses work under the direction of physicians but they are also independent professionals with their own professional ethics and experience in dealing closely with families. When a physician agrees with a parental decision to withhold (or to consent to) treatment for a seriously ill newborn, nurses are often not consulted about their views. This is unwise and frequently disastrous for physicians and family members, since the nurse, operating from her own sense of professional duty, may precipitate legal intervention. Physicians very often bitterly resent nurses's taking such action, seeing it as a mark of disloyalty or betrayal or overreaching of their abilities and duties. Nurses, however, see it differently.

When a physician agrees to withhold lifesaving treatment or to continue to provide it, it is the nurses who stay with the babies while they either die or continue their struggle for life. The nurses have a substantial emotional investment drawn from their clinical experience that needs to be taken into account when any decision is made. If they are not sympathetic to the decision, they are very likely to resent being expected to carry out the death watch or the life struggle. Nurses who are asked to watch over results of difficult decisions without being included in the decision-making process may justifiably question the moral quality of the decision and take independent action to alter it.

Ethics Committees' Perspectives

The 1984 congressional "Baby Doe" legislation recommended that hospitals create interdisciplinary infant care review committees to consider cases in which family or physician wishes to withhold life-prolonging treatment from an infant. Because there was a feeling that the physicians in the Indiana *Baby Doe* case and the New York *Baby Jane Doe* case had abused their discretionary authority to decide whether to treat, the Congress eliminated nearly all discretionary judgments. Except when treatment will only prolong the dying process, is virtually futile *and* inhumane, or when the infant is permanently unconscious, treatment must be provided. The law does not permit physicians or parents to consider the balance between the burdens and benefits of treatment for these infants as long as survival remains a genuine possibility. No decision about treatment is to be based upon the infant's predicted "quality of life."—

With such strict legal standards, it is not clear what the Congress thought ethics committees would do when faced with a decision about treating a seriously ill newborn. Although there are many difficult ethical questions in this area, the ethics committees are legally bound to a single ethical interpretation. It is possible that ethics committees will simply ignore the law, instead choosing to consider these cases carefully and making sincere and thoughtful recommendations that do not assume that preserving life is the only value that can be served. It is also possible that they will follow the law blindly, even though they believe that it requires them to make recommendations that they believe to be unethical. Either choice would be very unfortunate. Ethics committees ought not to operate under the shadow of lawlessness in their very initial stages; but, it is no better to have them sanction decisions that they feel to be unethical.

Legal Perspectives

Prior to 1982, the law appeared to be quite clear on the matter of providing treatment for handicapped newborns when lifesaving treatment was available, very likely to be successful, and not extraordinarily burdensome. Since parents are legally obligated to provide necessary care for their children, including medical care, the presumption would be that in the event of a life-threatening illness, parents would be entitled and obligated to consent to available treatment for their child. Normally, medical care for a minor would not be provided in the absence of parental consent. In the absence of a genuine emergency, physicians are obliged to obtain judicial authorization for treatment when parents refuse to consent to lifesaving treatment. If a child has a condition that is not life-threatening or if the threat to life is not fairly certain or fairly immediate, however, courts have permitted parents to make what may appear to be questionable decisions about medical care for their children. Thus, parents have been permitted to refuse treatment for cleft palate, limb deformities, and surgical correction of heart defects that would shorten the child's lifespan.

The decisions in the *Baby Doe* and *Baby Jane Doe* cases were thus rather surprising since they appeared to give greater weight to the parents' right to make decisions for their children than for the children's right to have lifesaving medical care. To many critics, these cases reflected the wider impact of legalized abortion, since both infants would undoubtedly have been aborted had their condition been determined prior to birth, as was possible. The courts were only permitting after birth what the U.S. Supreme Court permitted before birth: the destruction of imperfect infants.

The current law requires that treatment be provided in all cases where treatment can provide any benefit. In effect, it denies to these infants the right to decide (or to have decided for them by those who are acting in their interests) that some kinds of lives are not worth living, especially if they involve substantial pain and suffering. Similarly, it fails to acknowledge that the effects of some life-extending treatment may be so severe that the benefits are not worth the limited probability of benefit. This law assumes that all side effects of treatment are clearly known and that the effectiveness of treatment is well-known. In fact, in the cases of many seriously ill newborns, the doctors have little way of knowing what a specific infant's chances are. At best, they have access to statistics that show, for example, that at this time no infants who weigh below 500 grams have ever survived. The probabilities of a specific 750-gram baby living are more than zero, if all possible lifesaving treatment is used, but they are still not very good. Nevertheless, all possible treatment must be provided.

It is very possible that some parents, some day soon, will go to court and demand that the hospital stop treating their infant without parental authority. It is also possible that some court will refuse to consent to treatment in a situation in which the infant's interests do not seem to be served by continuing aggressive care. In either case, the congressional legislation may be challenged and even overridden ultimately, returning the problem of deciding when treatment should be provided to doctors and patients, subject to review by an ethics committee.

Ethical Perspectives

Ethicists, whether philosophers or theologians, have been writing extensively about the problem of treating handicapped newborns for the past fifteen years, especially since abortion was legalized in 1973. Some have argued that the acceptance of late—even third-term—abortions for fetuses with genetic or other abnormalities like Down's syndrome was simply the first step not only toward unacceptable eugenics policies but also toward infanticide. Ethicists who insist that lifesaving treatment must be provided for handicapped newborns argue that the Down's child must be treated exactly like the non-Down's child, because both are persons, entitled to life and to personal respect from their society. Thus, since the normal child with a life-threatening disease like intestinal or esophageal blockage would always be treated as long as effective treatment was available, then the Down's syndrome infant must also always be treated when he or she suffers from the same or a comparable condition. To withhold treatment from the handicapped infant in that situation would be the purest form of discrimination.

Other ethicists, however, argue that lifesaving treatment need not always be provided, because all people have the right to decide whether the potential quality of their life subsequent to medical treatment adequately meets their standards. Patients who can be kept alive only at the price of great pain or paralysis, for example, can refuse treatment, even if it means they will die without treatment. It is an accepted legal and moral principle that competent adult patients are entitled to refuse lifesaving medical care if they prefer death to a life that is compromised by either mental or physical impairment. Some ethicists have argued that infants ought not to be denied this right simply because they are infants and thus unable to make decisions for themselves about what quality of life is acceptable for them. By this reasoning, the parents, who have the duty to care for their children, are most likely to understand the best interests of the child. Therefore, the parents could choose to withhold lifesaving treatment for their child because they believe that the quality of life available to the child is too poor to justify the burdens of treatment. The assumption in these situations is that the burden of living will be a greater harm to the child than the entire loss of life.

Some of those ethicists who assert that quality-of-life arguments are acceptable in these handicapped adults and handicapped newborn cases take the argument further. Generally, it is claimed that a quality-of-life argument must apply only to the quality of life of the person under discussion, in these cases, the infant. Some ethicists, however, contend that the quality of the family's life may also be taken into account; that the family as a unit deserves as much consideration as the individual person, because the infant will be so dependent upon that family for all his or her needs. In support of using the family's well-being as the guiding value, proponents cite the high incidence of families who abuse handicapped children because they are seen to be the source of the family's difficulties and the high incidence of divorce and familial distress among families who are unable to withstand the strains associated with having a handicapped child. Although some families do suffer greatly under these circumstances, many others do very well and believe that the handicapped child brings a special joy and strength to them.

Policy Perspectives

Federal policy makers have acted on the issue of handicapped newborns, and have established guidelines for state and hospital policy makers. Many hospitals have policies about when treatment should be provided for seriously ill newborns. These policies, in many cases, are at variance with state and federal policies insofar as they acknowledge gray areas that should be left to parental discretion.

Federal law acknowledges "reasonable medical judgment" but not "parental preferences."

The state, rather than the federal government, has been the traditional regulator of family relationships, including parental responsibilities, and the federal government's invasion of this area is a troubling development. State legislatures, however, have avoided these kinds of questions because they are so controversial and because regulation breeds intolerance for diversity. The states may welcome federal legislators' preemptive actions, even if they do not much like the results, simply because it keeps them out of the controversy.

The state (and the federal government) may find that the current policy also creates problems for them in other areas. The treatment of handicapped and seriously ill newborns is extraordinarily expensive, with bills of $250,000 per child not uncommon. At a time when the government is striving to reduce health care costs, it has created a new source of costs: not only for the treatment itself but for the subsequent supportive services that these children will need as long as they live. The lack of funds for support services already makes the sincerity of the government's concern subject to doubt. Once the full financial impact becomes apparent, policy makers may begin to find new virtue in parental discretion.

What's a Family to Do?

To appreciate the plight of the parents who feel and think as individuals, as members of a family, and as guardians of their children, it will be useful to return to the case of the Merrills and their daughter Ellen. We can then explore some of the other practical problems parents may face. In this case, the infant—Ellen—was born prematurely but without any genetic abnormality or physical deformity. However, her physical development was so incomplete and her body weight so low that she was very likely to suffer from problems such as heart defects, seizures, excessive blood flow to the brain, and inability to breathe on her own. Despite the high technology (respirators, microsurgery, etc.) used to keep her alive and pull her through crises, she is likely to have suffered brain and eye damage, perhaps to a considerable extent. Although it is impossible to predict the extent of the damage in the individual case, it is known that premature infants constitute the largest group of handicapped newborns each year. Furthermore, those in the 500- to 750-gram range (Ellen was 800 grams) are at the greatest risk for severe handicaps.

The parents, having already experienced the loss of one child after a premature birth, were prepared for the possibility that Ellen would not survive. Yet they had wanted this child: when the physician recommended a cesarean, they agreed to do what was best for the child, even though it meant additional risk to Sara. After Ellen was born, they consented to all lifesaving measures that were required. After three weeks, however, with increasing signs of complications, they wanted to stop high-technology treatment. Relieve her pain, they asked, but stop treatment. At this point it was uncertain if Ellen would survive; it was also uncertain how disabled she would be if she did. The parents were willing to try, but they reached a point when they said, "This is enough." Should they be permitted to make such decisions? Prior to the 1984 Amendments to the Child Abuse Prevention and Treatment Act, they had such authority; with the new law, parents have lost that authority.

In this case, the pediatrician not only followed her initial and professional inclination to save the infant's life, but also her legal obligation to do so unless the infant became irreversibly comatose or would inevitably die. Although Dr. Beal sympathized with the parents' distress, her legal obligation was to her patient Ellen. The law demanded that efforts be made to save her life even if the lifesaving measures themselves caused further disabilities such as brain damage or blindness. This legal duty, however, overlooks the ethical conflict between doing what is best for the patient—here keeping her alive— and causing no harm—here a side effect of lifesaving treatment.

When Dr. Beal referred the Merrills to the hospital ethics committee, further complex considerations arose. One issue concerns the status and role of the ethics committee itself. Should the parents have been told of its existence earlier? Should they have access to the committee itself? How formal or informal should the committee sessions be? These and similar questions confront many of the 9000 hospitals in the nation who have or are considering forming ethics committees. Once the committees are formed, additional issues emerge. As in this case, the perspectives of physicians, nurses, attorneys, and lay members may differ. The value conflicts that pervade ethical debate are, for the moment, resolved in one way by the law. But laws change and conflicts will arise again. Even when the law is clear, it is not always obeyed. Although in this case the law appears to require continued treatment, the ethical conflicts were resolved by fiat rather than consensus.

For an area so filled with uncertainty and disagreement, it may be unwise for the government to sweep away the conflicts by rigid rule. In such cases, it may be more humane as well as prudent to tolerate the ethical ambiguity, to allow parents and physicians and other health professionals to share the responsibility for decisions with the law providing a presence and a limit on abuse of discretion. In this case, however, the physician and the ethics committee followed the law against the wishes of the parents and to the possible detriment of the patient. She may live, but is it a life worth living? Will she have the capacity to live a life with enjoyment or pleasures or only to endure pain and suffering? No one knows. In the absence of knowledge, decisions must be made, but it is not obvious that they should always be made either for or against further treatment.

Although parents have a general legal and moral right to decide what is best for their children, many parents are very uncertain about the extent of their authority in a medical setting. Parents may be intimidated by physicians for three reasons: physicians have superior knowledge about the medical factors in the case, they stand at the top of the power hierarchy within the hospital, and they enjoy a very high status position in the society. As a result of any (or all) of these reasons, parents in deep emotional crisis because of their newborn child's unexpected deficiencies frequently look to the physician for guidance. Often they lose the opportunity to assess the situation for themselves and, at least as far as is possible, to make decisions based upon their own perceptions of family interests.

Physicians generally understand the considerable power that they hold over the parents in these situations and sometimes justify it by arguing that it would be wrong to make the parents decide whether to provide or withhold treatment because the burden would be too great. By including the physician as a co-participant in the final decision, the responsibility is shared. Others, however, suggest that physicians actually shape the decisions for the parents; that is, they present all the relevant information, but do it in such a way that the parents are pressured to choose the path that the physician believes is right. Yet others point out that in many cases physicians make the decision about whether treatment should be provided or withheld and then inform the parents of their decision, without indicating that any choice was possibile. In this final instance, the physician apparently views the issue entirely as a medical or a legal decision, lacking any moral dimension that requires parental involvement.

Because the application of the new law is so uncertain, parents who have a seriously ill or handicapped newborn need to feel they can talk to someone about their own concerns. These may include matters ranging from career interruptions, personal inadequacy to undertake such a difficult challenge, and inadequate insurance coverage for the extensive medical care that will be necessary, to their own city's or county's inadequate child care support and education services. For most parents, the unexpected birth of a handicapped child is a severe shock. The child's imperfections affect their self-image, making them feel particularly helpless to control their lives, and often making them feel guilty, as if they had caused the disabilities. If they are able to make decisions about the child's future, with adequate information and reasonable support from health care providers, that may help them to regain some sense of control and acceptance of responsibility.

It is difficult for parents to make thoughtful, well-informed decisions if the infant has additional medical problems that require rapid decisions. They must immediately reassess all their plans and expectations, quickly trying to understand how (and whether) this child will fit into any imaginable future. Because of the press of time, parents will most often have a mixed set of perceptions and preferences, some of which are relevant to the situation, some of which are not. It would be asking a great deal of them to make carefully reasoned decisions that would suit the demands of philosophers or law courts. It would also be unrealistic to expect that parents would be able to make decisions based solely on the child's interests, ignoring their own interests or the interests of other children in the family. Although it might be desirable for them to separate their own interests from their child's in this instance, the interdependence of family living always requires an interweaving of interests. Under stress, parents are not likely suddenly to display new kinds of thinking.

Thus, parents who wish to withhold treatment may not know exactly why they are choosing this path, or may not know how their many reasons relate. If a career will be seriously disrupted or entirely derailed by the child's continued life, then such a consideration must inevitably be part of the parents' reasons to withhold treatment, although it might not necessarily be the primary reason.

The parents themselves are unlikely to know the "real" reasons and there is no way that others can determine or measure what is going on in the parents' minds.

Thus it is the responsibility of the health care providers to help the parents obtain the information they need. But parents may have to press for that information because the provider may not have it, or may be reluctant or unable to provide extensive social services for which the hospital will not receive payment. Some hospitals with considerable experience in dealing with handicapped newborns (such as university hospitals) may be better able to aid parents than a general community hospital that lacks such experience. Existing community services differ widely, as well. Large metropolitan areas are likely to have more services (though not necessarily better ones) than those in smaller communities. Such services include adoption, relinquishing custody to the state, home assistance, medical assistance, early intervention, special education, and the like. Gathering the facts and contacting the right persons, agencies, and service groups is difficult and time-consuming. Parents will need all the help they can get.

Because decisions to withhold treatment are so controversial, the parents must be able to articulate their reasons despite the great difficulty of doing so. Parents who have chosen or tried to choose nontreatment have found themselves explaining their reasons to the court, to newspapers, and to the public via national television. They are often resentful of this public intrusion in their family tragedy, this demand for accountability, and the implicit criticism of their moral sensitivities. This is understandable. Yet, although the parents may believe that no one has the child's interests more at heart than they themselves do, it may also be true that they have misconceived those interests. Or it may be that they do not actually have the child's interests foremost in their minds.

What can the parents do when they find themselves in this kind of situation? First, they should clarify their own feelings and values, long before the time of childbirth. They should discuss the risk of an abnormal birth very frankly with their physician. If they feel very strongly that they could not tolerate the birth of a child who is handicapped, they might seek amniocentesis even if they are not in a very high risk category. A decision to undergo amniocentesis, however, involves expense and real risk. Here is their first balancing test: are they willing to risk aborting their child in order to clarify its chromosomal correctness? Second, if they do not choose to take that risk, but would not want lifesaving surgery performed if it were needed for a defective child with life-threatening complications, then they should investigate the policies of their physician and of the hospital where the infant is to be born. Investigating one's own values and hospitals' policies beforehand when no one has any reason to confuse issues or is under exceptional stress or time constraints will make it far easier to act should action become necessary.

If parents have not undertaken any of these steps prior to the infant's birth and they must first consider the problem at that time, they should begin immediately to gather as much information as possible. It is difficult to take in information at a time of great stress, but decent, humane judgments cannot be made in the absence of accurate information. Parents can enlist the help of trusted friends or relatives at this time to help them keep track of all the information they need to have.

They need to insist upon adequate time with their primary physician and with any consultants that she or he has called in so that they can fully understand the risks and benefits of proposed surgery. Because medical language is so technical, many people are easily discouraged from trying to understand what they are told, and because risks and benefits are expressed in statistical terms their true meanings are frequently obscured. Parents need to have this information in language that they can understand, and they must insist upon having it.

Parents should try to speak with others who have had similar experiences. The knowledge that their tragedy is not unique to them is very important in helping them to understand that people can differ about how to make these decisions and that no decision is automatically correct or without its difficulties. Even here, however, different parents, children, and families are likely to have had different experiences of success and failure. If the parents speak to or are offered contact only with families who have done well with a handicapped child or only to families that have done poorly, what will they learn? It may not be possible to find representative families because each complex case is unique. Parents might at least learn from others with similar experiences what range of problems to anticipate. Hospital social workers and disease support groups can provide useful contacts.

Parents should try to join fully in the decision. Tension between them or a shifting of the decision-making responsibility to one of them only will almost inevitably be grounds for later problems. The parent who disagrees with a decision but "gives in" will have a long time to resent that action, whether the child lives or dies. If the parents are in disagreement or conflict, it may be helpful for them to seek individual or joint counseling from someone outside the hospital treatment team. In this way, the parents can think through the problems and attempt to clarify their feelings toward the infant and toward each other. No matter what the outcome is, the stress of dealing with a handicapped newborn can threaten even the most stable and secure family relationships. Obviously, when decisions must be made quickly, there is no time for counseling, but when there is a drawn-out series of decisions, counseling can be very helpful to strengthen family bonds through understanding.

Parents should not confuse decisions about treatment with decisions about the child's long-term care. Foster care, institutionalization, and adoption are all potential solutions for the family that cannot hope to cope successfully with the demands of a child with special needs. Many feel that adoption is impossible, but in fact there are adoption waiting lists for Down's and spina bifida infants in some parts of the country. Although it may be difficult for parents to accept that someone else is able to provide the care that they couldn't, they should realize that not everyone has the talent for this kind of heightened care. They might also feel gratitude for the sake of the child that others are able to do what they are not. Here again, the parents may find themselves in conflict. It will be necessary for them not only to obtain relevant information about the options available but also to explore their needs and their feelings. If they choose to keep a handicapped child in their home, they should do this with an awareness of the burdens and benefits. It may then be easier to tolerate the inevitable burdens. Similarly, if they elect not to keep the child at home, it is essential to understand the consequences (psychological and economic) of different choices. Psychological, moral, economic, and practical constraints may enter into any decision that is made. Such a decision is unavoidably difficult and complex. Social workers may be able to help or to recommend others who can help parents investigate these options fully before choosing.

Finally, parents should inquire as soon as possible about whether the hospital has an ethics committee or ethics consultant. If they feel that the information they are receiving from their physician or from consultants is inadequate or inaccurate, they should appeal immediately to the committee for assistance in getting clearer information. Regardless of the committee's role in the hospital, its members are likely to be able to act as intermediaries for the parents and to respond to their need for practical, understandable, and concrete information about the baby's prospects.

Under the new legislation, parents (even more than physicians) have lost a voice in decisions about the treatment of their seriously ill newborn children. Some parents may be relieved at not having to make such a momentous decision. Others will feel that their rights as parents have been violated and will want to challenge the law, either as individuals or as part of a group that represents common interests. Still others may recognize the problems of a political solution to a personal moral choice, but feel disinclined to fight a battle that seems already to have been lost. Whatever position parents take they most assuredly need to be aware of their legal status and restricted options concerning treatment decisions affecting their infants.

Conclusion

Despite Congress's attempt to resolve the handicapped newborn problem, they have not succeeded. The dilemma will continue to exist and to be experienced in hospitals by parents, physicians, and ethics committee members as they struggle to do what is right and to do what is legal. The problem of very small premature babies is a particularly difficult one, but there are others as well. It is unclear how the law is to be interpreted with respect to babies with Trisomy 18, a fatal chromosomal defect. These babies will not die immediately: are they to be kept alive at birth? If not, what of infants with hydranencephaly whose brains have been so damaged that they have no prospect of mental development? They can be kept alive for a very long time. What of infants who will never be able to take food by mouth? High-tech medicine can provide nutrition for years directly to the circulatory system by a new form of feeding called hyperalimentation. Are infants with Tay-Sachs syndrome also to be treated, despite the fact that they will live only a few years before dying a prolonged and painful death? Those who insist that parents provide treatment as a demonstration of their love and compassion when that treatment will sentence those children to brief but harsh lives and hard deaths are very certain that they are right in their moral judgments. Others are less sure, and may in fact believe that infants should not be sentenced to life just because it is possible to keep them going by technology. If they will never be able freely to experience relationships with others, to talk and to move about, even if that talk and movement is minimal or machine-assisted, if they never will have any sense of control over the smallest aspect of their lives, then we may seriously ask whether their lives are worth living.

America has long been known as the bastion of individualism and individual freedom. But it has also been considered a society devoted to fairness and justice for all people. Decisions to withhold treatment from handicapped newborns just because they are physically or mentally impaired cannot be defended, even if they are made by well-meaning parents and physicians. Decisions to impose treatment where none is wanted and where the benefits are minimal and unlikely cannot be defended either.

We have tried unregulated parental and physician discretion and found that unacceptable abuses occurred. Now we have embarked upon a course in which regulation severely restricts discretion. This solution, too, will eventually show itself to be intolerable and we will again face the question of when to choose life and when to choose death. As long as we are committed to simple solutions, we will be thwarted. It is only thoughtful, reflective, knowledgeable, and humane judgments that will permit tolerable, though often sad, decisions.

CHAPTER 7

The Tin Woodsman Was Just the Beginning
The Intractable Problems of Organ Transplantation

In 1954, a kidney was removed from one living person and surgically replaced in the body of the donor's twin: the first organ transplant ever performed in the United States. In 1983, a machine was placed in the chest of a dentist whose heart was about to give out: the first artificial organ transplant in the United States. In the twenty-nine years between those events lies a remarkable story about medical science's intellectual and technical achievements and mankind's severely limited ability either to orchestrate or to accommodate those achievements.

Organ transplants illustrate some of the most intractable moral problems in contemporary medicine. First, a belief in the wisdom of transplants forces us to think of ourselves and our bodies as separate entities. In order for us (the *real* us) to achieve immortality, science must develop good replacement parts for the inferior body pieces that don't stand up well to the rigors of contemporary life. The concept of organ transplants tends to make us think about ourselves as machines. It may ultimately encourage us to use and even abuse our bodies the way some people use and abuse tools or machines: repair and replacement are easy solutions. Second, organ transplants require a social vision that emphasizes human interdependence. Currently, Americans' social vision is dominated by ideas of independence and individual autonomy. Thus, transplantation fosters a different set of values about human relationships than those we now hold. Third, because of their very high costs, organ transplants

175

plunge us into the problems of allocating scarce resources—of specifically and pointedly choosing which person gets another chance at life—and of placing price tags on the value of individual lives.

Any one of these three problems would make a technology difficult to understand and use wisely; all three make it well-nigh impossible. Because the problems are so difficult, organ transplantation has, like Topsy, "just growed," not been developed or planned or thought through. Now, when the medical procedures have attained dramatic new heights of success as a result of technical breakthroughs with new drugs like cyclosporine,* we must—belatedly—think systematically about how we can handle this capacity. As with many other scientific advances, we blind ourselves to the implications of new technology until the problems are upon us. With transplantation, the problems are now upon us.

An increasing number of people believe that because this is the only life they are to have, they must make it last as long as possible. If we are to extend our lives, we need to be able to replace defective parts. Some parts are defective from birth; others wear out or run down as a result of everyday use; still others lose their usefulness due to environmental injuries such as air pollution, auto accidents, chemical food additives, or life-style irritants like excessive drinking and smoking. Right now we are actually replacing blood, corneas, kidneys, livers, hearts, lungs, pancreases, and bone marrow. Transplanting bone, as well as skin and other tissue, is now in the research stage. Lurking in the future, quite beyond our moral understanding but nonetheless the subject of monkey experiments, are human brain transplants.

Transplants on the grand scale require us to think about who and what we are. A cornea here and there; a pint of blood at a bad time—these are not enough to create concern about personal identity. But when we begin to think about major organ transplants and multiple organ transplants, when we begin to make promises to people who need and receive hearts and lungs and kidneys, or kidneys and livers, or more, then we need to think about ourselves in a way that will make sense of these substitutions. Are we spirits who happen to possess bodies and in fact need those bodies in order to manifest ourselves in this particular material world? If so, then it is of not much concern whether we are inhabiting a "pure" or mixed-parts

---

*The recently discovered immunosuppressant drug that has been very successful in reducing rejection problems in transplantation.

body. Are we, instead, minds-and-bodies, a kind of computer-like system in which the bodies are our hardware and the minds our software, our operating systems, as it were? If so, then the software, like any software, can run on any compatible body, although often not as well as on the body-hardware for which the mind-software was originally intended. Or are we individuals who consist of a mind and body that have shaped and been shaped by one another throughout our lives? We may see ourselves as single, unified beings with mind, body, and spirit inextricably intertwined. The individual is unique and of a piece, not a system of modular and indifferent components.

The logic of transplantation, on the other hand, is not very compatible with this last view. Here, individual integrity lies presumably in the brain or in the more complex parts of the nervous system culminating in the brain (although even here a serious problem lurks as researchers investigate the transportability of brain tissue). The rest, outside and inside, is mere packaging or operating parts, to be used and, when exhausted, to be replaced. A gummed-up heart is thus not much different from a gummed-up carburetor; a defective liver no different from a defective fuel filter. The concept of transplantation proposes that medicine deals only with appearances, whereas we—our identifying unique selves—are somewhere beyond the reach of medicine and the merely physical. It offers us longer life at the cost of the wholeness of our being. If we are unified, whole beings and we walk about the earth with someone else's heart pumping our blood, we must realize that, however welcome it is and however grateful we are that it is in residence, nonetheless there is a stranger's heart in our chest. Alternatively, we may view our bodies as if they were dwelling places, and we the tenants who are obliged periodically to repair, clean, and replace worn and damaged fittings, and, eventually, to move out to some other dwelling. The pursuit of immortality through transplantation assures us of an unsettling relationship (or estrangement) from our own bodies.

Transplantation technology also forces us to look at our primary values. Individual independence and autonomy characterize American values. Of course, life actually requires cooperation, but our mythology seldom acknowledges that, and frequently our actions do not either. The process of transplantation requires heroes, both as physicians and as patients. Being the first (or the fifth) heart transplant patient was heroic, even though those patients faced sure death with or without the transplant. Being the first (or the fifth) heart transplant doctor was also heroic, for the probability of failure was great, even if only reputation rather than life was on the line for the physician. Nowadays, even when transplants are so much more successful, heroism continues to characterize the patient's role. The patient is out on the line no less than before, with death usually the only alternative. The financial burden is often borne alone, and even the job of locating the needed heart, pancreas, or liver may fall to patients and their families. We can only admire the patient who chooses this solitary road to survival (although in our less mythic moments, we may have some nagging questions about an overly tenacious refusal to let go of life).

Yet, this last lonely independence of the transplant patient also demonstrates his or her dependence on others. He or she always needs the heart or the liver or some other organ of another and frequently the money of many others. Few patients in need of transplants can afford the costs. In the past year, television broadcasters and newspaper editors have given extensive coverage to those pleading for financial assistance. The *Los Angeles Times*, for example, recently detailed the plight of a welfare family whose oldest son had already died of heart disease and whose next eldest son was beginning a downward decline with the same illness. Four other members of the family also showed symptoms of the debilitating and ultimately fatal ailment. In a brief time, sufficient funds were collected to send the young man to Stanford for a heart transplant. If the transplanted heart was rejected, there were enough donated funds to provide a second transplant, but the donations would not cover a third if it were needed. And what of the other four family members who are expected to need transplants in the future? When they need help, will the newspaper or the neighborly gifts be there again? Or will it by then be an old story, not really news? Will the givers be saying, "What, *you* again? We already gave to you!"

Those who need funds are not all able to reach the media and even if they could, the repetitive tale of 20,000 people in need of transplants would quickly grow stale to our ears. These individuals are able to reach us in their requests for assistance primarily because their plea is unfamiliar and heartrending. Very likely, our hearts are not able to be repeatedly rent, or at least not to the same charitable level once we become accustomed to the story. We are uncomfortable with the inherent unfairness of a system that allots lifesaving care on the basis of wealth or ability to get the attention of the media or the governor. Yet, the alternative is for transplant costs to be covered either by the federal government or by Medicare and private insurance companies. In either case, the public pays the costs. And the costs are very great.

Transplantation raises issues of independence and dependence on a second level as well. An organ transplant depends upon a donor: another person who is willing to give up organs for the sake of helping the patient. In the case of kidney donations, both live and cadaver donors are used. Because a person can live with only one functioning kidney, living persons, almost always close relatives, not infrequently donate a kidney when one is needed. In the future, this procedure may also be typical of pancreas donations as well since there is some evidence that partial pancreas transplants can be effective. For all other transplanted organs—hearts, lungs, livers, spleens—only cadaver donors can be used. Whether the donor is alive or dead, however, the patient in need of a transplant must depend upon that donor's generosity. In the absence of good will, donations do not happen (at least not at present).

It would appear that this gift of life would be an easy one to make, especially when the source of the gift is a cadaver who no longer has any practical use for heart, lungs, liver, pancreas, or kidneys. Yet, the need for organs far exceeds the supply. Six thousand to ten thousand patients wanting kidney transplants, for example, are currently awaiting a suitable donation. The supply is insufficient in part because the needy patients cannot use organs from just any cadaver. The particular organ needed must itself be healthy and have been housed in a healthy body. Thus, those who die of infections or other diseases, such as cancer, are not suitable sources of organ donations. Suitable donors are those who have died suddenly and traumatically: automobile accident victims are the primary supply. Child abuse deaths, as well, provide small-sized organs for children in need of transplants. Thus, the supply of donors is naturally constrained by the kinds of sudden deaths the society endures. When automobile accident fatalities or child abuse deaths decrease, for example, the number of organs potentially available for transplant also decreases.

The limited size of the pool, however, does not alone account for the insufficient number of donor organs available. Many bodies go to their graves with all their reusable parts intact. Surveys indicate that a large majority of American adults support the idea of organ donation at death. On the other hand, a very small percentage of Americans actually practice organ donation at death. What accounts for this great disparity between theory and practice? Many argue that it is a problem of insufficient sophistication. For example, they believe that families would agree to organ donation if anyone asked them to do so but they are in too great emotional distress to think about it themselves. Even if they did think about it, they would not know how to go about making such a donation. An additional argument is that health care workers are insufficiently trained to approach the family in such a crisis to encourage donations. This seems a reasonable account of families' failure to volunteer donations, and one that might perhaps be changed with sufficient educational efforts. However, it does not account for the overwhelming failure of individuals to sign organ donation cards, which are routinely supplied with driver's licenses in many states and which have been the subject of extensive public education efforts. Many lay persons have expressed fears that doctors would not work so hard to save the lives of those whose organs were potentially available for transplantation through a signed donor card. We might interpret this evidence to suggest that Americans believe organs should be donated, as long as the donation is made by someone else.

The third great difficulty with organ transplants is cost: having very expensive lifesaving medical procedures available means that we must decide whether specific lives are worth being saved. When the U.S. Congress faced this question in regard to kidney dialysis, it decided that each life was priceless and each life should be saved. The kidney dialysis program has taught us a bitter lesson, however, about our inability to predict the consequences and costs of high-tech lifesaving.

In the spring of 1983, when the kidney dialysis problem had safely secured a top spot on the national medical Big Problems list, cyclosporine was beginning to look like the program's salvation. The new drug, which had been discovered quite fortuitously in a scoop of Norwegian soil, appeared to be the immunosuppressant about which the medical transplant community had been dreaming. The fatal flaw in organ transplants is the recipient's immunological system. When this system recognizes the transplanted organ as foreign tissue, it attempts to reject it. For a transplant to be successful, the body's rejection system must be turned down. It can't be turned all the way off because the person would then have no way of resisting the myriad viral and bacterial entities that constantly invade the body, and would die from raging infections. Successful immunosuppression (turning the immune system down but not off) had been difficult to achieve, especially when cadaver donations were used since the tissue matches were usually much poorer than those of kidneys donated by close relatives. Cyclosporine, however, gave early evidence of being able to provide successful immunosuppression, at least when the patient's antibody levels were not exceptionally high. Cyclosporine did work but it also appeared to be nephrotoxic (kidney destroying) and perhaps carcinogenic. It was also very expensive, averaging $5000–6000 per year. Nevertheless, it gave new impetus to transplant physicians. The problem now became paying the medical costs and getting the organs. Similarly, for the individual who needed a transplant, the problem was paying the costs and getting the organ. Someone who needs a transplant and cannot find a way to it is like Job, suffering a punishment that he or she cannot really comprehend. If such patients have been given Job's destiny, it is to be hoped that they have also been blessed with Job's steadfastness and his patience.

Case Study

Jeff Marshall was a young, idealistic lawyer who chose to work among the poor and the powerless. He received far more psychic rewards than monetary ones, but he was happy with the fruit of his legal skills. His wife Rachel shared his goals and aspirations and, though constrained by financial insecurity, they and their two children lived the kind of life that suited them. Their chief regret was the loss of their past. Living in California, away from their families and their childhood homes, they felt particularly isolated, as if they had been newly created as adults. Both Jeff and Rachel had grown up on the East Coast. Rachel, an only child, had gone to college in California and then had chosen not to return home after her graduation. Jeff had been estranged from his own parents for a number of years as a result of disagreements with his father. His decision to go to California after law school had been a conscious attempt to put space between him and his father.

Jeff's father, Edward Marshall, was a well-to-do businessman who found idealism quixotic in a 20-year-old, foolish in a 30-year-old, and unspeakable in a 40-year-old. Jeff was now 38. Jeff's mother had helped to bring some kindness to their relationship, but her death eight years earlier, rather than bringing Jeff and his father together, had further separated them. Edward Marshall could not forgive Jeff's idealism, his rejection of his parents' values, or his failure to enter the family business. Jeff had been the oldest, favored child. He should have been his father's partner in maturity, his comfort in his old age. Instead, he had frittered away the energy of his youth and now the judgment of his maturity on those who neither appreciated his efforts nor paid for his work. While the unknown and undeserving benefited from Jeff Marshall's concern, Edward Marshall was forced to depend upon his younger son, Ronald, who pleased him no more than Jeff did. From Edward's perspective, Ronald was a weak, unimaginative, unaggressive person, ill-suited for the business world. To his credit, he had entered his father's business, but Edward was never sure whether Ronald would have survived in a less protective environment. If anything, Ronald seemed to take more watching now than he had previously. The help that his sons were to provide him was sadly wanting and he grew increasingly bitter with age. He tolerated Ronald's ineptness and was willing to keep the distance that Jeff had set between father and son.

Jeff and Rachel's life became difficult when, after a series of illnesses, Jeff was discovered to be suffering from progressive kidney disease. He did not inform his father of the situation. Treatment was only palliative, reducing the discomfort of the disease and slowing down the destruction of his renal system. He knew that his kidneys would eventually cease functioning entirely, and that without kidney function he was a dead man. He was also aware that once he was diagnosed as having end-stage renal disease, he would have the option of kidney dialysis. Dialysis, though inconvenient, life-limiting, and discouraging, would save his life. Furthermore, dialysis would be paid for by the federal government.

There was another alternative, however, although it was not a choice in his power: kidney transplantation. If a donor could be found, he could undergo transplant surgery and, if it were successful, he could return to a life that, if not normal, was at least less restricting than a life on a dialysis machine and had some semblance of normalcy. The government would also pay for a transplant, but only for the first three years, and only for hospital and doctor costs. The transplant patient had high medication costs and these were not reimbursed, for the government supported dialysis treatment better than it did transplantation. Jeff's own medical insurance would not underwrite the additional costs, and asking his father for help seemed too bitter a pill to swallow on top of the illness itself. When the time came, dialysis seemed to be the only possibility.

Despite Jeff's diligent cooperation with the available treatment, his condition began to deteriorate seriously. He was not surprised when his physician, Dr. Spenser, told him that dialysis would soon be inevitable. Although Jeff had previously thought the matter through and decided that a transplant was out of the question, when the actual moment arrived, he found that transplantation, not dialysis, was what he wanted. Spenser suggested that Jeff not yet think about the possibility of transplantation. First they must begin with the dialysis and see how it progressed. Once the dialysis was working, they could consider transplant possibilities if Jeff were still interested, knowing that the machine was an available, workable fall-back position. Arrangements were made to begin the dialysis treatments as soon as they were needed. Jeff continued to think about transplants and began to learn as much about the subject as he could.

Jeff and Rachel adjusted to the dialysis process quickly. Within a few months, they were switched to home dialysis and it became an accepted if tedious part of their lives. Jeff tired of the rigid dietary restrictions and was uncomfortable with the new changes in his body. He became irritated by the travel difficulties that necessarily involved extraordinary arrangements to provide dialysis in other hospitals. Soon, he gave up any prospect of moving freely about the country. He deeply regretted the loss of camping trips and long treks into the wilderness, either alone or with his family. His recalcitrant and ailing body now dominated his life, and he resented that domination, as he resented all attempts to dominate him. Predictably, his mood progressed from weariness, anger, regret, and resentment to acute depression. The expensive and elusive possibility of kidney transplant first became his waking companion, and then began to invade his dreams in fantastic forms. Transplantation or death became his watchword.

Dr. Spenser was encouraging about the possibility. The dialysis had progressed well from a technical point of view, but Jeff's psychological state suggested that he might be the kind of patient that would be better served by taking on the risks of transplant. Dr. Spenser had found that some patients were not only able to adapt to the intrusions of dialysis but genuinely preferred them to the risks and uncertainties of transplant where the possibility of rejection was always so near. Dialysis provided something like certainty at the price of grinding dependency; transplant offered something more like independence, accompanied by risk and uncertainty, soaring hopes and crushing despair when the rejection came. For Jeff, dialysis totally controlled his life; transplantation seemed to give him the opportunity to regain some control.

Initially, Jeff wanted to pursue cadaver transplant, since his brother and father were his only living relatives, and he had no desire to ask for their assistance. Spenser counseled him, however, that he should at least ask both of them since the results with related, live donors were so much better. Several more weeks of dialysis passed while Jeff struggled with the issue. Rachel, motivated by a desire for the surest, most reliable treatment, urged him to ask them, arguing that this was not the moment for foolish pride. When she reminded him of his feelings for his own children and his desire to help them, she provoked some sense of identity with his father that he had not considered. When she spoke of the loyalty and love that their own children had for one another, she evoked memories of his own childhood relationship with Ronald. When she asked whether he would want to help his father or brother if the situation were reversed, whether he would feel wronged if he had not been asked or even told of the situation, he reluctantly agreed. After telling Dr. Spenser of his change of mind, he wrote to both his father and brother, explaining the problem, asking whether they might consider donating a kidney to him if it were medically feasible.

When Jeff wrote his father, he assumed that his father would write back. Since they communicated so seldom, it seemed more natural and far less awkward to ask for help or to receive it through the impersonal assistance of the U.S. mails. Instead, his father called. They spoke uncomfortably, neither sure of what tone preserved the other's sense of dignity. Edward, worried but holding back his concern for fear of angering his son, responded formally to Jeff's request. He was sorry, but it was impossible. He had spoken that morning with his physician who had told him that, because of his heart condition, a donation would be out of the question. Jeff, suddenly embarrassed even to have requested a functioning part of another human being's body, quickly smoothed the matter over. His father should think nothing of it; he had asked only as a formality, really; his physician had insisted; there were other possibilities, and in any case dialysis was workable. The call ended with the same stiff awkwardness. Each expressed concern about the other's health; information about the children was solicited and conveyed. Edward assured Jeff that Ronald would get in touch with him soon. Jeff assured Edward that he would let him know if there was anything he could do to assist him with his medical situation. When Jeff hung up, he felt the weight of the father-son relationship heavily upon his heart. He recalled his long-time conviction that what was done so poorly ought not to be done at all, and cursed his failing body that had brought him yet another mouthful of defeat and ignominy.

Ronald called that night, his sympathy and dismay spilling all over the conversation. When he got down to the bottom line, however, his dismay seemed equally to apply to himself. Never able to create an artful cover for his basic impulses, he blurted out his fears directly. He didn't know anything about what it would mean to lose one of his kidneys, though it didn't seem to be a very good idea. It made him anxious to think about it or to talk about it. He was not comfortable with the thought of operations and blood and medical machines. He understood Jeff's plight, however, and thought that it would be best if he consulted a specialist right away and got more information before he decided whether he could do it. As with his father's conversation, Jeff concluded this phone call with a black cloud over his head. He was not sure that dialysis was any worse than this.

Ronald spoke with his physician and, after much fretting, agreed to go through preliminary testing to see whether he would be a suitable donor. His wife Susan was opposed even to pursuing the matter that far. A woman of strong opinions, she could see no reason why Ronald should undertake the risks of surgery as well as give up his kidney when Jeff already had dialysis. It wasn't, after all, as if Ronald were going to be able to save Jeff's life. He would only be able to change the kind of inconvenience with which he lived, and only then if the transplant worked. There was a chance that it would not. Dialysis might be unpleasant, but transplants offered only a different set of difficulties: constant risk of infection, drug side effects, substantial expense, and long-term uncertainty. Ronald's fears combined with Susan's opposition promised an unsuccessful outcome.

The tests were completed and the results returned. The match was good. Ronald lay awake at night, gazed out windows into the middle distance during the day, and felt the question churn through his whole body. The pieces of his puzzle went round and round, but he had no idea how to lay it out, how to find a solution, how to organize his thoughts. Finally, in desperation, he went to his father and told him of his vacillation and of Susan's opposition. Edward unhesitatingly advised him to call Jeff immediately and offer to go through the operation. Ronald would never forgive himself if he were to turn his back on his only brother, Edward counseled. Ronald called directly and, momentarily filled with his father's certainty, triumphantly told Jeff that he should make arrangements for the transplant as soon as possible.

Arrangements, however, were not altogether easy. Ronald wanted the procedure done right away in Boston so that he might not be far away from work and home. Jeff preferred working with his own doctor in Los Angeles but he quickly realized that his illness did not enable him to ask that his brother do more than he had already agreed to do. Ronald was, after all, risking his life because of the surgery; he could at least risk it on his own ground. Several months passed before everything could be worked out. As Jeff grew accustomed to the idea of asking for and receiving his brother's kidney, he felt less burdened by the entire situation, and when he and Rachel flew to Boston, he felt exhilarated about his prospects.

Edward met them at Logan Airport and took them out directly for dinner. Jeff watched Rachel and Edward eat and drink what they wanted, as much as they wanted, and thought about the freedom that this operation would restore to him, both in little matters, like eating, and in big ones, like living. The initial stiffness with his father eased and they spent an unusually convivial evening, able to steer clear of those topics that created animosity. Edward even grew a little sentimental, openly wishing his wife were there, privately missing her ability to find calmness even in the midst of medical chaos. When they parted at the end of the evening, Jeff realized that these were perhaps the kindest moments he had spent with his father in all his memory. He spoke with Ronald before he went to bed, arranging to see him in the morning before he was to check into the hospital. Ronald would not be there until the next day. Both he and Ronald slept restlessly that night; Jeff with the uneasiness of anticipation, and Ronald with the wakefulness of distress.

When Ronald arrived at the hospital, he felt fatigued and uncomfortable. Almost immediately, a nurse took his temperature and noted that it was slightly elevated. A flurry of conversations took place and a second temperature was taken. The temperature had increased slightly. Within three hours, Ronald had a headache, a temperature of one hundred degrees, and a slight feeling of nausea. Blood tests showed a clear infection. The surgeons were notified and the transplant was immediately postponed, since they could not put the kidney of an unhealthy person in the body of a man whose immunological system was turned way down. The patients and the family members were notified. Ronald and Susan were relieved at this respite; Jeff and Rachel depressed by yet another obstacle; Edward impatient at his inability to order events. The family members left the hospital and gathered again at Edward's home to consider what next to do. Edward suggested that Rachel and Jeff have the children fly out directly and spend the next few weeks with their parents; by then, the operation could be rescheduled. Dialysis could be scheduled in the meantime. Ronald, feeling worse by the moment as a result of the flu and the near-loss of his kidney, said little. Susan took him home and next morning, she called Jeff, asking him if he could come by their house sometime that day.

Ronald was still in bed, but looking less miserable, when Jeff arrived. In his customary way, Ronald scarcely gave Jeff time to say hello before he told him that he couldn't go through with the kidney donation attempt again. As Ronald explained that it had taken all the courage he had to get to the hospital yesterday, Jeff saw before him the little boy he remembered his brother had been. He recalled how he had once abandoned him when they were out together. It had been something of a joke. He had just meant to scare him a little, but when he came wheeling back to the street corner, he found Ronald lying on the sidewalk, dissolved in tears, and an anxious crowd of grownups circling around trying to find out what was wrong. When Jeff had gotten through to him, Ronald looked up at him through the tears, not with gratitude for rescue, but with the hard eyes of accusation. It was a look that Jeff had never forgotten. Now, as Ronald told him that he could not, would not try again, the same look was there, though this time there were no tears. This time, Jeff understood the hardness. This time it wasn't a joke; it was for real, but nonetheless, once again he had forced Ronald to display his fears and his failure.

Comforting his brother as best he could, Jeff returned to his father's home and explained Ronald's position. Edward insisted that he would talk to Ronald immediately and straighten things out. Trying hard not to provoke his father's anger, Jeff insisted that he stay out of it. The matter was done and finished and no more was to be said. He and Rachel would make immediate plans to return to the West Coast. There remained the possibility of a cadaver donor for a kidney; dialysis remained as a lifelong option. He would continue to live and that was enough.

Edward tried to pursue the topic of other options, but when Jeff continued to resist, he left for his office where he called several prominent physicians of his acquaintance. To each, he explained Jeff's problem, asking them outright whether money—a substantial amount of money—could ensure a kidney donation for his son. Each in turn told him that a donation would expedite consideration, but that certainty was a matter of medical fit, and that was up to fate and the volume of donated kidneys. Edward sat in his office, vexed by his helplessness. He had seen parents on television, pleading for livers and hearts for their hapless small children. He could not very well go on television and plead for his middle-aged son. He could not force Ronald to contribute; he could not offer his own body; he could not buy either medical promises or organ donors. His son would, at least, not die. He knew that if it were a heart or lungs, pancreas or liver that was needed, the shortage of organs would mean death to Jeff, disaster to Jeff's children. Although the outcome would be worse, his impotence would be no less than it was now. His helplessness was anathema to him. At the end of the day, he returned home and listened to Jeff's detailing of their plans to return to Los Angeles. He had no advice to offer, no countersuggestions to make. A powerful man, not broken nor humbled by having his wishes thwarted, Edward was angered, but he tried to suppress that anger as he drove Jeff and Rachel to the airport. Afterwards, returning to work, he felt his anger rise but used it, like energy, to run himself for yet another day.

Jeff returned to Los Angeles, to his dialysis machine, to his unemployed and often unemployable clients. He watched more closely their constant struggle with the vagaries and the cruelties of urban living in twentieth century America. They carried their burdens; he carried his.

The Decision Makers: Their Perspectives and Interests

Medical Perspectives

With respect to transplantation, physicians may be filling one or both of two roles. The first is that of a doctor, primarily concerned with the best interests of the individual patient. The second is that of a researcher, with a primary interest in carrying out procedures that will provide better information to make transplantations more successful. The individual who occupies both roles inevitably has a conflict of interests, no matter how subtle the understanding, how sensitive the handling of the patient.

The researchers' motives may be pure, noble, and humanistic rather than egoistic. They may be primarily concerned with saving, extending, and improving human lives in general. Especially in the early stages of research, where little is known for sure, the researcher has little to offer; but the patient also has few options. The doctor may make a miracle, although probably will only acquire a fragmentary bit of information that can be added to other bits acquired in the treatment of other desperate patients. The patient is interested in a miracle; the researcher would not object to a miracle, but expects and is happy with just another bit of information.

Researchers were very careful to ensure that the first recipient of an artificial heart, Barney Clark, understood the experimental nature of the procedure, and although Clark probably knew that he was only a guinea pig, he doubtless hoped for a miracle. The artificial heart project had very high visibility, however, and the institution was very concerned about providing adequate informed consent. In research projects that do not appear regularly on the evening news, researcher or institutional concern with the patient's level of understanding is likely to be much less thoroughgoing. Barney Clark knew he was a hero because he was on the front pages of newspapers across the country. Ordinary patients in experimental transplant operations may not realize that they, too, are heroes, contributing generously to greater medical understanding of the body's rejection system. In their own eyes, they may only be desperate men, women, or children, grabbing at what chances there are.

The physician who is not also a researcher does not, of course, have the same conflict of loyalties. There may be, however, a different kind of conflict. At a time when there are inadequate resources—both money and spare organs—the primary care physician must make a "first-cut" decision about whether his or her patient *deserves* a chance at a transplant. Doctors do not often talk about *this* conflict, this moral appraisal, but when they do, they frequently refer to it as the necessity for "medical selection criteria." Both courts and doctors often cite the need to make *medical* decisions. Customarily, when they do so, they do not mean decisions that have a technical content involving medicine; rather, they mean decisions that are made by doctors and that have some connection

with medical procedures. Thus, for example, abortion is often referred to as a "medical decision," although only in a tiny number of
cases would the decision to have an abortion have any primary medical content. "Medical selection criteria" similarly invokes the *idea*
of medical content, although the criteria themselves tend to be
moral judgments.

Thus, for example, personal wealth, character traits like self-
control and self-discipline, age, and mental capacities might all be
considered relevant "medical" criteria for a transplant recommendation. If the primary care physician believes that a patient would
have no way of financing a transplant operation, the physician may
never mention the possibility of transplant. As a result, indigent or
welfare patients are unlikely to have access. Similarly, patients who
do not appear to be well-disciplined or highly cooperative with physicians may never hear about transplants for their conditions. Because successful transplants require the patient to follow a restrictive regimen, the patient who is uncooperative or appears
undisciplined will not be considered "medically suitable" for a
transplant. Nor will the elderly patient or the patient with limited
intellectual capacities be recommended for such high-tech treatment, although in their case it may be as much because their lives
are valued less as because increased age or limited intelligence
makes successful treatment more unlikely. The latter judgments
might more accurately be described as medical judgments. That is,
the treatment will not work.

Finally, physicians may fail to recommend transplant procedures simply because they do not know how to connect their patients with institutions that provide transplant services or because
they do not believe that, in general, the enormous effort expended in
gaining access to transplant services is justified by the results. In the
case study above, the physicians are not operating in a research atmosphere or in a scarce-resources atmosphere because kidney transplant is the oldest and most successful of the major transplant operations and because its costs are covered by government programs. As
a result, the physician's "medical criteria decisions" are more likely
to *be* medical. There are still not enough kidneys available for transplant, however. As a result, allocation problems continue and physicians must make nonmedical judgments about who deserves an
available organ when tissue-matching or antibody-level considerations do not alone provide a genuinely medical answer.

Legal Perspectives

Currently, legal regulation specifically concerned with organ transplantation exists almost exclusively in the area of informed consent from live donors. Within the next few years, however, much more attention will be directed to other areas. A federal law now prohibits the sale of organs offered either by living individuals or the families of deceased persons. Some legal writers have also proposed the introduction of legislation that would establish the state's right to claim all organs of any deceased person who has not, during his or her lifetime, refused that claim. This would reverse the current legal situation in which cadaver donations cannot be made unless the deceased individual had agreed to do so while alive or unless the family agrees to the donation at or after the individual's death.

Only kidney transplants use live donors because the kidneys come in pairs and a single healthy kidney appears to be adequate for the conduct of ordinary life (although not entirely without problems and risks). All other organ transplants—at least at the present time—require a whole organ: a heart, a liver, a pancreas, the lungs (which, although they are paired, operate as a single unit). A cadaver donor runs no risks (not in this world, anyway) from a donation. A live donor, however, is a different matter. When kidney transplants were in their earliest stages, physicians were uncertain about the implications for the donor. Even now, thirty years after the first successful kidney transplant, there are unresolved questions about whether donors suffer increased risks of illness and early death as a result of their generosity. The law has taken this uncertainty very seriously and has been concerned to ensure that live donations not be made unless competent individuals are fully informed of known risks and the possibility of unknown risks. In addition, the law has extensively addressed questions of prospective donors who are incompetent, whether because of mental disorders or handicaps, or because of their age.

Donations by competent individuals are legally permitted as long as the donor receives adequate information about the known risks and benefits. Living donors are almost always family members. This is partially accounted for by the need to match tissues as closely as possible, matches that could more easily be provided within the genetic group. An additional and powerful reason, however, is our belief that a request of such magnitude can be made only to a family member. Donations between family members do, however, create the potential for significant legal and interpersonal problems.

When a member of the family needs a kidney donation, the atmosphere tends to be crisis-ridden. It is obvious that the circumstances in which a request is made may be extremely coercive. Requiring informed consent does not protect anyone from the pressures that may be exerted within the family. The law is unable to protect family members in that instance and has made no attempt to do so. Physicians sometimes step into this breach and release the family member from a perceived obligation to donate by giving the person a "medical" excuse. If the physician is aware that one person does not want to donate but is unable to tell the other family members because of psychological pressures within the family, the physician can publicly disqualify that person as a donor for such reasons as poor tissue match. In this way, physicians can eliminate the need either to display the true reasons or to have an organ donation that is not a genuine gift. Although deception is involved, the deception does reflect the spirit of the law, which insists that the donation be made freely.

Live kidney donations by those who are mentally ill or mentally retarded provide another problem. In many instances, parents of these adult incompetents have obtained legal guardianships that entitle them to consent, among other things, to medical care for their adult children. When another member of the family needs a kidney donation, these parent-guardians have tried to consent to the removal of the organ from the incompetent "child." The courts have not, however, permitted this: they have insisted that some neutral third party be appointed to consider whether there is any possibility of benefit to the donor. For example, the incompetent person might be permitted to donate a kidney because there would be a psychological benefit in having saved a family member's life. Benefit need not always be psychological, however. A mentally retarded or disturbed person might be permitted to donate a kidney to a family member because that person, if alive, would be able to provide care or financial help to the donor. Where no benefit can be found, no donation may be authorized.

The courts have also dealt with the problem of forced donations. Although no one has yet tried to compel another person to donate a kidney, several such cases have arisen in the context of bone marrow transplantation. In bone marrow donation, the donor faces very little risk and loses nothing, for one's own body will manufacture new marrow to replace the donated bone marrow. Although more complicated and more painful, the procedure can be better compared to blood donation than to organ donation. Nonetheless, courts have refused to order bone marrow transplants when consent was not freely forthcoming, even though the patient's death was inevitable without the bone marrow transplant.

Ethical Perspectives

Philosophers who have discussed transplantation have primarily focused on two questions: first, the acceptability of experimenting on patients when the prospect of success is relatively small; and second, the "gift" aspect of organ donation. Debates about the former have diminished considerably as transplant procedures have become more successful, but the second issue continues to be frequently discussed.

The first human heart transplant, the first animal-to-human heart transplant, and the first artificial heart transplant had very little prospect of success. Adam Washkansky, the South African who received the first human heart transplant, lived only eighteen days, and it was immediately clear that his days were numbered. After his recovery from the initial surgery, Mr. Washkansky was promptly interviewed by excited reporters from around the world. In his hospital bed, his new heart pumping immunosuppressant drugs throughout his body, he smiled his delight at still being alive, thanks to the miracle of modern medicine. Had Mr. Washkansky's doctor expected him to live, he might not have exposed the patient to the world at a time when he was so extremely susceptible to disease. The immunosuppressant drugs were not only keeping his body from rejecting the heart; they were also keeping his body from rejecting the multiplicity of bacterial and viral agents that filled his hospital room turned newsroom. Those in the advance guard of experimentation, including Adam Washkansky, Phillip Blaiberg, and Dr. Barney Clark, survived only briefly. Their short, additional lives were far less of a benefit to them, trapped as they were in hospitals amidst constant observation, than a benefit to future heart transplant patients.

Human experimentation provides us with very difficult questions. Certainly those persons who take on the risks of experimenta-

tion when they are unlikely to benefit personally act with great no-
bility. Yet, the person who, in the face of certain death, is persuaded
to attempt the grand experiment may not intend a noble or selfless
act. The terminal patient is very susceptible to the promise, usually
only implicit, of a miracle. Ethicists have seriously questioned
whether any person in that position can legitimately be described as
having made a free choice. Death or experimentation . . . with the
possibility of a miracle? Unlike earlier periods of medicine when
doctors quite frequently experimented on themselves, nowadays the
subjects are desperate patients. Their contributions are noble, but
we might question whether their intention was to sacrifice themselves for scientific progress and the good of mankind.

Ethical debates about giving and selling body pieces and products first arose in connection with blood. The argument against selling blood posited that the "gift of life" ought to be freely made as a
symbolic statement about human relationships and human interdependence. By permitting the sale of blood and blood products, the
government was discouraging desirable expressions of compassion
and generosity. In England, this argument was politically very successful and the purchase of blood became illegal. In the United
States, it was less successful and, in most states, blood continues to
be purchased from donors. Sperm, too, is purchased, by sperm
banks.

The uneasy balance about what ought to be donated and what
could be sold has recently received a sharp jolt by the contention
that people ought to be allowed to sell major organs, like kidneys,
and perhaps even nonpaired organs like hearts and livers. A poor,
unemployed man from the hill country of West Virginia wishes to
sell a kidney for $20,000 because it will give him the opportunity to
be retrained for employment. He will be a kidney poorer, but he
will have a chance for work and an income sufficient to feed, clothe,
and house his wife and four children. From his point of view, the
kidney is his and he should be able to do what he wants with it. In
many respects, his argument differs little from that of the pregnant
young woman who argues that her body is her own and only she can
determine whether she should have an abortion. It is a privacy claim
and a property claim.

Philosophers have not been very sympathetic to the West Virginia man, however. They have, instead, been appalled at the suggestion that organs should be sold to the highest bidder. They object
because the existence of such a market would mean that transplan-

tation would be available only to the rich. They object because they believe that such a market would place the poor under inhuman pressures to sacrifice their health, their well-being, and perhaps eventually their lives to benefit their families. And finally, they object because such a market would encourage a view of the poor as a source of spare parts for the rich, whether the poor were white hill farmers from West Virginia or, as would be more likely, black or brown peasants from third-world countries. Donation, like experimentation, is a gift, they argue; and the procedures that surround both practices, whether requiring informed consent or forbidding organ sales, must continually stress compassion and generosity.

Policy Perspectives

Policy makers, too, have concerned themselves with problems of informed consent and organ sales. Their primary concerns at present, however, revolve around the desirability of increasing the available supply of cadaver organs for transplant and methods of funding the increasing demand for transplant services. Although these two subjects appear at first glance to be disparate, they are in fact closely intertwined since the overall cost of organ transplants (other than kidney transplants) is a direct function of the number of organs available for transplant. If the government acts to increase the number of organs available, the pressures to provide government funding for the operations will be much greater.

Organ transplants are expensive. Pancreas transplants are estimated to range from $18,000 to $50,000; liver transplants from $55,000 to $238,000; and heart transplants from $37,000 to $110,000. For policy makers who worry about the astronomical costs of the Defense Department budget, $3 billion for transplants may seem small stuff. But it is not small when health care costs already consume almost 11 percent of the gross national product and federal budget deficits have given new meaning to the phrase *far out*.

Elected officials at county, state, and national levels are under increasing pressure from their constituents to ensure medical or financial assistance for transplant operations. President Reagan has made national appeals during televised and radio press conferences for cadaver donated organs for children in need of liver transplants. California's Governor George Deukmejian, a conservative Republican, ordered MediCal (the state medical reimbursement program) to pay for a liver transplant after a personal appeal from a family whose child faced death without the surgery. Members of Congress recount numerous stories of their constituents pressing them for assistance; many of these individuals have appeared at congressional hearings, telling their heartbreaking stories of unrequited waits for organs or funds, stories that frequently end with the death of the family member.

Transplantation places policy makers between the proverbial rock and the hard place. Lives can be saved and the still living are literally beating on their doors; yet the policy makers cannot bring themselves to authorize funds to save those lives during economic hard times. As a peculiar compromise, they are first attempting to find ways to increase the supply of donor organs. They are also considering state laws that establish presumed consent for organ donation. Under such laws, cadaver organs would be available for donation unless the person, during life, specifically refused consent for donation. Since most people don't think about such matters—or even like to think about them—most people will not have refused consent. This would substantially increase the pool of available organs.

If the pool increases, however, demands for the service will rise. Then overall costs, too, will rise. Transplant experts estimate the yearly demand for heart transplants to be as little as 1000 or as much as 75,000. The extreme range results from variable patient criteria. If funding is available, transplants will be desired by and recommended for far more patients than are now considered medically eligible.

Eliminating that kind of escalation will be difficult, but already there are suggestions that transplants ought not be provided at public expense (whether through government or private insurance) to those whose condition results from their own behavior. Thus, alcoholics or heavy drinkers in need of new livers, for example, are already shown the door. Similarly, the three-pack-a-day smoker who wants a better functioning heart, lungs, or both may not be welcome. There is considerable evidence that most health care expenditures are directly related to life-style choices. How, then, will decisions be made about what costs should be paid and what costs should not? There are some questions that are better not asked, and if policy makers are heading toward this one, they might be advised to avoid the entire subject, even in the face of lost lives.

What's a Patient to Do?

Jeff Marshall's unhappy experience with dialysis and his own psychological makeup make him an appropriate candidate for kidney transplantation. His preference for seeking a cadaver kidney reflected his strained and distant relations with his family. The reluctant request that his father and brother consider donating a kidney added additional stress for the principal participants as well as for their families. His father's ineligibility increased his impotence and frustration; his brother's compatibility created anxiety and fear, and renewed old resentments. The stress on family members casts doubt on the voluntariness of consent, even if it is well-informed. Ronald was under pressure from several sides. One can understand his vacillation between consent and refusal.

Similarly, Jeff is concerned that a request for a kidney donation is an impossible burden. Yet he also believes that such a gift is also an act of great love, and Rachel convinces him that he cannot deny others the opportunity to help. Had Ronald expressed his doubts to the physician, it is possible that he would at least have been offered the protection of a medical excuse. Waiting so long to express his reluctance places everyone in an extremely difficult situation. The law, however, will go to extraordinary lengths to protect Ronald's right to use his body as he sees fit. Ordinarily, only when there is a need to protect public health do we require people to undergo medical interventions (e.g., vaccinations). In this setting, the law demonstrates its inclination to establish a minimum moral threshold: neither the law nor most moralists would deny that for Ronald to give his brother one of his kidneys would be a morally praiseworthy act. But a great distance exists between what is praiseworthy and what is required. Ronald's donation is not required; his refusal is legally and morally permissible within the framework of individual rights.

Jeff has made a point of educating himself about the transplant procedure itself and the risks and benefits he can reasonably expect. His physician, as well, has insisted that he experience the quality of life that dialysis provides so that he will fully understand his options with respect to transplantation. The patient who needs a heart, liver, or pancreas has no alternatives, and ensuring informed consent for such a person is much more difficult. In addition, Jeff understands that in asking his brother for help, he is making a burdensome request that love alone can justify. When help is denied, he accepts the limitations of that love. He can more easily accept that, however, because of the availability of dialysis. The parent whose child needs a liver from a cadaver donor may be hard pressed to understand the failure of others to extend their compassion and aid.

This case demonstrates how the complexity of interpersonal psychology and relationships interacts with the uncertainty of the human mind and the unpredictability of the human body. One is tempted to speculate that Ronald's resistance was reflected in his physiology. In any case, it is clear that such variables are not easily controlled. The ambiguous outcome in this case probably mirrors the mutual ambivalence of Jeff and Ronald.

We might also consider the complications that might have occurred if Ronald had donated a kidney and it had been rejected by Jeff's body. Both Jeff and Ronald would suffer significant psychological effects. Jeff might feel resentment and anger that would override his gratitude toward Ronald. Ronald, however, might feel guilt that his underlying hostility toward Jeff somehow caused the rejection. Whatever psychodynamics existed among the family prior to the transplantation episode would be amplified by the additional demands of Jeff's illness.

The professionals are charged with the responsibility of being sensitive to, anticipating, and managing the psychological nuances of their cases. However, neither human emotions nor conduct is susceptible to tight control. Furthermore, Jeff's physician, at least initially, has no direct contact with Jeff's distant family. An extremely sensitive physician might alert Jeff to potential problems or even mediate this delicate situation. But the problem of coordination among physicians is considerable and, as it turned out in this case, circumstances arose that were beyond anyone's control. Even a psychologically astute physician could only help regulate the emotional tension; the personal physicians of the brothers cannot control the moral choices or the psychological capacities of their patients.

When patients contemplate transplant, they must realize that life with a transplant is not the same as life with one's original body part. Despite the apparent level of success that organ transplantation now has achieved, it is still a very risky business. A large percentage of patients will not survive five years after the transplant operation. Many patients who survive are obliged to undergo second transplants as a result of rejected organs. The side effects of new immunosuppressants are unknown or only suspected and may include high risks of cancer and of kidney destruction. The news media, anxious for the dramatic story, tend to focus on the transplant operation itself, leaving the implication that if the operation works, the patient is back to normal. This is not true. As one physician has said, "When you talk about transplant, you always have to consider the *misery ratio*; that is, how much misery do you get per additional month of life?"

Body parts, whether kidneys, hearts, pancreases, or livers, are simply not interchangeable. The body's insistence upon rejecting foreign bodies is a deeply rooted biological necessity. In order to keep transplanted organs from being rejected, patients must undergo a lifetime of immunosuppressant medication. Suppressing the immune system keeps the transplanted organ from being rejected but it also makes the patient an easy prey for every passing disease-producing organism. In addition, the medication's side effects can dramatically alter the patient's quality of life. Finally, the fact that the transplant can fail at any time means that patients must live under a lifetime of anxiety. Some kidney transplant patients have found the anxieties and rejection episodes impossible to live with and have gratefully returned to the more predictable difficulties of dialysis. For patients in need of heart, lungs, liver, or pancreas, no such artificial organ is now available. For them, it is transplant or death. Before choosing transplant, however, patients need to understand fully the probable future *if the transplant is a success*. Dr. Barney Clark, who was the first recipient of an artificial heart implant, expressed concern to his physicians before the operation that the procedure might extend his life but leave him extremely ill. That was an option he did not want. Unfortunately, that was what the operation gave him. Although the expected results of organ transplants are better known than the results of artificial heart implants, patients need to take this issue very seriously. In Clark's case, other physicians have stated that they believe the transplant team seriously underestimated the amount of stress Clark was going through, primarily because transplant teams have become accustomed to seeing the procedures and the attendant difficulties. For the patient who is experiencing them, they are brand new, very uncomfortable, and very stressful.

If patients are prepared to choose transplant, it is well to consider in advance the timing of the operation. Because transplants are still relatively experimental, they are not usually done except as a last resort. By that time, patients are usually very ill. Many transplant specialists assert that transplants would be more successful if the patients were not so weakened by their disease before they reach the transplant stage. That is, if they operated on stronger patients, the patients would be better able to tolerate the stress and thus be more likely to survive the operation. This is always a problem with experimental procedures but now that transplant is becoming more widely accepted as a nonexperimental procedure, patients are in a better position to take the option sooner. For individual patients, of course, there is an important risk: they are gambling the certain time they have left for a chance of a better life, but with a risk of no life at all. Transplant physicians who are anxious to improve their overall survival statistics (and that is a concern of all physicians in this field) may well tend to encourage patients to undergo transplants at an earlier stage. Nontransplant physicians may tend to encourage patients to wait until the last possible moment. Patients who want to control their own decisions need to ask their physicians about the range of time in which a transplant is possible and discuss the implications of having it both sooner and later.

The costs of transplantation are of enormous importance to the patient. For those who seek kidney transplants, government payment is available through the Social Security End-Stage Renal Disease Program if the patient is covered by Social Security (i.e., has contributed through employment to the Social Security system) or if the patient is a minor whose parents have contributed to Social Security. Long-term costs of care are not covered, however. Although reimbursement is extensive, patients should be sure they understand the kinds of costs that will be reimbursed and the kinds that will not. Costs of immunosuppressant drugs are not covered, and cyclosporine, the most promising drug, costs between $5000 and $6000 per year, perhaps more. Immunosuppressants must be taken as long as the person has the transplanted organ functioning in his or her body.

For other transplant candidates, reimbursement is spottier. Some state governments reimburse for some transplants as a matter of policy. Some state governments have ordered transplant costs covered in individual cases in the absence of a payment policy. Some insurance companies are now covering transplant costs if the transplants are done at specifically designated centers. Each insurance company decides whether to cover transplant costs, so patients will have to find out what is the case with their carriers. Only a few now provide coverage, but that number is likely to increase. In the future, insurance companies may offer separate coverage for transplants (much as maternity coverage used to be offered as an option, usually paid for directly by the insured individual). Even if patients have coverage, they need to be very clear about what that coverage includes. Does it, for example, include the costs of retrieving the organ from the cadaver and transporting it to the appropriate hospital? Organ retrieval costs may or may not be included in standard coverage.

If patients have no insurance coverage, they must seek other alternatives. A research program may cover some or all costs whereas a program in which research is not the primary focus might require that all hospital costs and professional fees be paid in advance by the patient. At California's Loma Linda Hospital, where Baby Fae received the baboon heart transplant, all costs were reportedly paid by the hospital. Had the infant been sent to a standard heart transplant center, the costs would not have been paid by the hospital. Patients who cannot personally afford the costs have frequently gone to newspapers, television stations, and institutional employers to ask for community assistance. Some have been successful; others have not been. Those cases involving young children appear to have greater public interest, but some adults have also been able to finance transplants in this way.

Transplants are available only at a limited number of hospitals, so patients may want to consider where they would like to have the transplant performed. Some hospitals have long-term transplant programs; others may have begun to perform these procedures only recently. Transplant operations are reasonably complex and patients are likely to do better when the transplant team is highly experienced. Patients should be concerned not only about the experience of the surgeon but also about that of the support staff. For example, is there good nursing care? If patients can choose between experienced and inexperienced teams, they would probably be better off with experience, all other things being equal. Unfortunately, all other things are seldom equal. Patients may need to consider whether they are better off staying near home and receiving treatment at a relatively new transplant center or traveling to a more established center but being separated from family members. They may not be able to make that choice because of payment considerations, but they ought to know how much experience each team has had as well as their survival rates (as compared to national survival rates) for the operation. Survival rates are usually given at one and at five years. A new center will, of course, have no long-term and perhaps very few short-term figures.

Patients facing transplant have the benefit of national organizations that provide information about all aspects of transplantation. Twenty years of therapeutic research have produced private organizations that assist current patients, and act as lobbyists for patients, urging government assistance for payment, insurance coverage for the procedures, freer access to organs of persons who die from traumatic injuries, and increased research into artificial organs that can be used, like kidney dialysis, as a backup until the real thing is available. They are, however, supporters of transplantation and may be less worried about the risks and problems of transplantation than with providing more and better services. Nevertheless, patients who understand the risks and the downside may be able to get assistance from organizations like the American Liver Foundation, the National Kidney Foundation, the Organ Procurement Foundation, and the Juvenile Diabetes Foundation International. These groups can provide information about the complexities of organ procurement or of funding, and can help patients to develop a realistic sense of the life changes that transplantation demands by putting them in contact with individuals who have received successful transplants. Local chapters of these organizations can, as well, provide understanding and comfort for the families of those who die without the chance that transplant offers or who die despite the use of transplant. These organizations represent a vast store of information about transplantation and, as such, they are a critical link between patients in need and doctors and policy makers in a position to help.

Transplant patients are usually chronically ill and in deteriorating condition. This kind of illness is almost inevitably accompanied by psychological disturbances within the family. Because the process of transplant is likely to be long and drawn out, these emotional conflicts may be especially exacerbated. Many families can rise to noble psychological heights for brief periods of time, but to do so for months is well-nigh impossible. Patients who undergo treatment, as well as their families, should realize that family dynamics are likely to change. They should be prepared for emotional outbursts and unusual behavior. When the transplant involves live donors, these disjunctions can be especially severe.

The problem of live donation is a considerable one. On the one hand, there is a feeling that people should give "the gift of life." On the other hand, American law and logic insist that a gift is a gift only if it is freely given. The family of a patient in need of a kidney is in a difficult position because the situation can be too coercive for genuine giving. Family members who do not wish to be donors but do not feel that they can refuse in the face of family pressures can make their positions known to the physician. They might be advised to point out specifically that they are speaking in confidence to the doctor and do not want the information to be given to anyone else. The physician, too, may try to persuade the reluctant family member, but if this is not successful, physicians will ordinarily cover the situation by stating that the family member is not a medically appropriate donor. However, physicians cannot protect potential donors if they are not informed of the person's reluctance prior to testing.

Procuring informed consent for a hazardous procedure from an acutely ill patient is always problematic. In kidney transplants, patients should be very clear about the different risks and benefits of transplant and dialysis. End-stage renal disease patients have time to talk with other patients in order to find out how patients (as opposed to physicians) evaluate the difficulties of these alternative treatment forms. Heart, liver, and pancreas candidates need to be sure that they understand the kinds of risks they are undergoing. Not everyone who is faced with the need for a transplant will choose that route, even if it is open to them. For some people, the prospect of being attached to a hospital, even if on a long line, for the rest of their lives is unacceptable. Part way through Barney Clark's 112-day ordeal, he begged his physicians to let him die. They did not, and perhaps correctly so since they believed him to be mentally incompetent to make that request. Nevertheless, the fact that the request was made obliges us to consider whether continued life, in some situations, might not cause more suffering than any person need rationally accept.

Providing consent for infants may be among the most difficult areas. Families should be very certain that they understand the risks and the probabilities of success before they consent. Published interviews with Baby Fae's parents suggest that they did not actually understand how extraordinarily experimental the baboon heart transplant was and how little prospect of success there was. Parents' extreme desires to do everything they can to save their infant's life make them easy to manipulate. As long as organ transplants are considered experimental, no parent can be required to consent to a transplant. Kidney transplants are standard treatment; heart transplants are approaching that status; liver, pancreas, and heart-lung transplants are experimental. Heart transplants are seldom performed on very young children. Parents who face choices about transplants for their children need to be sure they know the statistics for patients like their children, rather than the overall statistics. That will give them a better understanding of the risk they are accepting for their child. A transplant operation is an extraordinary assault on the body and one could genuinely question whether an infant or young child should be subjected to such pain and suffering if there is little chance that it will benefit by more than a few days or months of hospital life. In some cases death may be a better alternative.

A child is very vulnerable and many ethicists have argued that no vulnerable patient should ever be subjected to experimental treatment when there is little probability that the patient will benefit. But the sincere desire of the physicians and parents that the child should live—even if the treatment is a long shot—should not be discounted or disparaged. In order to perfect techniques and understand physical processes, experimentation is necessary, but parents may not want to contribute their children to the cause. The question that parents need to ask is what is best for the child? Researchers and transplant teams may have difficulty sorting out their concerns for the patient and their concerns for the advancement of medicine. Parents need be concerned only with seeing that their child does not endure pain and suffering without compensating benefits.

Conclusion

Organ transplantation remains a very risky, very halfway measure. It prolongs life, but does not fully restore health. It prolongs life, but it subjects the patient to new risks. It prolongs life—at least some lives—but it takes money and deflects time and effort from other health care needs that would benefit more people and that might even encourage people to live lives that didn't result in the need for organ transplantations.

But it is not only a problem of money. Even if we had the money, there would not be enough organs. If we had access to the organs of half the 20,000 yearly victims of brain death (a very optimistic figure), there would still not be enough extra pieces to go around. We would have to choose which patients deserve to live—or at least to have another chance at living—and which would have to die. When the demand for organs constantly exceeds supply there are other curious questions about the worthiness of recipients. The question has already been raised as to whether organs donated by Americans can be used for foreign nationals or whether, as one interested party suggested during congressional hearings, "organs donated by deceased American citizens or their next of kin are inherently intended by the donor to benefit a fellow American citizen. . . . When a suitable American recipient cannot be identified, transplantation to a foreign national is entirely appropriate." If cadaver organs are simply spare parts, how can they have nationality?

How then to think about organ transplantation but as a perilous wood, fraught with known and (worse) unknown dangers? In the individual case, however, the wood looks very different, for the forest hides the only chance at life there is, even if that chance is not sure, the life not as good as the old one (and perhaps not very good at all), the costs very high, and the burden of gratitude to the unknown donor considerable. Those who have the choice may want to take it. In the future, the choice may be less available. Policy makers might now wish they had turned their collective backs on this new medical frontier with its grave economic and moral dangers. Yet they did not and will not. The public is too attached to the idea that medicine can defeat death, making each of us immortal: an entire nation of Six-Million Dollar Bionic Men, Women, and Children.

CHAPTER 8

Research and Experimental Therapy
Bone Marrow Transplantation and the Cruelest Death

Because of the enormous advances recently made by medical science, both doctors and patients psychologically expect cures to be available when illness strikes, even if reason tells them otherwise. The great scourges of fifty or so years ago—pneumonia, influenza, scarlet fever, tuberculosis, poliomyelitis, smallpox, and diphtheria, to name but a few—have practically vanished. Nowadays, patients who are visited by a disease that cannot be cured or even effectively controlled are likely to feel much more desperate than they would have only a short time ago, when most serious illness could not be effectively treated and fate, not the patient or doctor, chose life or death. It is not only patients, however, who have been affected by these advances. Doctors, too, feel particularly helpless and even resentful in the face of illness that they cannot control. For many years, critics of medical practice have commented on the fact that, once it is determined that a patient is terminally ill, doctors tend to ignore the patient. Some have argued that this results directly from physicians' focusing on diseases instead of patients: when the disease cannot be treated, the physician no longer has any role. Care is the responsibility of nurses. Others, more sympathetic to the doctors' behaviors, suggest that this tendency to withdraw from the terminally ill patient merely reflects physicians' own acute discomfort with their inability to be of any further help.

There is, however, a third alternative to cure and abandonment. When there is no sure cure for a fatal disease, the patient's only hope may be in research, in experimental therapy. There, on the front lines of medical investigation, the patient donates himself or herself to scientific inquiry. Perhaps the patient will benefit; perhaps he or she will be cured by the new methods of treatment under investigation. In all probability, the patient will not benefit, but the knowledge the researchers gain from the patient's experience may, in the long run (perhaps a *very* long run), benefit others who suffer from the same disease. All research does not bear fruit, of course. Patients may offer themselves to projects that ultimately benefit no one; they cannot know in advance whether life, a noble death, or a vain one lies ahead. It would help if they knew the odds, but even that information is frequently unknown.

Concern about whether patients understand what it means to participate in research has grown in recent years. For most of the twentieth century, doctors themselves regulated medical experimentation. It was assumed that either physicians would possess moral sensibilities that kept them from doing anything inappropriate (self-review) or they would be discouraged from doing research that was unethical by their fellow doctors, who would readily express professional disapproval (peer review). Self-review and peer review work well so long as all parties agree about what constitutes ethical standards for research. When those standards are not well articulated or when varying standards are held, self- and peer review are likely to produce uneven results. In the 1970s, uneven results were appearing in American medical research. Three very questionable, large research projects—the Jewish Chronic Disease Hospital case, the Tuskegee syphilis study, and the Willowbrook study—surfaced over a ten-year period, leading to the establishment in 1974 of the National Commission for the Protection of Human Subjects of Biomedical and Behavioral Research.

In the Jewish Chronic Disease Hospital study, cancer researchers had been interested in finding out the effect of injecting live cancer cells under the skin of patients with chronic diseases who did not have cancer. They had already performed the study with patients who had cancer and with patients who were healthy. Their strong expectation was that patients with diseases other than cancer would reject the cancer cells, just as the healthy patients had. It was not enough, however, to theorize or to present a few anecdotes; they needed to demonstrate scientifically that the cells would not survive. Elderly patients at the Jewish Chronic Disease Hospital in new York were used in this research. The patients did not agree to participate in the research; for the most part, neither they nor their families had any idea that they were involved in a research project. The public was distressed when information about this project was revealed in the press. The research-medical establishment, on the other hand, did not see it the same way. They believed that the procedures carried no risk and that the information gained was vitally important. The principal investigator of the Jewish Chronic Disease Hospital study was, subsequent to extensive and disapproving media publicity about the project, elected president of the American Association for Cancer Research.

Nine years after the Jewish Chronic Disease Hospital case was widely discussed, the Tuskegee syphilis study was revealed. This long-term study, which the U.S. Public Health Service had begun early in the century, traced the effects of untreated syphilis on a large group of black males in the southern United States. When the study began, no effective treatment was available. Over time, however, effective treatment with antibiotics became standard medical care. The researchers neither informed the men in the study that such treatment was available nor gave it to them. Instead, their condition was preserved: a long-term study of effects of untreated syphilis was pursued even though untreated syphilis no longer needed to exist in the United States. The researchers defended their practice on the grounds that antibiotic treatment would have been of little or no value to subjects with thirty- and forty-year histories of the disease. Furthermore, the study was almost complete (or would be when the last patients died) and since so much time and effort had been invested, it was only reasonable that the final work be completed. This latter rationale did not explain why the research had been continued thirty years earlier, when penicillin first became widely available.

The third research project, the Willowbrook study, used mentally retarded children as its subjects. It had long been known that institutionalized children were at particular risk for hepatitis. The researchers suggested that it would be reasonable to inject a group of young, retarded children with hepatitis virus—that is, to infect them purposely—to see whether a low-level hepatitis infection could be induced, thereby saving them from a much more virulent form of the disease. The idea that these vulnerable children—even with their parents' consent—would intentionally be given a harmful illness offended many people. The researchers explained that the children were bound to get hepatitis anyway, since virtually every child in the institution eventually did. Furthermore, there was at least the possibility that the injections would leave them better off since it might stave off a much more devastating version of the disease.

These three cases in particular activated a new level of concern about research ethics and how research should be regulated and controlled. The fact that the subjects of all three studies were people who were particularly powerless focused concern on vulnerable subjects, including children, the mentally ill, and prisoners. the National Commission for the Protection of Human Subjects of Biomedical and Behavioral Research issued a series of lengthy reports on recommended ethical standards for various kinds of research. In the Commission's reports, the vital role of informed consent and the importance of the potential benefit to the research subject were repeatedly emphasized.

Research standards have become much more specific as a result of the work of the National Commission. Every institution conducting research now has an institutional review board (IRB) that must review and approve every research protocol. It the board feels that the research is too risky, they may refuse to approve it. If they do not approve it, it cannot be done and will not be funded. If they think that the procedure for obtaining consent is inadequate or that sufficient information is not provided, they can insist upon changes. These procedures have bureaucratized research to some extent and may have slowed down the initiation of many research projects. Many researchers believe that the boards not only have eliminated some risky research, but also have discouraged many projects from ever being suggested because of the risk factors. Researchers who do not maintain the standards established by the institutional review board are likely to lose access to funds, suffer institutional censure, and may lose their positions.

Although the review boards have developed good procedures for many kinds of research, they have difficulty with therapeutic research. The greatest risk-balancing problem lies with those diseases for which there is no probable cure or even palliative treatment. If there is little likelihood of known methods working, many people think that patients and their doctors should be able to try anything—not just what a review board permits. It is at the edges of research that a miracle may occur.

When a physician tells a patient that he or she is suffering from a disease such as acute leukemia, the news is bad. The cure rate is very low; the treatment has many unpleasant side effects, significantly reducing the patient's quality of life. The patient is likely to be devastated by the diagnosis. What the patient needs—or wants—is a miracle, a lightning strike of luck, one last chance to draw to an inside straight. At this point, the patient may meet the researchers, if he or she is in the right town and in the hands of a family physician who is inclined toward experimental treatment. Bone marrow transplantation for some diseases, including acute leukemia, is one such experimental treatment. The adult patient who opts for bone marrow transplantation is a gambler, looking for "a card so high and wild he'll never have to draw another."

Almost thirty years have passed since the first clinical use of bone marrow transplantation. During those thirty years, numerous research projects have been initiated and completed, numerous patients have been treated, and numerous articles have been published in medical journals. It has been successful in treating aplastic anemia and immunodeficiencies, and is now the treatment of choice for those diseases. Its use in other areas, especially with the acute leukemias, has not been as successful.* Despite the research, medical interest, and clinical practice, bone marrow transplantation remains one of medicine's most controversial therapies when used for acute leukemia. Professionals disagree about *whether* bone marrow transplantation should be used, *when* it should be initiated, *whether* patients or their families can actually give informed consent (especially considering that many patients are young), and *how* (or whether) physicians can provide the kind of information necessary for informed consent.

In order to understand bone marrow transplantation, it is first necessary to understand the disease it seeks to remedy. Acute leukemias result from the proliferating presence of cancerous white blood cells. White blood cells are produced in the bone marrow and, the theory goes, if the patient's own cancerous cells can be destroyed and new bone marrow (from a donor) introduced and encouraged to grow ("engraft"), then the new marrow will produce normal white blood cells. In this way, the cancer will be "cured." In effect,

---

*The reader should note that the figures and procedures described in this chapter apply only to bone marrow transplantation when used to treat acute leukemias, particularly acute lymphocytic leukemia. Its use in aplastic anemia and severe combined immunodeficiency is quite different in many respects, not the least of which is that it is widely regarded as the preferred treatment, with one-year survival rates of 50 to 75 percent. In younger patients, the success rate is very high.

it is not a "cure" as much as it is exactly a transplant. The patient's diseased bone marrow is replaced by healthy bone marrow from a donor, just as a diseased kidney is replaced by a healthy kidney from a donor.

Bone marrow transplantation is not, however, exactly like other forms of transplantation. The greatest medical problem with any transplant procedure is that the transplanted organ will not engraft, that it will be rejected and destroyed by the patient's body when the body recognizes the new part as foreign, not its own. In organ transplantation, the physician attempts to reduce the body's ability to recognize, reject, and destroy new tissue by suppressing the cells that do the identifying. White blood cells bear the responsibility for identifying, rejecting, and destroying foreign tissue in the body. In bone marrow transplantation, it is the white blood cells that are being transplanted. The transplant itself is both the patient's greatest hope and his or her greatest threat. If the transplant works, the white blood cells may recognize the patient's body as foreign, as different, and then attempt to destroy that body. Therein lies the great problem of bone marrow transplantation.

When a leukemic patient chooses to undergo bone marrow transplantation, the physician's first job is to try to destroy as many of the patient's white blood cells as possible. If a significant number of the patient's white cells remain functioning, then they will try to reject the new bone marrow, resulting in a failure of the transplant to engraft. If a significant number of the patient's cancerous white cells are left alive, then even if the new bone marrow engrafts successfully, the patient is likely to suffer a relapse of the leukemia. The leukemic white cells will then overwhelm the healthy white cells generated by the new bone marrow. Ensuring engraftment and avoiding a recurrence of the leukemia means that the physician must use methods that will effectively destroy the patient's own bone marrow, as well as the white blood cells it produces, which range throughout the body. Two methods are available for such destruction: radiation and cell poisoners. In bone marrow transplantation, both are used. The patient is frequently given chemotherapy, which consists of very high doses of cytotoxins (cell-poisons), and then subjected to total body irradiation, which will (it is hoped) destroy those white cells that lurk in parts of the body that the cytotoxins do not easily reach.

At the end of this preparation, the patient is, in a very real sense, at death's door. In order to save life, it has been necessary first to kill it. If the procedure succeeds, the patient no longer has any functioning immunological system and, thus, is easy prey to the most innocuous microorganism. Patients without a functioning immunological system will soon be dead. Patients who have received total body irradiation and high doses of cytotoxins will also be acutely nauseous in the short run and incapable of reproduction—if they live—in the long run. They must remain in a highly sterile environment while the new bone marrow attempts to find a home and begins producing new and healthy white blood cells that will be able to fight off germs and viruses.

The bone marrow transplantation itself is fairly simple. Bone marrow is drawn from the donor's pelvic bones through a needle. It is then transferred to the patient through the veins. In the following days, while the new marrow is attempting to relocate itself, the patient is likely to be stricken with severe infections, fevers, and hemorrhages. Pneumonia is common and antibiotics are of little use. Death's door remains open. Then, if the patient survives this period and the bone marrow transplant engrafts successfully, a new immunological system begins to function that can counter these opportunistic infections. The transplant has succeeded. It is at this point that the patient faces the most severe challenge of bone marrow transplantation.

One important function of the white blood cells is to recognize foreign cells, foreign tissue, and foreign bodies and then to destroy them. The donated bone marrow has some important similarities to the cells of the patient who has received it because it is matched before donation. It is not identical, however, unless the donor and patient are identical twins. When donor and patient are not identical twins, the donated marrow's white cells look about and identify the patient's cells, tissues, and organs as foreign and begin to set about destroying them. In ordinary transplants (e.g., heart, kidney, liver, etc.), this process is known as rejection or host-versus-graft disease. That is, the host (the patient) rejects the graft because the patient's white blood cells reject the foreign organ that has been transplanted. In bone marrow transplantation, the process is reversed and is known as graft-versus-host (GVH) disease. Here the graft (the bone marrow) attempts to reject the host (the patient). When a heart or lung is rejected, it dies; when the patient/host is rejected *by* the transplant, the rejected patient, too, may die. Thirty to fifty percent of patients attempting bone marrow transplantation die from graft-versus-host disease, primarily during the first year.

Death from GVH disease can be lingering and agonizing. It has been described as the cruelest possible death. The patient will slowly but thoroughly be attacked by the new white blood cells, an attack that will result in ulcerations of the inner and outer surfaces of the body, fevers, hemorrhagic bleeding, infections, and wasting away.

Graft-versus-host disease is not always fatal, however. It may only be mild or moderate and short-lived. Yet again, it may be chronic, the constant companion and reminder of the bone marrow transplantation procedure. Approximately 20 to 30 percent of those who survive bone marrow transplantation do have chronic graft-versus-host disease. If the reaction is chronic, the patient may continually suffer from skin disorders, gastrointestinal disturbances, and infections. In order to diminish the graft-versus-host disease, the patient's newly installed and operating immune system may be suppressed somewhat, just as is that of any transplant patient. Such suppression is risky, for it promotes any lingering leukemic cells' opportunity to proliferate and again gain control of the patient's system. Bone marrow transplantation physicians are now using cyclosporine, the immunosuppressant drug that revolutionized the transplant industry, with their patients and finding that it almost entirely eliminates serious or acute graft-versus-host disease. Cyclosporine appears to be as good for bone marrow transplantation as it has been for organ transplants.

For years, when graft-versus-host disease seemed the greatest barrier to successful bone marrow transplantation, researchers hoped, even prayed, for such a drug. Now that they have it, however, things look different. The current belief is that some degree of graft-versus-host disease may be necessary for bone marrow transplantation to be successful in combating leukemia. Although it is too soon to be certain, there is some suggestion that a *decrease* in graft-versus-host disease leads to an increase in recurring leukemia. This new insight only heightens the ethical and medical problems of bone marrow transplantation, especially in patients who are over 30 years old. Among these patients, the success rates are low indeed.

The standard treatment for acute leukemia is chemotherapy, not bone marrow transplantation. The success rates of the two therapies are almost impossible to compare. Until recently, the patient with acute leukemia was usually given chemotherapy and if the leukemia recurred, he or she was given a second regimen of chemotherapy. A third reoccurrence of the disorder opened the gates to bone marrow transplantation if the patient consented, since the chemotherapy was clearly not working. The experimental therapy didn't work very well either and deaths at the 70 percent level were common. The researchers argued that patients failed to do well on bone marrow transplantation because they received the procedure so late in the disease process. The poisoning involved in the repeated chemotherapy treatments had already seriously weakened the patients. If they were to receive the transplant earlier, say after the first chemotherapy relapse or even as the initial treatment, then the results would be better.

Researchers persuaded those seeking to beat the odds and draw inside straight cards that bone marrow transplantation as initial or at least very early therapy was advisable. The patients entered the research projects and the death rate dropped, as the researchers had predicted. It did not drop entirely, however. The death rate for bone marrow transplantation held at about 30 to 50 percent during the first two years. Better than previously, better than 70 percent or 100 percent, but still not very good. The deaths were grim, approximately half from graft-versus-host disease, the rest from interstitial pneumonia and recurring leukemia.

Standard chemotherapy survival figures were very difficult to determine. Certainly there was nothing like a 50 percent death rate within the first year or two. If there had been, no one would have considered it the standard therapy. Long-time survival rates look about the same for both forms of treatment according to some researchers, but cancer specialists use so many different forms of chemotherapy (with differing results) that it is difficult to tell just how good (or how bad) chemotherapy is. In any case, standard chemotherapy wasn't promising any significant improvements. For an outside chance for cure, the bone marrow transplantation unit was the place to go and patients were increasingly persuaded to go there.

The available research figures make it difficult to tell whether bone marrow transplantation or chemotherapy constitutes a better choice for the acute leukemia patient. The best results for both methods come with young patients: for chemotherapy, those under eighteen, for bone marrow transplantation, those under age 20. Only 20 to 40 percent of patients over 30 who choose bone marrow transplantation survive two and a half years. With chemotherapy, the patient is likely to live longer (or less likely to die as quickly), but still not very likely to live a long time. With bone marrow transplantation, patients who survive for twenty-four to thirty months are likely to continue surviving. But they are not very likely to survive that long in the first place. With such grim data, great consideration ought to be given to the quality of life that the patient is likely to have while continuing to live, if he or she lives. The comparisons here are very difficult: graft-versus-host disease is certainly the worst possible death, far worse than dying of recurring leukemia. Standard chemotherapy has unpleasant side effects, but chemotherapy—often in even stronger forms—is used in bone marrow transplantation as well, with the same side effects (nausea, hair loss, lassitude). Bone marrow transplantation additionally uses total body irradiation with its accompanying side effects of acute nausea and permanent sterility. Chronic graft-versus-host disease afflicts a significant number of patients who survive bone marrow transplantation. The positive side of bone marrow transplantation is that if the patient survives the first two years or so, he or she is very unlikely to have recurring leukemia; with chemotherapy, a similar period of survival still brings with it the likelihood of recurring leukemia. Measuring the quality of life provided by these two treatments is even more difficult than assessing which gives a better chance of survival.

When there are such difficulties, how does a patient give informed consent to an experimental procedure like bone marrow transplantation? Many have argued that, since patients are placed under such severe stress, they can neither process the murky data nor grasp the implications of risks like graft-versus-host disease. Physicians, it is argued, merely lead their patients to whatever option the physician is inclined to choose. If they have chosen an aggressive doctor, patients are likely to find themselves signing up on the bone marrow unit very soon after diagnosis. If, on the other hand, they have a more conservative physician, the experimental treatment may never be offered, or may be offered only as a risky gamble. Others—especially researchers—have argued that patients and their families can and do make these choices intelligently. Bone marrow transplantation programs frequently have very involved procedures for obtaining informed consent, including films of the procedures and interviews with patients who have undergone the procedure successfully and with families of patients who died. Advocates of bone marrow transplantation believe that only by continuing to treat patients in experimental protocols will new information be gained; when there is little hope, patients ought to be encouraged to participate in therapies that may lead to better knowledge about the disease process, so that their deaths will not have been in vain.

Experimental therapies are always uncertain and frequently bear significant risks. Seldom, however, does the therapy itself create a disease and death. The grimness of graft-versus-host disease, which many doctors describe as the very worst death, makes bone marrow transplantation a very special kind of experimental therapy. Only the patient can decide whether he or she is willing to undergo the risks of this treatment. Yet, the patient may be psychologically unable to assess those risks, because of age, stress, or both. A desperate patient falls easy prey to a zealous researcher. One physician, defending researchers, said that at his institution, no patient had died as a result of questioned (and questionable) research practices who would not have died anyway. The issue is not, of course, that the patients died: it is how they died and whether they genuinely chose to gamble their remaining time or to contribute their lives to science and the hope of saving the lives of others, or whether their fear of death led them to sacrifice themselves without thinking on the altar of someone else's scientific research.

Case Study

Raymond Darrow awoke abruptly, just before sunrise, on the morning of his thirty-fifth birthday. He moved about restlessly in bed, trying not to disturb his wife Connie who slept soundly beside him. He felt again the faint nausea and the skin sensitivity that had plagued him off and on for the past three or four weeks. He was not feverish yet, but he knew that he would be shortly if the pattern were to continue. Just awakening, he already felt tired. It was beginning to seem like a chronic case of flu. He had had a rotten spring, with one minor illness after another. Being sick again today was bad news, though. Connie had planned a big birthday party for him that evening, an after-dinner affair with music to which all their friends were invited. She had gone to so much work and was so pleased with her efforts that he couldn't possibly think of cancelling the party just because of a little illness. In any case, by the end of the day he might be feeling better. He would take it easy, spend the rest of the weekend catching up on paperwork for his pottery business, and let the kiln repair that he had planned for that day wait until the beginning of the week. If he was not feeling better by Monday, he decided, he would call the doctor.

Ray took it easy throughout the day, assuring Connie that he was fine each time she asked whether he was okay. By eight o'clock, when the guests started arriving, he was pretty sure that he could make it through the evening; but he would pass on the dancing, even if it was his birthday. By midnight, Ray was afraid to stand up for fear that he might pass out entirely. Thirty people must have asked him if he was feeling okay, and he had staunchly declared that he was doing fine for an old man, just a little tired after a hard week's work. He *had* spent the week rebuilding the drying shelves for the pots and repairing the roof of the shed where he worked during the hot weather, which was more physically exhausting than working with the clay. Ray made it sound good to his friends, but he himself could not believe that a week of demanding physical labor could account for how bad he felt. When the last guest left, he collapsed into bed, finally confessing to Connie that he was not feeling too well. Probably just too much to drink, he concluded, as he fell almost instantly into a deep and restless sleep. Later, Connie would recall Ray's party as the last normal event of their life together, and would be astonished yet again at how an ordinary, happy life can turn overnight into a continuous nightmare.

On Monday morning, Connie got an immediate appointment for Ray. He had arisen Sunday morning after the party feeling no better, and by Monday there was no denying that he was feeling very bad. He was so weak he could barely walk. Dr. Handley poked and prodded, asked questions, listened to the body before him, made some notes, and sent Ray down to the lab for a few tests. Ray was certain that if he just went to bed for a few days, he'd be feeling better. Connie was inclined to believe that some kind of antibiotic would do the trick. Ray wasn't a man to put up with much illness, so it seemed very unlikely to either of them that he could be *really* sick.

When the test results were available and they again spoke with the doctor, they were totally unprepared for his news. Ray's white blood cell count was sky high, and a high proportion of the cells were malignant; Ray had leukemia. Dr. Handley explained the nature of the disease to them briefly, pointing out as delicately as he could that leukemia is often fatal for there was no sure treatment. There were, of course, some things that could be tried and that worked for some patients. There was chemotherapy, first of all. And even if the chemotherapy did not cure the disease, it would probably get Ray into remission and he would have some time, perhaps a long time of feeling pretty normal. For some patients, chemotherapy provided long-term survival. Dr. Handley recommended immediate hospitalization and chemotherapy. By immediate, he meant that day. Both Ray and Connie were too stunned to really grasp the information, but they were also inclined to doubt that anyone could be certain about something as serious as leukemia that quickly. Nonetheless, they were overwhelmed by Dr. Handley's sense of urgency and, after a flurry of phone calls, found themselves at the nearby university medical center. Handley had referred them to a specialist at the hospital who would arrange for admission and then see Ray immediately. When they arrived, Ray was taken up to the ward while Connie was left filling out a multitude of hospital forms.

By the time she got up on the ward, Ray had been put into bed and he had already fallen asleep. As she passed through the door, she saw him with new eyes. In the starkness of the room and amid the starched sheets and the harsh light, Ray's big, athletic frame looked almost frail. His face was drawn, his complexion drained, his long and curly red hair limp. His right hand hung lifelessly over the edge of the mattress deprived of its normal energy. For a moment, she thought she might have come into the wrong room; that she was looking at someone else's husband. She did not know whether she was seeing him with Dr. Handley's alarm or whether she had been blind to his appearance in the past few days. When had he become so ill? As she sat down in the chair beside the bed, he awoke and life again flooded his being as he responded to her presence. Connie was both relieved to see him look himself again and haunted by the vision of devastation she had first glimpsed when he had not been aware that she was in the room. Connie explained the arrangements she had made for her mother to pick up their two children from school and they nervously awaited the appearance of the specialist. They did not discuss Handley's pessimistic diagnosis.

Dr. Martin Webster's first meeting with Connie and Ray was a long one and, when he left, they both felt much calmer, even hopeful. He had explained the leukemia thoroughly, made it easy for them to ask questions, and described the medical field's present state of knowledge about Ray's condition and about the disease's progress. They would do some more tests and if they came out as expected, would begin chemotherapy promptly. His sense of Ray's condition was that the chemotherapy would probably get him into remission. The therapy would, of course, have some uncomfortable side effects; perhaps some nausea, headache, even feverishness. The drugs they were using would be aimed at killing off the cancerous cells. The drugs were strong—they had to be or they wouldn't work—and you had to expect some crossover of the effects. Webster seemed to understand what they most needed to know, and he answered their questions as if they were his equals, not as if they were children who were only to do as told. He had even urged them to call him "Marty," rather than "Dr. Webster." "For better or worse," he had smilingly pointed out, "we're going to be seeing a lot of each other for a while. We might as well be friends."

He had left them with one consideration. He was firmly convinced that they could get Ray into remission with the chemotherapy, but was not sure how long the remission would last. If the leukemia recurred, then the chemotherapy treatment could be repeated. A second remission was possible, but the prospect of a third recurrence was very high. There was one alternative, however. You couldn't use it with everybody, because the patient needed to have a family member who had the right kind of tissue. There was a chance that one of Ray's siblings (two brothers and a sister) might be right, and if that one was willing to be a donor, then, if Ray was interested, they could consider trying him on a new bone marrow transplant therapy program.

Dr. Webster had been working in bone marrow research now for almost fifteen years. The results were a lot better now than they had been when he started, mostly because patients were getting the treatment sooner. Instead of waiting until the chemotherapy had failed them and severely weakened their systems, they were starting right away with the marrow transplant, when their bodies were still strong and could help with the recovery. Of course, there were no guarantees. A lot of people still didn't make it, but they didn't make it with chemotherapy either. Webster firmly believed that bone marrow was the best new direction medicine now had for leukemia treatment. Chemotherapy could achieve remissions—but it couldn't cure. Destroying all the old white cells and replacing them with new marrow was the only way to get a cure that lasted. That's why he had spent his professional career in that area of research. It wasn't enough just to keep people hanging on, waiting for the next attack of the disease. If medicine was to help, it needed to provide a cure.

Dr. Webster described with growing enthusiasm how bone marrow transplantation research would, in the long term, provide real possibilities of cure. For a moment, Ray and Connie forgot that they weren't there for the long term, that they were there right that minute. Webster paused, then suggested that if they had no more questions, they should stop for today. They could talk about it more the next day. There were other things they needed to know, of course. There were risks of the treatment that were different from chemotherapy risks, but first, he wanted them to think about it. It was a research project and the additional treatment costs would be covered by the project. It was a big decision, he assured them. They didn't need to make it right away. They would talk about it again tomorrow.

When he left them, they were emotionally exhausted but hopeful. Both were impressed with Webster, and felt an immediate confidence in him, born of their quick rapport. It was inspiring that a man who lived constantly with the death that trailed leukemia patients could himself be so hopeful and confident. If he was not intimidated by the disease, then perhaps they need not be either. It was the least they could do to merit his help. Ray was ready to sign up right away for the transplant, but Connie reminded him that Marty had urged them not to make a decision now.

In the following days, the three of them spoke often. Although Connie was uncertain at times about the wisdom of starting with the research therapy, Ray never wavered after that first conversation. Webster had given him a sense of how to fight a disease like leukemia. You didn't cower before it, wringing your hands and timidly hoping for the best. You came right out and stood up to it, gave it your best shot. It reminded Ray of an earlier time, when he was still playing semi-pro football on a very lightweight team, hoping he could make it to the big leagues. Every game, even every practice session, he went out and gave it everything, because you never could tell when doing it right would make a big difference, for the team and for oneself. The cancer also made him think of Gary Cooper in *High Noon*. It was as if he had to go out there and face it down, only he didn't have to do it alone. He had Martin Webster by his side. Ray was a fighter and a gambler, and he fancied the idea of teaming up with the dedicated Webster to try to beat the odds and get back his life, his real life, instead of some sorry invalid imitation of it.

The chemotherapy sessions began immediately while Ray's two brothers and his sister were undergoing testing to see whether they would be able to donate marrow. When Connie had called to ask them to talk to the doctor, it had not even occurred to her that they might not immediately agree. Sid and Elaine had offered to come to the hospital right away, but Richard had been more hesitant, even aloof. He wanted to talk to his wife Laura first, then he would call

Connie back about meeting with the doctor. When he did call back, the following day, he reported that Laura was very reluctant to have him involved in anything that included surgery. Connie explained to him as best she could what was involved, but she couldn't resist pointing out that Sid and Elaine hadn't hesitated to meet with Webster. Richard, too, finally agreed, but Connie bitterly resented his slowness. He was the youngest son and Ray was the eldest; they hadn't gotten along well when they were growing up because Richard always felt that Ray was trying to boss him around. But Richard was 26 now, not a child chafing under the direction of an older brother. She couldn't understand what was in his mind, didn't want to understand. All she wanted was to have him in Webster's office at the right time.

Sid, Elaine, and Richard met separately with Dr. Webster, who had explained to Connie that the policy on the bone marrow unit was to interview donors separately so that each person would feel free to ask whatever questions she or he had. In family groups, he explained, people often let someone, the oldest or the father or mother, take the lead. Donating marrow involved very little real physical risk, but it was very difficult psychologically and they needed to be sure that the donor fully understood what was involved, beyond the act of donating itself. It also gave the doctor on the case a chance to get to know the donor a little, to give him or her a pep talk if that seemed in order. People were often frightened of participating in any medical procedures if their own lives or health were not at risk, even for the sake of relatives. When they were uncertain, he could sometimes help them get rid of their fears and anxieties, help them to get through to the place where they could offer help without having to suffer much anxiety.

Webster met with Richard first, and the interview was a discouraging one. Richard had listened patiently to the explanation of the procedure, then responded, somewhat indifferently, that he didn't think he wanted to donate if it was possible for one of the others to do it. Throughout their meeting, the young man maintained a reserve that Webster found no way to break through. He didn't seem much interested in the descriptions of the procedures, and only nodded calmly when Webster described Ray's poor chances for cure by methods other than the bone marrow transplant. By the end of their meeting, Richard had made his position quite clear. He preferred not to donate and did not wish to discuss his reasons. If neither Sid nor Elaine were able to donate because their tissues weren't compatible, then he would do so if his were. But they should be considered first.

Webster found the meeting with Richard disturbing because it was unusual to find a family member who was so distant. They were often afraid or very anxious, but seldom as cold as this one had been. On the other hand, if he were to be the donor, he would be a good one because he would not be so wrapped up in the process. An emotionally disinterested donor was a blessing, but was unlikely among family groups.

The interviews with Sid and Elaine were very different; both were anxious to help Ray in any way they could. Elaine was obviously upset about the prospect of having to be out of work for a while since her husband was currently unemployed, but she gamely insisted that they would be able to work something out. Sid was even more responsive than Elaine. He clearly had a deep affection for Ray, and closely identified with him. The prospect of Ray's death was not only disturbing because it was the death of his beloved brother, but also personally threatening. It was as if Sid, too, had been struck with leukemia or expected to be very soon. Webster found that aspect of Sid's concerns unfortunate. It meant that Sid, as a donor, would probably be very seriously affected if the transplant didn't work, if Sid's bone marrow effectively killed his brother.

And the chances were, of course, that it would not work. At Ray's age, the prospects of success were pretty small. If he were 20 or even 25, it would be another matter, but for now, 35 was pretty old. The transplant process was hard on the older patients and they were much more likely to go under with graft-versus-host disease. The cut-off age for the unit was 40, and some of the new people thought it ought to be lowered, but Webster had insisted on keeping it up there. It was true that older people did poorly, but if they didn't keep trying with older people, they were never going to find a way for them to do better. In theory, at least, they could survive and some of them did. As long as some of them did, they needed to keep that age cut-off high. Besides, Ray was in good condition. He had maintained the physical pride, maybe vanity, of his football days. Even his first days in the hospital, he had been asking about whether he might get out on the grounds to do a little running. This when he'd hardly been able to walk. Webster wished Ray was younger, but since he was not, he was glad that he was a fighter.

When the sibling tests returned, the results were somewhat disappointing. No one of the three was a perfect match, but Sid and Richard were both good matches. Elaine was out of the running entirely. Webster was never really uncertain about what to do, but he spent a little time pondering the matter, considering using Richard despite his reluctance. Richard would be the better donor if Ray died; Sid the better donor if Ray lived. But better only for their sakes—not for Ray's. Either one was okay for Ray and it was Ray who was his patient, not Sid or Richard. If Richard had shown a better match than Sid, Webster would have gone with him, without a second thought. As long as a donor consented, Webster was not going to be overly concerned about how enthusiastic his consent was. He called Sid and had his nurse make the arrangements for the transplant. Ray was in pretty stable condition right now. They could put him on the pre-transplant chemotherapy protocol right away, then do a total body irradiation, get the marrow from Sid, and transfuse it. Getting the transplant set up and handling the patient after it was done were the hardest parts. This in-between part was easier: it was like reaching the saddle on a mountain climb. Looking up, you knew the rest of the way was going to be tough but for the moment you could rest a little, breathe easier.

Connie shuddered inwardly as she observed the results of the heightened chemotherapy regimen. Ray once again became feverish and nauseous, with constant headaches. Although he did not complain and seldom even mentioned his discomfort, Connie saw all the tensions mirrored in his eyes. He spoke about it gruffly; it was part of the price of getting better. He was no longer able to see the kids since his ability to resist any infection was dropping radically, and he missed that, objected to their absence more than to the presence of the drugs' side effects. A few masked, gloved, and gowned friends came to visit him and found him weak but apparently undaunted. The friends came hoping to give him courage, and left feeling they had learned something about bravery from him.

The night before the transplant was to be done, Ray and Sid spent several hours together, reminiscing about their childhood, talking about what they would do in the future when Sid's bone marrow was keeping them both alive. Ray remembered having read in the newspaper once about a woman who got a kidney transplant, and then it turned out to have a tumor in it, and they wouldn't give her another transplant because she had cancer. She insisted that the cancer wasn't hers; that it belonged to the original owner of the kidney. Ray wanted Sid to guarantee the quality of this bone marrow he was buying into at great personal inconvenience. Afterwards, Sid remembered those hours with amazement. They had seemed unaware that there was a good possibility, a good probability, actually, that Ray would die from the treatment he was undergoing. Ray had somehow made all that possibility vanish.

The next day, Ray was taken in for total body irradiation. The cobalt machine did its work quickly, relentlessly, ferreting out and destroying the lingering white cells. In a short time, Ray was returned to his room, where he endured a bout of continuous retching. Exhausted, he sank into the bed watching—with Marty Webster beside him—the bottle filled with the pinkish lifesaving liquid drawn that morning from Sid's pelvic bone. The marrow now seeped slowly into his own veins, the first leg of its trip to the hollows of his bones.

Then the waiting began. When his own bone marrow began to die off, Ray was transferred to a new room, totally sterile, totally protected, totally isolated. For two weeks, Ray's condition wavered. Infections ravaged him and pneumonia got a firm grip. Massive transfusions got him over that hump and the pace of complication slowed for a few days. Shortly after the twenty-second day, there was evidence that the bone marrow graft had taken and was growing in Ray's bones. A few days later, however, a severe rash appeared on his body and Webster knew that graft-versus-host disease would have to be fought off. Medications were increased but it appeared to be a severe case. Webster fought desperately, using all his strength of personality to inspire Ray, too, to resist the onslaught, and all his professional experience to help him. Connie stood by helplessly, barely able to recognize the shattered body that lay in the bed, moaning in unbearable pain. Sid, too, stood silently by, no longer able to make any connection with his dying brother, whose battered body valiantly tried to resist the efficient white blood cells that Sid had given to him. The white cells were winning, however, and Ray was bleeding to death.

Within a week, he was dead. He died in the night, with Marty Webster beside him, trying until the last minute to help him endure just a little longer, and to help reduce the pain. When Connie was awakened and told that the end had come, she had no tears left.

The Decision Makers: Their Perspectives and Interests

Medical Perspectives

One of the great medical practice controversies of recent years has been whether physicians should tell their patients the truth when it comes to terminal illnesses. Doctors' attitudes about truth-telling have undergone a very rapid change. In a 1961 survey of physicians, 88 percent of the doctors reported that they generally did not tell their cancer patients the truth about a cancer diagnosis. A repeat survey in 1977 found vastly different practices. By then, 98 percent of the physicians reported that their general policy was to tell the patient the truth. However, one can still wonder how much of the truth is really told.

As a result of the extended dialogue on the question of truth-telling, physicians nowadays are more likely to be candid with patients about their diagnosis and prognosis. Concern with giving the patient a sense of defeat still exists, however, and thus, their disclosures may not be total. Oncologists (cancer specialists) point out that they can never give a cancer patient definite information. In all forms of cancer, there is at least some chance, however minute, that the patient will go into remission. To tell the patient that death is inevitable would be inaccurate, even if 999 out of 1000 patients will die quickly. The patient before the doctor might be that one patient who will survive and telling her she won't does no one any good. Beyond that, neither patients nor cancers are static, uniform entities. Different cancers respond differently to different treatments with different people. Older people may respond more poorly than younger ones (or vice versa); those who have postponed diagnosis and treatment will probably fare less well than those who receive prompt treatment; optimists may do better than pessimists. What the doctors cannot tell their patients—because no such figures exist—is what the chances are for a person exactly like the patient now before them. Physicians can speak only of patients in general, if no other information is available for smaller, discrete groups of patients.

Researchers' Perspectives

The physician involved in therapeutic research has a potential conflict when he or she undertakes the care of patients. The physician's first obligation is to do what is best for the patient. The research-er's obligation, however, is to do what is best for the research proj-ect. A research project may, for example, attempt to discover which of two drugs more effectively reduces the white cell popula-tion prior to total body irradiation. The researcher may sense that drug A is working better, but is still obliged to give half the pa-tients drug B, since he or she cannot be sure of that conclusion un-til the project is completed and the data analyzed. On the other hand, the physician, who senses that drug A works better will sim-ply stop using drug B, even though he or she has no hard informa-tion. The doctor who occupies both researcher and physician roles will have conflicts, though these may be minimized by arguing, for example, that a personal intuition that one drug is better than an-other is no justification for using the drug when solid information is absent.

The researcher has another, more subtle area of conflict, how-ever. Bone marrow transplantation research has been conducted vigorously for twenty years. Many researchers have spent their pro-fessional careers in this area and they have a significant personal in-terest in having the treatment proved workable and effective. Oth-erwise, they have spent many years running up a blind alley, and they have taken many patients with them, patients who have died harsh and hard deaths in their hands. A researcher who is commit-ted to a specific line of research may have a hard time acknowledg-ing the merits of other lines. A researcher who is committed to bone marrow transplantation may have difficulty even considering che-motherapy alone as a reasonable treatment for a patient who has an available marrow donor. She or he may fail to give the patient ade-quate information to make a choice simply because the physician-researcher believes there is little, if any, real choice. For the re-searcher, the standard therapy is ineffective: a possible remission, but little real prospect of cure. The proposed research-therapy, on the other hand, has a chance of real cure, though a probability of rapid and agonizing death.

In the last few years, bone marrow transplant researchers have received national publicity on several occasions because of question-able research procedures, including failure to gain institutional re-view board approvals for treatment they provided to patients. In one instance, the researchers argued that the unusual bone marrow procedures were not, in fact, research but were simply the physi-cian's assessment of what offered the patient the best chance. Since the procedures in question were quite novel, it is clear that the physicians were arguing that since there was no hope, anything might provide a miracle. Researchers can argue that when everything known has been tried and all has failed, patients have nothing to lose by trying the unknown: the alternative is rapid death. Patients, too, may be persuaded by this assertion. The question remains, however, whether patients are psychologically able to make free and informed judgments or whether, under the threat of death and amidst pain and suffering, patients are merely pawns in the researchers' hands. The patients' goal is life, and researchers share that hope; but researchers may have a more distant goal as their first priority.

Legal Perspectives

The law's primary interest is in resolving conflicts between parties, and where patient, family, and doctor agree, there is little room for conflict. Thus, the law has taken little note of therapeutic research like bone marrow transplantation, except to require that informed consent be given by the research subject/patient. In addition, conflicts between patients and potential bone marrow donors can exist and at least two court cases have involved such conflicts.

A patient who wished to undergo bone marrow transplant filed the first case (*McFall* v. *Shimp*) when no suitable donor other than a cousin was available. The cousin agreed to undergo testing, but then refused to donate the marrow despite the fact that the only significant risk of being a donor was that of undergoing general anesthesia. According to newspaper reports, he offered no reasons other than his wife's reluctance to have him undergo the procedure. In the briefs filed with the court, no personal reasons were given for Mr. Shimp's refusal to donate. The Pennsylvania court concluded that Shimp had no legal duty to donate bone marrow and thus the state could not compel him to do so, even though McFall would certainly die if the donation were not made. The court stated its rationale very strongly: "[American] society and government exist to protect the individual from being invaded and hurt by another." The court acknowledged that, although other cultures and other societies believe that the individual exists to serve others, American culture does not hold that belief. McFall did not receive the bone marrow transplant.

In the second case, William Head, a 27-year-old Louisiana man with leukemia, had no family member whose tissue match was close enough to donate marrow. He contacted several hospitals that maintained tissue registries. One hospital informed him that its register did include one person with the appropriate tissue match. The hospital contacted the woman, both by letter and by telephone, and she informed them that she was not interested in becoming a donor. When pressed, she added that she would donate for a family member, but not for a stranger. The hospital declined to discuss the question with her further, feeling that additional conversations would be too coercive. Head argued that the hospital's approach had been too neutral and that the woman did not clearly understand that a specific person was in need of bone marrow that only she could supply. The hospital refused to release the woman's name on the grounds that it would breach the confidentiality of their records. Head sued the hospital, asking that they be required to release the woman's name to the court so that the court could make sure that the woman understood the nature of the request that was being made. Head's request for additional contact with the woman was denied by the court, however.

In these two cases, the law has taken a very strong position against requiring donations, especially considering that bone marrow donation is a low-risk procedure that is potentially lifesaving. (In McFall's case, the transplantation was not even experimental, for McFall had aplastic anemia and transplant in that disorder is the standard treatment when there is a suitable donor.) In the McFall case, the court protected the potential donor's bodily integrity even in the face of another's death; in the second case, where identification of a potential donor was sought rather than a requirement to donate, the court continued to protect the potential donor, even at the expense of the dying patient, on the basis of confidentiality of medical information.

Ethical Perspectives

With respect to experimental therapy in any life-threatening illness like leukemia, ethicists debate whether a patient ever has the ability to give genuinely informed consent. The problem of consent is intensified by the fact that many leukemia patients are children who have little or no ability to appreciate the nature of the choices being made for them.

The significant ethical questions for all high-risk research projects are these: (1) Is it possible for a patient to act freely in choosing to participate in experimental treatment when he or she is threatened by an otherwise certain or almost certain death and when therapeutic research contains the symbolic chance of a miracle? (2) Ought we to permit patients to choose experimental therapies that have little or no prospect of benefit to them, *and* that have a significant prospect of increased risk to them, *but* that will provide additional scientific information that may be of benefit to other ill patients?

Of course, any individual consenting to medical care is under some degree of stress, since illness inevitably creates stress. Whether the stress felt by the acute leukemia patient differs in kind rather than in degree from that felt by the patient facing gall bladder surgery is another question. The ethicist might argue that the significant threat of death with (and from) standard treatment, experimental treatment, or no treatment makes it more difficult for the leukemia patient than for the gall bladder patient to judge where his or her best interests lie. If so, then some degree of paternalism would be justified by ensuring that a neutral, third party at least reviewed these patients' decisions, even if the third party did not actually make them. Thus, for example, a 35-year-old acute leukemia patient who consented to bone marrow transplantation might be interviewed to make sure that he understood the therapy's risks to him, personally, as opposed to the risks to patients generally. Or, a 45- or 50-year-old patient with an incurable blood disease other than those for which bone marrow transplantation is currently used might not be permitted to undergo the treatment, even if the patient consented to it or even requested it. Such review would enable us to separate out consents based upon false beliefs that the therapy will be personally beneficial from those based upon an altruistic desire to submit to experimental therapy in order to provide others with scientific knowledge.

Those ethicists who give primary value to autonomy might argue that the patient's decision could never be overridden as long as he or she had been given accurate information. Concern with external judgments about the patient's best interests would be less important than the individual's right to make his or her own choices, even if those choices do not appear to be in the person's best interests. Autonomy arguments permit individuals to draw to inside straights, to make decisions by throwing pennies and interpreting the *I Ching*, to choose always what their parents oppose, or to make any other irrational choice, so long as the chooser understands the nature of the choice. Although American ideology gives very heavy weight to autonomy-based arguments, some kinds of irrational judgments are likely to fall before paternalistic claims (for example, nonstandard preferences of elderly patients, adolescents, the mentally ill, and social deviants). Patients' "irrational" choices are less likely to be paternalistically overridden with respect to experimental therapies, however. The patient, it is widely believed, ought to have the last word when the choice is between almost certain death and the unknown, perhaps greater, risks of experimentation.

Apart from the patient's capacity to provide consent, we might ask whether anyone ought to be encouraged or even permitted to take serious or unknown risks for the sake of adding to scientific knowledge when little or no benefit can accrue to them personally. Some years ago, a new intensive chemotherapy protocol was devised for use with bone marrow transplant patients. The researchers referred to the new drug regimen by its acronym, the SCARI protocol. Those patients who consented to the SCARI protocol died in substantially greater numbers than those who had used the earlier drug protocols, because the powerful drugs' high toxicity killed the patients. SCARI, indeed. Individuals who enter risky research projects without expecting personal benefit go substantially beyond what the culture expects of them. Because there are no societal expectations, they may be perceived as heroes, as fools, or as manipulated victims of scientific zealots.

Different ethical concerns focus on the donor's role. Although there is no legal duty to rescue another person, certainly most ethicists would argue that "Good Samaritanism" contains important moral values, and that one might have a duty to save the life of another when there is no significant risk to the person doing the lifesaving. A prospective donor might reasonably question, however, whether being a donor under experimental conditions does, in fact, constitute "Good Samaritanism." A distinction surely needs to be made between doing what another person wishes and doing what will save another's life. If the transplant succeeds, as it will in a proportion of cases, the life may be saved; but if it does not, the donor's contribution may cause the recipient's death through graft-versus-

host disease. Thus, being a donor is not simply a case of offering un-
alloyed benefits. The donor, in a very real sense, may kill the patient.

Policy Perspectives

If effective cures and treatments are to be found for diseases like
cancer, then research must be conducted on a fairly large scale. Inevitably, humans in these research projects will die, sometimes—
perhaps often—sooner than they might otherwise have done. As a
society, we have a strong belief in the importance of clinical research
and are thus willing to accept many of the problems that accompany it. In attempting to minimize these problems, policy makers
have largely depended upon institutional review boards (IRBs).

IRBs differ from peer review in that their members include theologians, attorneys, and public interest representatives in addition to
scientists who conduct applied and basic research. These non-
research members are included to diminish the potential of medical/
researcher bias, thereby giving the patient and the public some role
in deciding about what kind of research is acceptable, as opposed to
what kind of research will give the information that is wanted. Most
hospitals, universities, and other institutions engaged in medical research with human subjects have institutional review boards. These
institutions ordinarily require IRB approval for all research conducted by their employees.

Problems continue to arise about experimental therapy that is
not part of a formal research project, however. Review boards occasionally have had serious disagreements with physician-researchers
about therapeutic practices. In some instances, the IRB has con-
tended that the researcher has failed to get approval for a specific
form of treatment, and the researcher has donned his or her other
hat—that of treating physician—claiming that the treatment was
not research but simply an expression of the doctor's clinical judgment as to what would give the patient the best chance for recovery.
Policy makers have not been successful in sorting out this subtle distinction between research that must receive approval and innovative therapy that lies within the physician's sphere of discretion. If
the action violates research procedures, then the researcher is subject to institutional censure; if it violates good judgment in therapy,
then the patient has a right to complain and the institution a duty to

review it because the action is performed within the doctor-patient relationship under the auspices of the institution.

What's a Patient to Do?

In the case study, Ray Darrow is 35 years old. Treatment for acute leukemia is much more successful for those under 20, whether transplant or chemotherapy alone. Patients over age 30 have very poor prospects, and bone marrow transplant centers often restrict transplant to those under a certain age (40–45), on paper. These restrictions are not fixed, however, and older patients who seek the treatment may sometimes receive it. Because of his age, Ray Darrow is unlikely to do well on either form of therapy, but he is not told this by his physician. Instead, he is given overall statistics. The physician justifies this deception (or lack of full disclosure) by appealing to Ray's best interests. If Ray were to know how poor his prospects were, it might diminish his will to live. He has been informed that his condition is serious and potentially fatal; that is sufficient. To pinpoint the degree of "potential fatality" would be unnecessary, cruel, and counterproductive.

Dr. Webster does offer Ray the option of standard treatment, but he also downplays standard chemotherapy. He presents the information in such a way that Ray will be helped to choose the research protocol. It is probably the case that some patients will always choose the standard treatment, no matter how poor its chances, and that some patients will always choose the research protocol, regardless of how grim its risks. It is the patients in the middle that can be affected by the physician's presentation. Ray was able to identify with Webster and Webster could use that identification to bring Ray into research. It is possible, of course, that even a downplaying of the research protocol would not have discouraged Ray from pursuing that one lone chance back to a normal life.

An ethicist might argue that the physician had failed to respect Ray's autonomy by encouraging him to participate in the transplantation without sufficiently explaining to him the alternatives. Dr. Webster believed that transplantation was the best choice for Ray; as well, he believed that Ray was the kind of person who would choose transplantation, even if you tried to persuade him otherwise. Although it is possible that Ray would have chosen the experimental therapy even if he had known the extent of the risks, that does not morally justify undue assistance in reaching that decision, if the patient's autonomy is the primary ethical value. If, on the other hand, paternalistic decision making is appropriate because Ray was unable to act autonomously in the face of so much stress, then the individual who made or shaped the decision should not have been the physician whose own interests might be in conflict with Ray's best interests. Instead, Ray's personal physician, attorney, or a close friend might have been better able to help Ray assess the information relevant to his personal preference.

The selection of donors is ethically very difficult in this case. Ray's sister is willing but she will experience economic hardship as a result of donating. The youngest brother, Richard, is a reluctant donor at best. If he had absolutely refused to be a donor, then he could not be required, even morally, to do so, given the risks. He was, however, conditionally willing. If his tissue match had been superior to Sid's, then Webster would have been in a dilemma. He would have had to choose between a willing but less appropriate donor or an unwilling but appropriate donor. If such a choice had been required, Webster would have had to face the problem of truth-telling. Richard had claimed he would donate only if Sid or Elaine were inappropriate donors. Would Webster be required to tell Richard that only he had a perfect match, or that Sid was an acceptable but inferior donor compared to Richard? We have already noted that when there is an unwilling donor, physicians frequently conceal that information and simply report that the reluctant relative is inappropriate because of poor tissue match. When the donor is merely reluctant, however, the quality of the donation may be used to persuade him or her, and it is in those instances that the physician faces an ethical quandary as to whether to protect the sensibilities of the reluctant donor or to promote the patient's best chances of recovery. Similarly, if both brothers had been inferior to Elaine, the physician must consider whether the hardships she will undergo prohibit using her as a donor if Sid is equally willing, but somewhat inferior with respect to tissue matching.

In this case, Ray has no doubts. Perhaps no amount of talking would have given him uncertainty about his choice. Ray's wife Connie, however, suffers with her unacknowledged doubt. Moved along by Ray's certainty and Webster's confidence, she is never able to pull back and consider the choice. She is devastated not only by his death but by the manner of his death and she is likely to be haunted for many years by the fact that she never pursued the possibility of al-

ternative treatment. The bone marrow unit that swept up their lives
focused intensely and unswervingly on its fight against leukemia,
but to her its concern seemed to be with the disease, not with the patients and their families who suffered from the disease. Looking
back, she fears that Ray did not die his own death; instead, he died
the death of a statistic, one more subject in yet another research paper on the effectiveness of bone marrow transplantation.

The patient with acute leukemia has few options, none of them very
good; the older patient with acute leukemia is even worse off. At
this time, only one in three patients is likely to have a suitable family
donor and thus to be eligible for bone marrow transplantation. Researchers have had some experience with unrelated donors and this
line of inquiry may prove fruitful. At present, there is at least some
suggestion that neither bone marrow transplantation nor standard
chemotherapy can be demonstrated to be a superior treatment for
all leukemic patients. The long-range survival curves appear to be
similar (although the research is difficult to compare). The patient
must choose between a therapy that is likely to result in temporary
improvement and then a return of the leukemia, and a therapy that
is likely to result in even more acute illness with a significant probability of death from the treatment itself, but a possibility of "cure."
It is, perhaps, a choice that no human ought to be given, and surely
not one who is ill and hospitalized, estranged from the ordinary setting of his or her life.
    What the patient needs is information, hope, and caring com-
passion. The research setting may provide all three, or it may emphasize only one or two of these qualities. Some patients will prefer
to take risks; some patients may be manipulated into accepting risk
taking; some patients may abhor risk taking. That middle group of
patients may need time and calmness to decide how much risk they
want, but experimental therapy units may not be geared to provide
either of these. For the unit to work effectively, the staff must believe
in the treatment. For believers, doubt is a waste of time. Yet, the patient may need the opportunity to doubt before choosing, even if she
or he chooses to pursue the experiment.
    Procedures for informed consent are rigorous (at least on paper)
in most institutions that conduct research with experimental and
risky therapies. Unfortunately, requiring specific procedures to gain
consent does not necessarily assure that consent is informed. It
merely assures that procedures exist and perhaps have been fol-

lowed. Research into consent has shown that many patients have very little understanding or recollection of information given to them prior to medical treatment, even though they signed elaborate consent documents and were given extensive information. Even when thorough information has been given, patients who face terminal illnesses with uncertain treatment may not retain the information or may interpret it in unusual ways. They are very likely to experience a considerable amount of denial, with respect to both the seriousness of their condition and the risks of the proposed experimental therapy. They may believe that the experimental treatment they have consented to is actually superior because it is new, or that being in a research project means they will receive better and more intense care from the research physician. A physician who tries to ensure that her patients understand what they are consenting to may find that her best efforts are circumvented by the active minds of worried patients who invent explanations more to their liking.

Approved informed consent procedures do not guarantee that the patient will retain the correct information. Worse than that, the procedures do not even guarantee that the patient will receive the information. Very sick patients frequently do whatever their physician tells them to do. Doctors, nurses, and administrators may give patients papers to sign, explaining that the papers are simply a formality, and they may sign without reading any of that carefully prepared, IRB-approved text.

Physicians may provide only the most positive information. Thus, if the overall recovery rate is 60 percent, but most of that percentage is accounted for by the fact that more children than adults survive, the adult patient is likely to hear the *overall* statistics for survival, while the family of the child patient is likely to hear the survival statistics only for children.

When information is given verbally, it may be selectively stressed. The patient may be given detailed information about the evidence that bone marrow transplant patients who survive for thirty months are very unlikely to suffer any relapse of leukemia, but much less information about the prospects of surviving those thirty months. They may be given elaborate information about the details of the experimental therapy, but little information about the alternatives to the experimental therapy. Patients frequently do not understand that once they enter a research protocol, treatment decisions will be for the most part based upon the research design, not upon their own individual needs. Whether this lack of understanding results from the researcher's failure to educate the patient/ subject or from the patient's unwillingness or inability to process such information is not clear. It is, nevertheless, one of the most severe problems of the informed consent process in experimental therapy. Patient/subjects are always entitled to withdraw from a research project at any time they wish, and should do so if they feel that their individual needs are being sacrificed to the demands of the research. This entitlement is, however, not always very useful, for once the patient has begun a therapy like bone marrow transplantation, there are very few exit stations. The train stops only to bury its dead.

Patients need information but often fear receiving it, and that makes it hard for physicians to decide how much patients should be told. Patients who want to control their decisions cannot do so in ignorance, however. They must seek out the truth and it may hurt. Patients who are receiving adequate emotional support are probably better off knowing the truth, however, because then they are able to consider the real risks instead of having to struggle through the myriad fears that bloom in the absence of knowledge.

Even patients who want accurate information are vulnerable to being misled and manipulated both by their physicians and by themselves. The physicians are anxious to keep the patients' hopes alive because in that way the psychological mechanisms that affect healing can be effectuated. Patients who are candidates for experimental therapy have fears that stimulate psychological denial and thus allow them to have unrealistic expectations about how probable the benefits of the treatment will be. The cards tend to be stacked against these patients with respect to informed consent in therapeutic research. Even those who try hard to gather adequate information and then rationally to consider their choices may find themselves swept away by others' enthusiasms or their own ungrounded hopes.

Thus, patients should consider having an advisor or advocate to help them go through the decision process. Whether a friend, family member, or counselor, this advisor's role would be to provide balance and to protect the patient from others' enthusiasms. Considering modern medicine's capacity to create suffering while it prolongs life, a decision not to pursue further treatment can be very rational. An advisor's function is not to advocate that position but to help the patient consider priorities and values in light of that possibility.

Patients who are contemplating research participation may want to ask to read the research protocol. Has the researcher published any papers on this topic? If patients are going to run considerable risks for the sake of future knowledge, they may want to consider whether the knowledge is likely to be forthcoming or whether the project is only a stepping stone in someone's research career. They should clearly understand the design study before signing on. Well-designed research studies will involve control groups in order to be able to tell whether the treatment makes any difference. Many quality projects will be designed to be double-blind (that is, neither patient nor physician knows what group the patient is in); some will involve a placebo group (that group of patient/subjects receives only an inert substance or some other kind of noncontent treatment). Much of medical research proves to be of little value because it is poorly designed. If patients want to contribute their discomforts or deaths to science, they should have some sense that the project will be legitimately useful. Although they cannot be expected to become experts in research design, they can be sure that they understand at least what the researcher expects to be accomplished and can ask what need there is for that accomplishment.

Therapeutic research provides more conflicts of interest than any other area of medicine, and patients will have to work hard to understand this and take it into account when making decisions. They must keep in mind that therapy is primarily intended to benefit them, but research's benefit is primarily to science and to other patients at later times. Experimental therapy can, at best, provide patients only with statistical expectations about large groups of people. Unfortunately, the patient is only one individual. It is usually stated that there is, for example, a 50 percent chance of the therapy's failing to work. That does not state the situation accurately, although it is an ordinary way of talking about statistics. What is meant is that the therapy will fail for 50 percent of patients who try it. If it doesn't work, that patient will endure the failure at the 100 percent level: that is, all of the patient will suffer all the failure. When the risks are that high, patients should understand that they are bearing those risks for the hope of further medical knowledge rather than for personal benefit, although some personal benefit may occur.

The major successes of modern medicine (and of bone marrow transplantation itself) have come because of research. Research has

saved lives and continues to do so. Nevertheless, individual patients
need to consider seriously whether they want to participate when
the benefits are not primarily intended for them. Researchers have
devoted their lives to unraveling the mysteries of specific disease processes. As a result, they are often zealous about what they are doing
and are anxious to have the patients who are potential subjects become as zealous as they are. The intensity of their commitment is often contagious but patients need to realize that the commitment is
not to their being cured but to the disease being cured. The patients
are, however, foot soldiers in that army, not fellow officers. Their
own lives are not the crucial battle: the war will go on without them
should they fall in the line of duty.

Patients should be aware that agreeing to enter into a research
project does not mean agreeing to stay in it. Patients are always entitled to withdraw at any time. If they do try to exercise this option
for withdrawal, they are likely to meet resistance from researchers
both because this slows down the research and because they may believe that the research-therapy best serves the patients' interests. Patients need to be prepared to persevere in their desire to withdraw,
and in this instance, too, an individual advisor may help patients to
exercise their preferences. It may be psychologically difficult for
patient/subjects to withdraw from research projects because they
fear alienating or disappointing the physician who is providing their
care. Patients should, however, remember that it is they who are
sick and in need of help, not the clinician/researchers.

When patients with terminal illnesses consent to participate as
subjects of therapeutic research, they should also make plans for
their eventual incompetence. Different states have different ways of
handling this, but even if a state has no legally binding document,
patients can write out their wishes, stating whether therapy should
be continued if they no longer are competent to state their own
wishes. Signing a living will, a natural death act, or a durable
power of attorney for health care will require a rational consideration of the risks of the therapy, but this does not preclude or eliminate hopefulness.

Choosing among a variety of very poor options is always difficult, and there needs to be great social tolerance for whatever patients choose as long as they clearly understand what choices they
have made. These are very personal value choices, and life need not
always be sought nor suffering always be avoided. Hospitals and
clinician/researchers are not always in tune with patient autonomy

as a primary value when therapeutic research is considered. It is an area where physician paternalism is often exercised very freely. Patients who wish to control their own choices must be sensitive to the psychologically coercive environment of hospital research, realizing that they may have to fight for their autonomy even as they fight for life or death.

Conclusion

Like most problems in biomedical ethics, therapeutic research does not yield to a simple analysis. If treatment advances are to be made, then they must ultimately be attempted on human subjects whose illness makes them vulnerable to manipulation by others. There may be a tendency for some to believe that those who are fated for death might as well take greater risks since, as the researcher pointed out, "they all would have died anyway." Autonomy values urge that those who wish to take such risks should be permitted to do so if they understand their choices. Nay-sayers argue that people cannot genuinely understand such choices, especially when the potential research subjects are facing death. Communitarian values argue that those who generously give their lives to benefit others, even if only indirectly by contributing to scientific knowledge, are to be praised. Another view, and one more directly paternalistic, suggests that we ought not to permit our fellow humans to make such sacrifices for us because the gift is too great, its benefit too uncertain. Therapeutic research poses these dilemmas daily to dying patients and their families, and to physician/researchers and institutional review boards. The questions are clear; the answers are not.

CHAPTER 9

A Look Forward
Essential Facts of
Health Care Financing

For thirty years, changes in health care have been so overwhelming that patients could only adapt. In the last few years, patients have struggled to gain an independent voice in decisions about their own medical treatment, thus forcing further change in the system. The previous eight chapters explain the ethical debates, the legal concerns, and the medical factors so that patients and their families can maximize their own ability to act autonomously when dealing with the health care system. This final chapter will look at further change: to see where health care is now going and how those changes will affect the hard-won rights that patients now have.

The most important change in health care in the 1980s is how we pay for it. Health care financing is a complex topic, lacking the drama and human engagement of issues like organ transplantation, kidney dialysis, and innovative cancer research. Because it cannot be explained quickly or simply, many people will fail to see how financing changes will affect their choices or their ability to make choices.

As Paul Starr has so successfully shown in *The Social Transformation of American Medicine*, health care is now undergoing a major revolution driven by medical costs. This, in turn, may drastically alter the organizational structure of health care, hospital ownership, and provider-patient relationships. Health care financing seems remote from problems of patient autonomy, but that is because the patients (as well as doctors and hospital administrators) have been shielded from cost issues for so many years. Now, hospitals that cannot function in this new economic climate will close or be taken over by hospitals that can. Physicians who are indifferent to treatment costs may find themselves abandoned by patients or rejected by hospitals. Patients who do not understand how policy decisions about funding affect their own decision making will also face frustration. They will again find their decisions being made for them. This time, however, it will be the government, their insurance company, or the hospital administrators that exercise primary power, not the doctors.

Many policy makers have urged that if health care is to be rationed, it should be done so that the rationing decisions are not apparent to patients or to the public as a whole. So far, that has been the direction of most cost-containment efforts. If cost-reduction policies continue to encourage hidden or implicit restrictions, patients will need to be even more sophisticated about how the system works in order to choose the care they want. If patients pursue health care knowledgeably, however, reduced spending need not mean reduced quality of care.

The Funding Crisis

In the 1960s, the political struggle was for increased access to health care for the poor and for minorities. The moral concerns of the civil rights movement were applied broadly, and Medicare and Medicaid were established to ensure that the poor and the aged would have access to the fruits of health science. In the 1970s, there was a period of relative quiet, optimism, and even self-congratulation as these publicly funded programs took root and expanded. The creation of the open-ended dialysis and kidney transplant program under Medicare demonstrates the tide of optimism that health care rode during those years. The dominant ideology was that if treatment existed, everyone who needed it should receive it. The substantial expansion of medical schools and the rate of hospital construction during this same period reflected the belief that more and better health care was the birthright of all Americans. By 1984, over 85 percent of the public had either publicly or privately funded health care coverage (35 million people were uninsured). Now, there is a drawing back and a questioning of our previous achievements and even of our goals. Should all Americans have a right to all the health care they want or even all they need?

Since about 1980, health care policy discussions have been dominated by worries about health care costs. The source of the financing problem is variously attributed to technological advance, public belief in full entitlement to all available care regardless of its degree of benefit, and a financing structure with no incentives to cut costs because those who paid (the government and third-party insurers) made none of the decisions about use. Whatever its causes (and they are doubtless multiple), by 1984, it was economists—not physicians or philosophers or lawyers—who were being asked for advice about solving health care problems.

There is general agreement that we have a real problem: health care costs are high, perhaps too high. It is important to remember that every dollar spent on health care is a dollar less spent on housing, food, education, defense needs, and other products and services. The concern with costs is not only that they have risen. We have, of course, recently been through a period of high inflation, and costs for everything have risen dramatically. Health care costs, however, have risen far more than the costs of other goods and services. In 1960, health care expenditures accounted for 5 percent of the gross national product. Twenty-three years later, health care expenditures had risen to 10.6 percent of the gross national product. Although a country can, at least in theory, spend a significant percentage of its gross national product on health care, it cannot spend all of it that way. The current 11 percent figure is not too great if we choose to spend that much. Nor would 12 percent be too much, as a political choice. The percentage must be stabilized, but health care costs have shown no sign of stabilizing. The increase will taper off only if government, consumers, insurance companies, doctors, and hospitals exert some kind of restraint.

A second concern is that our expenditures are not buying better health. Although statistics can be made to demonstrate almost anything, it is hard to prove that the enormous investment in health care over the past twenty-five years has translated into longer or healthier lives for Americans. Other Western, industrialized countries pay far less per capita for health care than America does, and many of those countries have lower infant mortality rates and higher life expectancy figures (the two primary measures of the effectiveness of health care). Thus, it is apparent that spending less might not necessarily lead to worse outcomes. Other evidence strongly suggests that preventive measures—especially those under individual control—will do far more to improve health than will medical care. The recent decrease in heart disease is attributed not to the availability of bypass surgery or heart transplants but to reduced smoking, increased exercise, and better diets. If patients take more responsibility for their health as well as their medical care choices, then reduced expenditures may not pose a threat to the average, well-informed individual.

Cost-Cutting Reforms and Patient Choice

There are many changes now being made in health care financing that will affect patients' options concerning health care. Patients and their families should be aware of them so that they can understand the treatment implications of the economic choices they make. These changes include providing less money for publicly paid health care, instituting capitation* costs for reimbursement, reducing the numbers of doctors and hospitals, increasing the use of nonphysicians for health care, increasing use of outpatient care, decreasing hospital care and unproved routine care, changing research patterns, socializing physicians to provide less treatment (and, in effect, to eliminate it for some patients), educating consumers to want or to need less care, taxing health care benefits, developing health maintenance and preferred provider organizations (HMOs and PPOs), strictly reviewing both hospital and physician patterns of providing services (PROs—peer review organizations—and physician profiles), requiring patients to pay for more of their health care, reducing physician incomes, and reducing or restricting benefits by insurers. These practices affect patient/consumers in different ways.

1. Reduced Government Expenditures

This is the simplest but least sensitive method of cutting costs. When state and local governments reduce their health expenditures, they

---

*Capitation costs are cost per unit, as opposed to costs of specific services provided. Thus capitation might involve flat payment rates for each medical condition treated or for each patient treated.

may reduce services, shut down hospitals or clinics, or raise eligibility requirements for health care benefits, thus providing public care for fewer low-income people. If they reduce their costs simply by reducing allocations of funds, then the hospitals, clinics, or agency heads are in a position to decide what kinds of care to eliminate or reduce. If the reductions are made more specifically (i.e., eligibility requirements or hospital closures), then overall costs will be reduced, but many people will no longer receive basic health care. If consumers want protection from this kind of cost cutting, they need to be sure that they have insurance coverage, whether employer- or self-paid, and that they keep it. The number of uninsured people who are not eligible for public assistance is increasing. More and more frequently, hospitals will provide them only with the minimum care necessary in an emergency.

2. *Use of Capitation Reimbursement*

Traditionally, medical care has been paid for on a fee-for-service basis. That is, the physician and hospital have been paid (either by the patient, government, or insurer) for whatever services were provided. Beginning in 1983, the federal Medicare program instituted a new capitation program called DRGs (Diagnostic Related Groups). Under capitation reimbursement, hospitals and physicians are paid a specific amount per person or per treated diagnosis. DRGs currently apply only to hospital reimbursements for Medicare patients, but a bill to extend the system to physician payments is already before Congress, and before long the DRG system or something very similar will also be used by private insurers throughout the country to pay hospital and physician claims.

Under the DRG system, every hospital patient is assigned to one of 467 categories. The categories are mutually exclusive and are based upon the patient's principal diagnosis, complications and other disorders, and, in some cases, age and sex. The hospital is paid a preset amount for each patient in a specific category. If the payment rate for DRG 467 were $2500, and a patient were in that category, then the hospital would receive $2500 for the treatment provided. The government does not care whether the actual cost of treating patient Mary Smith, DRG 467, is $1000, $2500, or $10,000. It pays $2500. The rates are based upon the average cost for treating a patient with that diagnosis and it is assumed that some patients will cost more and some will cost less. The purpose of the DRGs as they now exist is to reward hospitals (and eventually doctors) for providing care that costs less than the average (they get to keep the difference), and to punish them if care costs more than the average (they must make up the difference themselves). Although in the ideal system the rewards and punishments would even out, it is probable that there will be a significant desire to end up with a profit, since more and more hospitals are now private, profit-oriented corporations. The DRG system provides hospitals and physicians with economic incentives to provide slightly less care than is ideally necessary.

Even if everyone acts with noble intentions, there will be problems. In large hospitals, these high-cost and low-cost patients will presumably average out because there are enough of both kinds each year in each DRG. Small hospitals, on the other hand, can easily have an insufficient number of patients in each category to have the payments average out. Small hospitals will therefore be reluctant to provide treatment at the high end because they cannot guarantee that they will have enough patients at the low end to balance out their losses on the high-treatment patients. Approximately 40 percent of all the hospitals in the United States are in the small hospital range (fewer than 200 beds), Their occupancy rate is already low and they tend to have greater financial problems. When care is paid for under a DRG system, patients who have very serious illnesses would be likely to receive more care at a larger hospital than at a smaller one since the smaller hospital has a greater need to reduce the high-treatment end of the spectrum.

The hope of capitation payments is that unnecessary care will be eliminated. The prospect is that some care will be eliminated. Unfortunately, we do not always know what care is unnecessary. Hospitals that try to reduce their costs by eliminating "unnecessary" care may use their own administrative judgment, rather than the physicians' or the patients' judgments, about what is unneeded. Care may be reduced for patients who are old, disabled, or socially unconnected. Whereas the present assumption is that life-extending care for terminally ill patients should be provided unless the patient refuses it, we may find a subtle shift so that life-extending care is *not* provided for the terminally ill patient unless he or she requests it. Under such circumstances, it is increasingly important that patients make known their requests about treatment in the event of their incompetency, and that they write their preferences down and entrust the document to their physicians and trusted family or friends.

In recent years, many patients and their families have struggled to *refuse* treatment. The court cases that have resulted in disconnecting respirators, in withdrawing naso-gastric or gastrostomy feeding tubes, and in not applying standard cardiopulmonary resuscitation have made refusal legally possible. In a cost-cutting climate, people may have to go to court to *get* treatment. Dollar cutbacks may benefit those who want to avoid the excessive medical care that has been imposed upon unconsenting patients in recent years. It is, however, unfortunate that the right act may be done for the wrong reason.

3. *Reducing the Number of Hospitals and Physicians*

The laws of supply and demand do not appear to operate very effectively when it comes to health care. Unfortunately, the increased supply of physicians and hospitals that was fostered by the federal government in the late 1960s and early 1970s has been accompanied by increased costs *and* demand. When there are fewer medical school graduates, rural and ghetto residents have less access to physicians. However, the enormous increase in numbers of hospitals and doctors did not benefit underserved areas nearly as much as planners hoped. Nevertheless, reducing those numbers will mean reduced access. For patients who want easy access to physicians and high levels of medical care, that means staying in the affluent areas of cities and suburbs and staying out of rural America.

4. *Increased Use of Alternative*
Health Care Providers for Primary Care

Some have argued that costs could be reduced if physicians provided less of the care. Unfortunately, this argument is likely to run head on into the growing physician surplus. Doctors have long been effective protectors of their turf, whether they were fighting off chiropractors, nurse practitioners, midwives, or snake oil salesmen. The medical profession will oppose any attempt to encourage alternative care providers. This political battle could have significant effects upon consumer/patients who want to choose their own form of health care. Alternative providers may not be permitted to offer care, even if patients want it and the providers want to give it. Nurse midwives who want to practice independently and nurse practitioners and psychologists who want to be able to prescribe a limited number of medications have not been very successful. Midwives have been denied licensure in many states and prescription authority, which requires statutory approval, has not been given. Unless citizens insist upon access to alternative methods of health care through political action, individual choice is likely to be minimal or nonexistent. On this matter, the potential for cost reduction is likely to be ignored.

5. Increased Outpatient Care

In 1982, 42 percent of all health care dollars were spent on hospital services (not including physician care). Thus, major cost-reduction efforts are likely to focus on this area. Health maintenance organizations (see pp. 251–253) effectively discourage hospital care and encourage ambulatory or outpatient treatment. Any plan that focuses on preventive health measures also will tend to encourage outpatient care and reduce hospital care. One of the most interesting developments in this area, however, was neither designed nor encouraged by health policy planners. Instead, it probably flows from physician oversupply. This is the "Doc-in-the-Box" phenomenon. Because consumers have used hospital emergency rooms for primary medical care, medical entrepreneurs have created free-standing physician offices, often in shopping centers, to provide acute care treatment. Although they are not equipped to handle genuine emergency medical cases (those are transferred to hospitals), they are capable of treating many of the kinds of acute care needs that normally surface in hospital emergency rooms.

Doc-in-the-Box operations are private corporations, with salaried physician employees. They operate rather like fast food franchises: they are fast medicine (thus the appellation). They are often open twenty-four hours a day and no appointments are necessary. Organized medicine has not been friendly to this new development and in some states, medical associations have tried to force the offices to be licensed as genuine emergency rooms. These onslaughts have, so far, been successfully fought off by the medical entrepreneurs and these "emergi-centers" are considered doctors' offices, not emergency rooms.

The major effect of changes like these (and one that also applies to the current shift from nonprofit and not-for-profit to profit hospitals) is that patients may have more choices about where they receive health care. Outpatient care, however, is frequently less fully covered by insurance (except in HMOs), so patients will be responsible for more of the costs. The fact that patients must pay more of the costs, combined with the fact that some of these new health care forms are businesses, means that care will be based upon whether the services are worth providing: that is, whether someone is willing to pay for them. Consumer/patients may be willing, for example, to have their eyes tested regularly if someone else pays for the services but not willing to do so if they themselves must pay. Routine health care may once again become the province of the home rather than the physician or hospital. In any case, patients can expect additional control over treatment decisions if they have a greater financial investment.

6.   Changing Research Patterns

The possibility of changed research patterns may be the most important of all possible alterations. Research funds could either be cut (leading to fewer high-tech medical developments) or they could be used to fund a different kind of research. This would alter the health care system and patients' choices only in the long run. A decision, for example, to reduce research funds for cancer "cures" and palliative treatments could be complemented by a decision to increase research funds for consumer education programs that instruct people on how to avoid cancer in the first place. On the other hand, research funding patterns might emphasize scientific demonstrations of the effectiveness of current treatments, rather than creation of new ones. If preventive treatment were to be seen as the appropriate direction for research, then the investment in basic research might increase so that causes of disease could be determined.

These kinds of changes would affect the health care that patients were offered but would not have much effect on individuals' power to choose from what is available. However, if changing research patterns led to depending upon patient education as the primary mode of avoiding illness, then patients who knowingly engaged in behavior that was likely to lead to injury or illness might receive less care or might be required to pay more for the care they received. This might include seriously injured patients who were not wearing helmets when involved in motorcycle accidents, patients with smoking-related lung cancer, and alcoholic or heavy-drinking patients with kidney or liver disease. This approach could also extend to reducing health care and welfare benefits to parents of children with genetic defects who chose to give birth with the knowledge that the child would be handicapped. America's long-term struggle with welfare, trying to determine the identity of the deserving poor as opposed to those undeserving of assistance, suggests the depth of the attraction that such a system might have. Not content with trying to identify the deserving poor, we could move on to pinpointing the deserving ill.

7. *Socializing Physicians to Offer Less Care*

This method has recently been recommended by Lester Thurow, one of America's most prestigious economists, as a desirable way to reduce health costs. The "socialization route" is best demonstrated in the British National Health Service, where physicians are taught by peer pressure and role modeling not to provide care that physicians, as a group, feel is not justified, given the limited resources of the health service. The best example of this is renal disease. According to Aaron and Schwartz's recent book, *The Painful Prescription*, National Health Service patients over the age of 55 are seldom offered dialysis by physicians, nor are they told that dialysis would significantly extend their lives. Instead, since physicians as a group have decided that older people don't have as much claim on this limited resource as do younger people, the older patients are told that nothing more can be done for them and are sent home to die. It should be noted that there is no government or National Health Service policy that dialysis is unavailable to those over 55. It is, instead, a kind of gentlemen's (and, increasingly, gentlewomen's) agreement among physicians.

Allowing doctors to make these decisions may sound reasonable enough because that is how many similar decisions have been made in the United States. Nevertheless, permitting physicians to decide who will receive effective care means making decisions that depend upon physicians' values, not upon patients' values. Physicians who felt that the quality of Down's infants' lives did not justify lifesaving treatment were making this kind of judgment. Physicians who feel that quadriplegics' lives are too burdensome may neglect to provide lifesaving treatment when it is necessary, even though some quadriplegics lead extraordinarily productive lives. Encouraging physicians to make quality-of-life decisions generally defeats patient autonomy and patient control of decisions. Professionals' decisions about when to extend life and when to allow death may conflict with patients' decisions about what is best for them.

8.   Requiring Individuals to Pay
    a Greater Share of Their Health Care Costs

Those who seek to provide more efficient health care urge the creation of incentives for patient, physician, and hospital to use or provide less expensive care. There are many ways to do this, including taxing health care benefits, increasing insurance deductibles, and increasing patients' co-payments. These methods all encourage individuals to take a more active role in deciding what kind of health care they want and what kind of health care they believe they genuinely need. Thus, although these strategies may require individuals to pay more than they previously did, their willingness to pay can increase their power to choose.

Taxing employee health benefits means that the amount that employers pay for health insurance will be treated as taxable income to the employee. The logic of this strategy is that requiring employees to pay tax on their benefits will encourage them to look more carefully at what they are getting for the money that their employers are paying. Assuming that the employer pays all the costs of whatever health insurance plan the employee chooses, then employees will have to pay more in taxes if they choose an expensive insurance plan than if they choose a less expensive one. If employees choose more expensive plans, they will probably have access to more services. That will not, however, necessarily increase their power to choose. When services are provided at no cost to the patient, the physician may be more inclined to insist that the patient receive the services.

With less expensive plans, however, consumer/patients are likely to have to pay a larger amount of initial costs (deductibles) and/or a larger percentage of all costs (co-payments). It is reasonable to believe that physicians pay little attention to the costs of care that they recommend for patients as long as they do not think that the patients have to pay all or most of the costs. If patients have no financial obligation, physicians are more likely to recommend all beneficial treatments, from highly to minimally beneficial, because they might help. If physicians are aware that their patients have to pay more of the costs, they may be more cautious when there is less to gain from treatment. Thus, consumer/patients who have chosen insurance coverage with higher co-payments or higher deductibles should inform their physicians of their financial stake in treatment. A considerable amount of care is discretionary, but physicians are not used to thinking of it in that way. Their attitude tends to be "the more the better," either because care is "free," because it might help the patient, or because this offers them some protection from the possibility of malpractice charges. Physicians' inclinations to overtreat sharply reduce patients' choices because patients are not clearly informed of when choices can usefully be made. When patients are paying more of the costs themselves, then they and their physician may have a better opportunity to think about whether the care is worth the cost. But that will not happen if patients are not straightforward with their physicians in explaining their own financial stake.

9.   Health Maintenance Organizations (HMO) and Preferred Provider Organizations (PPO)

Costs can be reduced by providing appropriate incentives for patients; they can also be reduced by providing incentives for physicians. HMOs and PPOs are intended to capitalize on both these incentives. Overall, HMOs and PPOs probably serve to reduce many patient choices.

HMOs are health care groups that are paid a fixed amount per patient each year to provide a fixed set of benefits. All treatment must be provided by the HMO's physicians and, usually, in the HMO's facilities. Kaiser-Permanente is one of the oldest and largest HMOs in the United States, but such groups are becoming increasingly common in large cities throughout the nation. HMOs may require co-payments and deductibles, but they are usually very small (e.g., $3 per physician visit). The principle behind HMOs is that they are operating on a fixed budget and, since they are obliged to provide all necessary care with those funds, they will have to perform efficiently in order not to lose money. HMO physicians are paid salaries, not fees-for-services. They will receive the same income no matter how many operations they perform so there are no incentives to perform unnecessary surgery in order to increase their income. In some HMOs, if the group spends less than it takes in in membership fees, physicians receive a proportion of the profits. Thus, there may be incentives for physicians to supply slightly less care than is needed.

This incentive was discussed widely in connection with the 1983 California case in which two physicians promptly disconnected the respirator and intravenous tubes of a patient who had fallen into a coma after routine surgery. There were widespread allegations that the physicians had been motivated not by the patient's interests but rather by the costs to the hospital of keeping the patient alive when he had little chance for recovery. With traditional medical care, patients may have to fear that they will be receiving more care than they want because physicians are inclined to recommend it even if its benefit is doubtful. In HMOs, the fear is that patients will receive too little care because physicians are inclined not to recommend treatment if there is doubt about its usefulness.

HMOs are similar to the DRG system in that both involve capitation payments. In any capitation system, patients may do far better than they have in the fee-for-service system in having their preferences honored if their preference is for less treatment. If they are interested in receiving *more* treatment (that is, all that medicine can do for them), then they may need to be very insistent with their physicians to find out about alternative forms of treatment and may want to seek second opinions in the case of any serious illness. The second opinion should always be sought from a physician outside of the HMO or PPO structure.

Preferred provider organizations (PPOs) are a recent variant of HMOs. PPOs are, in part, a product of the emerging oversupply of physicians. Insurance companies like Blue Cross and Blue Shield are beginning to offer PPOs as a means of reducing insurance costs. These plans continue to permit insurance holders to go to any physician they choose, but if they go to one of their company's "preferred providers," then the patient pays less. The preferred providers, for their part, have agreed to accept specific levels of payment for patients. The PPO system resembles DRGs in that it pays per capita, although the agreed upon payments may be negotiated individually with each provider rather than set as a fixed rate for all providers.

Despite the differences, PPOs (like HMOs and DRGs) are designed to encourage physicians to provide less care. If less care is provided, patients may benefit because they will not have to argue about whether they can refuse specific care: it will never be offered to them. On the other hand, the aged, the disabled, and the poor are at risk for being the primary vehicle by which the amount of care and overall costs are reduced, regardless of whether they wanted to refuse the care.

10.   PROs and Physician Profiles

Professional review organizations (PROs) and physician profiles are both methods for monitoring hospital and physician efficiency. PROs are responsible for ascertaining whether a particular hospital is, for example, providing an unusually high number of procedures and for ensuring that those procedures be reduced or justified. Thus, a hospital that is performing twice as many gall bladder operations as the typical hospital might be required to reduce the number by means of some kind of internal review procedure or to receive approval from the PRO before performing each operation. The implications of this for patients might be good in that unnecessary treatment will be eliminated or that treatment will be maintained at the appropriate level (e.g., some kinds of surgery might be handled on an outpatient rather than inpatient basis).

On the other hand, it might also lead to situations in which PROs, in reviewing use of life support equipment, might urge termination of that support in the absence of authoritative patient desires to continue the care. The idea that permanently unconscious patients can legally have life-extending care withdrawn if this would be their preference has been accepted only recently. That position has quickly shifted to one in which care could be withdrawn if the family thought it appropriate. It is easy to imagine that soon care will be withdrawn from permanently unconscious patients *unless* someone objects. PROs could help in making that shift and consumers should make sure that life-prolonging care is not being withdrawn precipitously in order to improve the monitoring picture.

Some hospitals now maintain "physician profiles" to keep track of their individual physicians' style of practice. Those doctors who appear to order more tests, perform more procedures, and generally run up higher bills for patients are encouraged to provide less care under the threat of losing their hospital privileges. Whenever a squeeze is placed on health care services, vulnerable patients are most likely to be affected: the poor, the elderly, and the physically and mentally disabled. The use of physician profiles can place doctors in very difficult positions with respect to making recommendations. They may sincerely desire to do only what is in their patients' interests, but if the hospital is second-guessing their decisions, self-interest may win out over patients' interests.

11.   *Reduced Insurance Benefits, Required Second Opinions*

If patients pay a greater share of costs, they will be in a better position to insist upon making their own decisions. Third-party providers (whether government or insurance companies) are also likely to try to exert some control over what is purchased. They are more likely to want to make sure that second opinions are sought for costly treatment. An automatic requirement for second opinions will help patients to identify options and to understand them better. Furthermore, the fact that the opinions are required by the insurer, not sought out by a distrustful patient, will eliminate patients' fears that asking for a second opinion will alienate the primary physician.

Third-party payers will probably resist extending coverage to new, expensive forms of health care interventions. Alternatively, they may extend limited, optional coverage, paying only if the procedures are done in certain centers and if the customer chooses the optional coverage. Whether the treatments in question are fetal surgery, organ transplants, artificial organ implants, nonstandard methods of dealing with infertility, genetic surgery, or sex-change surgery, patients are likely to have to bear the costs themselves if they want the services. This, of course, will sharply limit patients' choices since access will depend upon financial status. If limited coverage is provided, then patients may have to decide whether a heart transplant is worthwhile if it means relocating permanently in another city in order to receive extended treatment. Local care will not be available for most new, expensive treatment.

If the government (or private business, as in the case of embryo transfer and the artificial heart implant) continues to fund research for these big ticket health care interventions, there will be a continuing public demand for full access and probably a continued resistance by insurers. Although many people are offended by the idea of placing a value on life, that is what will be done and must be done in these areas. If third-party payers conclude that a particular form of treatment provides, on average, six extra months of life at $400,000 per month, it would be unwise for the society as a whole to underwrite that kind of treatment for everyone. It is not, consumers must realize, that the treatment provides *no* benefit but that it fails to provide *enough* benefit to justify the cost. In the private market, those who have sufficient funds may find that it is worth it to them to spend that kind of money for a minimal return. American democratic feelings may find it hard for many people to accept the fact that the rich will have access to heart transplants or artificial hearts and that the middle class and poor will not. The alternative, however, is no transplants or artificial hearts for anyone, and that goes against the grain of America's capitalist and progress-oriented ethos.

What's a Patient to Do?

In the past, the issue was the doctor-patient relationship. The hospital was a place where doctor and patient met. In the future, the relationship will be more crowded, for the hospital administrators and third-party payers will be there too. Doctors will lose their preeminent position as captains of the ship and will find themselves caught between the patients' demand for more and better care and the hospitals' and insurers' insistence that costs be reduced and profits increased. Physicians have written eloquently of how they are caught between the hospital's interests and the patient's interests. There are, as well, their own interests in high incomes, technological gadgetry, and psychological authority. As they themselves have said, they were as gods. We may now be seeing them in their twilight.

In the revolution that health care is now undergoing, what's a patient to do? Many will be tempted to throw up their hands in frustration. Even the simplified analysis we have provided may seem hopelessly complex. Such patients will passively endure the impact of changes in health care financing as they have endured changes in medical practice resulting from modern technology. The increased costs or decreased services in health care can be viewed as a product of forces beyond human control, as a fate to be accepted stoically, railed against, or complained about, but about which nothing can be done. These patients will continue to be passive recipients of whatever health care is given to them.

Others will want to protect and preserve their autonomy, to exercise rational control over their health care options. In previous chapters we have indicated the steps that patients must take to retain and exercise their personal preferences when health care choices must be made. These steps include (1) getting clear and detailed medical facts and treatment options; (2) obtaining additional opinions when appropriate; (3) formulating, communicating, and documenting their preferences; (4) anticipating bureaucratic and administrative obstacles; (5) enlisting support of consultants, advocates, ombudsmen, courts, ethics committees, and the like; (6) becoming sensitive to hospital politics and psychodynamics; and (7) establishing a consensus and univocal position, if possible, within the immediate family. Similarly, patients must learn essential facts about health care financing that will affect their opportunity to have and exercise personal preferences.

First, just as it is necessary to develop some understanding of medical diagnosis, treatment options, and prognosis, so also it is necessary to have a clear idea about economic facts that pertain to health care. Although most people have some kind of health care insurance, they rarely choose to change or modify insurance coverage, even though the coverage they have very much affects the kind of care they will receive. Many people don't even know how extensive their insurance coverage is until they face hospitalization. We have discussed such matters as DRGs, HMOs, PPOs, and the like. Consumers need to find out the facts germane to their situation. For example, a person on Medicare is subject to DRGs, but a person with Blue Cross falls under PPOs. Such persons must know how they are classified; their options are in part determined by their status. An understanding of financing can help a patient determine what options are available. It is important to know who pays for dialysis, organ transplantation, or hospice care. Patients should weigh the implications for treatment before choosing or rejecting a particular kind of insurance.

A third consideration is the more elusive issue of health care financing policy. At the time of writing this book, considerable controversy exists about what policies should prevail. Patients cannot possibly be fully informed about the shifting winds of economic and political doctrine, but they should be able to obtain the information they need when they need it.

One way to do this is through judicious use of additional opinions about financing options in a given situation. A person with acute leukemia might want to contact a university research hospital to find out about eligibility for treatment under a research protocol that pays patient costs. An elderly patient with cardiac problems might want to avoid that same university hospital, thereby avoiding high-technology intensive-care treatment in the event of a cardiac arrest, especially if he or she has insurance beyond Medicare. State regulations also may affect choices. In some states, a patient whose medical care is covered by state welfare funds may retain ownership of a home but the state has a claim against the person's estate for medical costs incurred for terminal care. Such a patient might wish to limit those costs by signing a natural death act directive, by executing a durable power of attorney, or by documenting personal preferences in writing.

Patients who are unsure about how health care financing affects treatment options may need to consult others. Persons with Medicare coverage may need to penetrate the bureaucracy; those with substantial economic resources may employ an attorney, a mediator, or even a health economist as a consultant. Some hospital administrators may be able and willing to help patients; other patients may turn to organizations to which they belong for assistance. Personal physicians may understand the nuances of financing, but how many patients still have personal physicians? Patients may need to search for outside consultants appropriate to their particular needs. Although the process may be complex and at times frustrating, it is in principle no different from other areas where financial matters are at stake—buying a house or car, selecting a college, choosing a job. Health care may be as economically important as any aspect of one's financial planning. If one waits until a crisis occurs, it will be too late for rational, reflective analysis of the options that are available.

Many Americans are reluctant to talk about money, especially when it comes to health care. If a person takes financial matters into consideration in making health care choices, it is essential that such factors be made explicit, communicated, and documented. A person can reject a high-priced, high-technology treatment just because of its costs; some patients have even gone so far as to instruct their attorneys and families to notify the hospital that they will refuse to pay for expensive treatments that promise no therapeutic benefits, and then have gone to court over it. Threatening such a course of action is likely to get the attention of an appropriate hospital administrator.

Patients who want treatment but have financial difficulties can enlist the aid of patient support groups. They can even try to negotiate with hospital administrators or insurance companies, or enlist media support to raise funding. These are long shots, but a particular patient may succeed where others have failed. Just as it is necessary to know how hospitals operate in order to avoid unwanted treatment, so may this knowledge help to obtain treatment that is desired. Physicians, like hospitals, are susceptible to subtle as well as overt pressures. Because of the visibility of hospital care, hospitals often elect to provide care and pay the costs themselves rather than face an unpleasant confrontation, either in court or the news media. Other times, there are solutions to cost problems that benefit both patient and hospital, as when patients want to leave but their physicians want to continue treating. The high cost of hospital care may make it advantageous for the hospital to help the patient leave the hospital and obtain effective assistance with home care. Similarly, hospice care will be more available to patients because it looks to be less expensive. Although this is a poor reason for providing it, it is better than not having it at all.

The changing patterns of health care financing will inevitably have an effect on the physician-patient relationship as well. Physicians are facing a new generation of patients who want to know what is going on and who expect to be given that information. Furthermore, those patients plan to participate actively in their health care decisions. Physicians will be expected to translate technical medical information into language that patients can understand and to provide more information than ever. Insurance companies and other payers, however, will pressure physicians and patients to spend less time talking to each other because talking takes time and time means added costs. This conflict will lead to increased use of technological patient education (videotapes, interactive computers, etc.) and a reduced doctor-patient relationship.

Physicians and patients may find that a new alliance needs to be created between them. At present, the doctor-patient relationship is strained and both members sometimes feel alienated. They may find a new relationship as they together try to promote professional and personal autonomy and responsible health care decisions amid the maze of financial constraints. As the patient has lost autonomy by increasing technological development, so now the physician is losing autonomy as a result of economic problems. Both can regain their proper authority, but the task of creating a new relationship will not be easy. If it is achieved, patients could benefit greatly.

We have argued throughout this book that many factors affect, restrict, and shape the scope of patients' personal autonomy in health care. We have tried to show that patients have a right to exercise control and can do so much more than they often do. Some patients don't want this freedom. Those who do must cultivate clarity of thought and show persistence in getting relevant information, and should make judicious use of available consultants and resources and the moral and emotional support of friends and family. Choices may be hard; options may be unpleasant; but those who want autonomy can choose their own fate. Physicians are sometimes willing to help and to share decision-making responsibilities. Paternalism can be pushed back, though there are consequences for the patient. Although patients cannot choose their diseases, they can take some steps to avoid them. Although they cannot completely control health care options, they do have choices about who will be their physician and they can find physicians who will accept their desire to make treatment choices according to the patient's values. Although patients cannot decide health financing policy, they can choose rationally among the alternatives offered. Choices may be constrained; options may be limited; but within the limitations, autonomy can flourish, whether choosing life or death.

Bibliography

Below are listed the primary journals, the most widely used anthologies of articles, and a selected number of books that address bioethics issues. Publication in this field has increased enormously within the past five years and an exhaustive listing of relevant works would be impossible. Current journal articles on bioethics topics are indexed in *Index Medicus* (which can be found in all medical school libraries); in the *Bibliography of Bioethics*, which is published yearly (Vol. 10, the most recent volume, by the Center for Bioethics, Kennedy Institute of Ethics, Georgetown University, Washington, DC 20057); and in *New Titles in Bioethics*, a monthly publication of the Center for Bioethics. Both the *Hastings Center Report* and *Law, Medicine & Health Care* also include current bibliographies in each issue. Computer-based bibliographies are available through *BioethicsLine*, National Library of Medicine, Medlars Management Section, Bethesda, MD 20894; and *Med-Line*, also located at the National Library of Medicine.

Journals

Hastings Center Report (published every other month). Institute of Society, Ethics and the Life Sciences, 360 Broadway, Hastings-on-Hudson, NY 10706.

Law, Medicine & Health Care (published six times a year). American Society of Law and Medicine, 765 Commonwealth Ave., 16th Floor, Boston, MA 02215.

Ethical Currents (published quarterly). Center for Bioethics, St. Joseph Health System, 440 S. Batavia St., Orange, CA 92668.

Anthologies of Selected Articles on Bioethics Issues

ABRAMS, N. AND BUCKNER, M.D. (eds.). *Medical Ethics*. Cambridge, Mass.: MIT Press, 1983.

BEAUCHAMP, T. AND WALTERS, L. (eds.). *Contemporary Issues in Bioethics*, 2nd ed. Belmont, Calif.: Wadsworth, 1982.

GOROVITZ, S., MACKLIN, R., JAMETON, A.L., O'CONNOR, J.M., AND SHERWIN, S. (eds.). *Moral Problems in Medicine*, 2nd ed. Englewood Cliffs, N.J.: Prentice-Hall, 1983.

HUNT, R., AND ARRAS, J. (eds.). *Ethical Issues in Modern Medicine*, 2nd ed. Palo Alto, Calif.: Mayfield, 1983.

REISER, S., DYCK, A., AND CURRAN, W. (eds.). *Ethics in Medicine: Historical Perspectives and Contemporary Concerns*. Cambridge, Mass.: MIT Press, 1977.

General Works

AARON, HENRY, AND SCHWARTZ, WILLIAM B. *The Painful Prescription: Rationing Hospital Care*. Washington, D.C.: The Brookings Institution, 1984. (Health care financing)

BLANK, ROBERT H. *The Political Implications of Human Genetic Technology*. Boulder, Colo.: Westview Press, 1981. (Genetic screening)

FOX, RENEE C., AND SWAZEY, JUDITH P. *The Courage to Fail: a Social View of Organ Transplants and Dialysis*. Chicago: University of Chicago Press, 1978. (Kidney dialysis and organ transplants)

JAMETON, ANDREW. *Nursing Practice: The Ethical Issues*. Englewood Cliffs, N.J.: Prentice-Hall, 1984. (Nursing dilemmas)

JONSEN, ALBERT, SEIGLER, MARK, AND WINSLADE, WILLIAM J. *Clinical Ethics*. New York: Macmillan, 1982. (Patient autonomy)

KATZ, JAY. *The Silent World of Doctor and Patient*. New York: Free Press, 1984. (Informed consent)

LAX, ERIC. *Life and Death on 10 West*. New York: Times Book Co., 1984. (Bone marrow transplantation)

LEAR, MARTHA. *Heartsounds*. New York: Simon and Schuster, 1980. (Being a patient)

LERNER, GERDA. *A Death of One's Own*. New York: Harper Colophon, 1980. (Being a patient)

Lyon, Jeffrey. *Playing God in the Nursery.* New York: Norton, 1985. (Treatment of seriously ill newborns)

Mullan, Fitzhugh. *Vital Signs.* New York: Dell Publishing Co., 1984. (A doctor as patient)

Murray, T. H., and Caplan, A. (eds.). *Which Babies Shall Live? Humanistic Implications of the Care of Imperiled Newborns.* Clifton, N.J.: Humana Press, 1985.

President's Commission for the Study of Ethical Problems in Medicine and Biomedical and Behavioral Research. *Defining Death,* 1981; *Making Health Care Decisions,* 1982; *Screening and Counseling for Genetic Conditions,* 1983; *Securing Access to Health Care,* 1983; *Deciding to Forego Life-Sustaining Treatment,* 1983. Washington, D.C.: U.S. Government Printing office.

Reich, Warren (ed.). *Encyclopedia of Bioethics.* New York: Free Press, 1978.

Rettig, Richard A., and Marks, E. L. *Implementing the End-Stage Renal Disease Program of Medicare.* Santa Monica, Calif.: Rand, 1980. (Kidney dialysis)

Robertson, John A. *The Rights of the Critically Ill.* Cambridge, Mass.: Ballinger Press, 1983. (Patients' legal rights)

Robin, Eugene D. *Matters of Life and Death: Risks and Benefits of Medical Care.* New York: W. H. Freeman & Co., 1984. (Patient education)

Sidel, Victor, and Sidel, Ruth. *Reforming Medicine: Lessons of the Last Quarter.* New York: Pantheon Books, 1984. (Medical reform)

Siegler, Miriam, and Osmond, Humphry. *Patienthood: The Art of Being a Responsible Patient.* New York: Macmillan, 1979. (Patients' role)

Starr, Paul. *The Social Transformation of American Medicine.* New York: Basic Books, 1982. (Medical history and reform)

Stinson, Robert, and Stinson, Peggy. *The Long Dying of Baby Andrew.* Boston: Little, Brown: 1983. (Treatment of seriously ill newborns)

Thomas, Lewis. *The Youngest Science: Notes of A Medicine-Watcher.* New York: Viking, 1983. (Medical reform)

Weir, Robert. *Selective Nontreatment of Handicaped Newborns: Moral Dilemmas in Neonatal Medicine.* New York: Oxford University Press, 1984. (Treatment of seriously ill newborns)

Index